Honoré de Balzac

LA COMÉDIE HUMAINE

THE CAXTON EDITION

ADOREMUS IN ÆTERNUM

They saw then, in the antechamber of the cell, the dead body of the duchess lying on the floor upon a plank.

Caxton Edition

HISTORY OF THE THIRTEEN

FERRAGUS, CHIEF OF THE DÉVORANTS
LA DUCHESSE DE LANGEAIS

BY

Honoré de Balzac

WITH ILLUSTRATIONS

LONDON
THE CAXTON PUBLISHING COMPANY, LIMITED
CLUN HOUSE, SURREY STREET, STRAND, W.C.

COPYRIGHTED, 1896, BY G. B. & SON
All rights reserved.

The Human Comedy

PARISIAN LIFE

HISTORY OF THE THIRTEEN

PREFACE

There were brought together under the Empire and in Paris, thirteen men all equally possessed by the same sentiment, all of them endowed with sufficient force to remain constant to one idea, sufficiently honorable not to betray one another, even when their individual interests conflicted, sufficiently politic to conceal the sacred ties which united them, sufficiently strong to maintain themselves above all law, courageous enough to undertake anything, and fortunate enough to have almost always succeeded in their designs; having encountered the greatest dangers, but never speaking of their defeats; inaccessible to fear, and having trembled neither before the prince, the headsman, nor innocence; accepting each other for such as they were, without taking into account social prejudices; criminals undoubtedly, but certainly remarkable for some of those qualities which mark great men, and recruiting their number only from men of distinction. And, finally, that nothing might be lacking to the sombre and mysterious poetry of this history these thirteen men have remained unknown, though all of them have realized the strangest chimerical ideas which are suggested to the imagination by that fantastic power wrongly attributed to the Manfreds, the Fausts, the Melmoths; and all of them are to-day crushed, or at least dispersed. They have quietly returned to the yoke of the civil law, as Morgan, the Achilles of pirates, transformed himself from a destroyer to a peaceful colonist, disposing without remorse by the light of his own fireside, of the millions gathered in blood by the red glare of incendiarism.

Since the death of Napoléon, an accident concerning which the author should still preserve silence, has dissolved the bonds of this life, as secret and curious, as the darkest of the romances of Mrs. Radcliffe. The permission, sufficiently remarkable in itself, to relate, in his own manner, some of the adventures of these men, always with respect for certain proprieties, has only recently been given him by one of these anonymous heroes to whom all branches of society were secretly subject, and in whom the author believes himself to have discovered a vague desire for celebrity.

This man, in appearance still young, with light hair and blue eyes, whose voice, soft and clear, seemed to reveal a feminine soul, was pale of complexion and mysterious in his manners; he conversed affably, pretended to be only forty years of age, and might have been a member of the highest class of society. The name which he had assumed appeared to be a fictitious one; in the gay world his person was unknown. Who is he? no one knows.

Perhaps, in confiding to the author the extraordinary things which he revealed to him, the unknown wished to see them reproduced in some manner and to enjoy the emotions which they would be certain to awaken in the bosoms of the populace; some feeling analogous to that experienced by Macpherson when the name of Ossian, his creation, was inscribed in all languages. And it was, certainly, for the Scottish lawyer one of the keenest sensations, or at least one of the rarest, that man can give himself. May it not be said to be the incognito of genius? To write the *Itinéraire de Paris à Jérusalem*, is to take one's part in the human glory of a century; but to endow one's country with a Homer, is it not to usurp the privileges of God?

The author is too well acquainted with the laws of narration to remain in ignorance of the engagements which this short preface causes him to assume; but he also knows sufficiently well the story of the Thirteen to be certain of never falling below the interest which this programme would seem to promise. Certain dramas blood-curdling, certain comedies full of terrors, certain romances through which roll human heads secretly struck off, have been confided to him. If any reader has not been satiated with the horrors coolly served up to the public recently, he could, if but the slightest desire to hear them were manifested, reveal to him quiet atrocities, marvelous family tragedies. But he has selected in preference the mildest adventures, those in which pure scenes succeed the storms of the passions, in which woman is radiant with virtue and beauty. For the honor of the Thirteen, such scenes may be met with in their history, which perhaps some day may be judged worthy of being published as a pendant to that of the buccaneers, that race apart, so curiously energetic, so attractive despite its crimes.

An author should disdain to convert his recital, when that recital is truthful, into a species of jack-in-the-box, and to lead his reader, after the manner of some romancers, from one subterranean crypt to another through four volumes in order to show him a withered corpse and to say to him, by way of conclusion, that he has been keeping him in constant terror of a secret door in the tapestry or of a dead man left inadvertently under the floor. Notwithstanding his aversion to prefaces the author has felt obliged to place these sentences at the beginning of this fragment. *Ferragus* is a preliminary episode which is united by invisible bonds to the history of the Thirteen, whose power, naturally acquired, alone can explain certain energies, apparently supernatural. Although it be permitted to story-tellers to have a kind of literary coquetry, on becoming historians, they should renounce the benefits which they might derive from strangeness of titles, which in our day procure certain slight successes. Therefore the author will explain here briefly the reasons which have obliged him to accept certain titles for his books which at first sight may not seem quite natural.

Ferragus is, according to an ancient custom, a

name taken by a chief of *Dévorants*. The day of their election, these chiefs adopt for themselves those of the names of the *dévorantesque* dynasties which please them, just as, of the pontifical dynasties, the Popes do, at their installation. Thus the *Dévorants* have *Trempe-la-Soupe IX.*, *Ferragus XXII.*, *Tutanus XIII.*, *Masche-Fer IV.*, in the same manner as the Church has its Clement XIV., Gregory IX., Julius II., Alexander VI., etc. Meanwhile, who are the *Dévorants? Dévorants* is the name of one of the tribes of "companions" that issued formerly from the great mystical organization formed among the workmen of Christendom to rebuild the Temple of Jerusalem. The *compagnonnage* still exists in France among the people. Its traditions, powerful for the unthinking and for those who are not sufficiently-well educated to break these oaths, might serve for formidable enterprises if some rough-hewn genius were to seize the direction of these various societies. In fact, there, there is no lack of blind instruments; there, from one town to another, has existed, for the *compagnons*, from time immemorial an *obade*, a species of halting-place kept by a *mother*, an old woman, half gipsy, having nothing to lose, knowing all that passes in the country, and devoted—either from fear or from long custom—to the tribe which she lodges and feeds in detail. Finally, these people constantly changing, yet submitting to immovable customs, may have eyes in every locality, execute everywhere a will, without a judgment thereon, for the oldest companion is still in an age when one believes in something. In addition, the entire body professes doctrines sufficiently true, sufficiently mysterious, to electrify patriotically all the adepts, if they but receive the slightest development. Then the attachment of the companions to their laws is so passionate that the various tribes wage bloody combat among themselves in order to decide some question of principle. Fortunately for the existing public order, when a *Dévorant* becomes ambitious, he builds houses, makes a fortune, and leaves the *compagnonnage*. There would be many curious details to give concerning the "Companions of Duty"—*compagnons du Devoir*—the rivals of the *Dévorants,* and all the different sects of workmen, their customs and their fraternity, the relations which exist between them and the Freemasons; but these details would be out of place here. Only, the author will add that, under the ancient monarchy, it was not unknown to find a Trempe-la-Soupe in the king's service, having secured a place for a hundred and one years in the galleys; but from there still directing his tribe, still consulted religiously by them, and if he quitted the chain-gang, certain of finding aid, comfort and respect everywhere. To see its chief at the galleys is, for a faithful tribe, only one of those misfortunes for which Providence is responsible, but which in no way relieves the *Dévorants* from the duty of obeying the power created by them, above them. It is the temporary exile of their legitimate king, always a king for them. Here may be seen, then, the romantic prestige attached to the name of *Ferragus* and to that of *Dévorants* completely dissipated.

As to the Thirteen, the author feels himself sufficiently strongly supported by the details of this history, almost romantic, to renounce again one of the finest privileges of the novelist of which there can be an example—and which, on the Châtelet of literature, would be awarded a high prize—and to impose on the public as many volumes as have been given them by LA CONTEMPORAINE. The Thirteen were all of them men of the same quality as was Trelawny, the friend of Lord Byron and, as it is said, the original of the *Corsair;* all of them fatalists, men of heart and poetical, but wearied of the monotonous life they led, strongly drawn towards Asiatic enjoyments by those forces which awoke in them all the more furiously, having been so long suppressed. One day, one of them, after having re-read *Venice Preserved,* after having admired the sublime union of Pierre and Jaffier, fell into contemplation of the peculiar virtues of those who find themselves thrown outside the social order, on the probity of the bagnios, on the fidelity of thieves to each other, on the privileges of exorbitant power which these men know how to conquer by concentrating all ideas in a single will. It appeared to him that man was greater than men. He thought that society in its entirety might belong to those distinguished ones who, to their natural abilities, to their acquired enlightenment, to their fortune, would join a fanaticism furious enough to cast into a single jet all these different forces. Thus equipped, immense in action and in intensity, their occult power, against which the social order would be defenceless, might overthrow in it all obstacles, overwhelm all wills, and give to each one of them the diabolical power of all. This world isolated in the midst of the world, hostile to the world, admitting none of the ideas of the world, recognizing none of its laws, submitting only to the conscience of its own necessity, obedient to devotion only, acting altogether for one of the associates when one of them claimed the assistance of all; this life of buccaneers in kid gloves and in carriages; this intimate union of superiors, cold and mocking, smiling and cursing in the midst of a false and mean society, the certainty of being able to make everything bend under a caprice, of contriving a vengeance skilfully, of living in thirteen hearts; then the continual satisfaction of having a secret of hatred in the face of men, of being always armed against them, and of being able to retire into one's self with one idea more than even the most remarkable men could have;—this religion of pleasure and of egoism fanaticized thirteen men, who reconstituted the Society of Jesus for the profit of the Devil. It was horrible and sublime. And in fact the compact was made; and in fact endured, precisely because it appeared impossible. There were then, in Paris, thirteen brothers, who belonged to each other and who did not recognize each other in the world; but who came together in the evening, like conspirators, hiding none of their thoughts from each other, using alternately a power like that of the Old Man of the Mountain; having a foothold in all the salons, their hands in all the strong-boxes, elbow-room in all the streets, their heads on any pillow, and, without scruple, making everything serve their fantastic will. No chief commanded them, no one could arrogate to himself the supreme power; only, the most vivid passion, the most exacting circumstances, assumed the initiative. They were thirteen unknown kings, but really kings, and more than kings, judges and executioners who, having made for themselves wings with which to traverse society from the top to the bottom, disdained to be something in it because they could be all. If the author should learn the causes of their abdication, he will relate them.

At present, he is permitted to commence the recital of the three episodes which, in this history, have most particularly attracted him by the Parisian flavor of the details and by the extravagance of the contrasts.

Paris, 1831.

FERRAGUS, CHIEF OF THE DÉVORANTS

TO HECTOR BERLIOZ

FERRAGUS

CHIEF OF THE DÉVORANTS

*

There are in Paris certain streets as dishonored as can be any man convicted of infamy; then there are noble streets, also streets that are simply honest, also young streets concerning whose morality the public has not yet formed any opinion; then there are murderous streets, streets older than the oldest possible dowagers, estimable streets, streets that are always clean, streets that are always dirty, workingmen's streets, students' streets and mercantile ones. In short, the streets of Paris have human qualities, and impress us by their physiognomy with certain ideas against which we are defenceless. There are streets of bad company in which you would not wish to dwell, and there are others in which you would willingly take up your residence. Some streets, like that of Montmartre, have a fine head and end in a fish's tail. The Rue de la Paix is a wide street, a grand street; but it reveals none of those gracefully noble suggestions which surprise an impressionable soul in the midst of the Rue Royale, and it certainly lacks the majesty which reigns in the Place Vendôme. If you walk about in the streets of the Ile Saint-Louis you will require no other cause for the nervous sadness which oppresses you than the solitude, the gloomy air of the houses and of the great deserted houses. This island, the corpse of the Farmers-General, is like the Venice of Paris. The Place de la Bourse is chattering, active, prostituted; it is only handsome by moonlight, at two o'clock in the morning; in the daylight it is an abridged presentation of Paris; at night, it is like a dream of Greece. The Rue Traversière-Saint-Honoré is it not an infamous street? There are in it wicked little houses with two window-casements, in which, from story to story, may be found vices, crimes and misery. The narrow streets facing north, into which the sunlight only comes three or four times in the course of the year, are streets of assassination which kill with impunity; to-day, Justice does not interfere with them; but formerly the parliament would perhaps have summoned the lieutenant of police to reprimand him accordingly and would at least have issued a decree against the street, as one was directed formerly against the *perruques* of the Chapter of Beauvais. Meanwhile, Monsieur Benoiston de Châteauneuf has demonstrated that the mortality of these streets is double that of others. To sum up all these ideas in one example, the Rue Fromenteau, is it not at once murderous and profligate? These observations, incomprehensible outside of Paris, will be doubtless appreciated by those men of study and thought, of poetry and pleasure, who know how to gather, whilst idling in Paris, all those enjoyments which float continually within her walls; by those for whom Paris is the most delicious of monsters;— there, a pretty woman; farther off, old and poor; here, brand-new, like the coinage of a new reign; in that corner, elegant as a woman of fashion. A monster so complete, moreover! His garrets, a species of head, crowded with science and with genius; his lower stories, comfortable stomachs; his shops, veritable feet,—from them issue all the comers and goers, all the busy people. And what a ceaselessly active life is that of the monster! Scarcely has the last rattling of the last carriages from the ball ceased in his heart when already his arms are moving at the barriers, and he shakes himself slowly. All the doors open, turning on their hinges, like the members of a great lobster, invisibly set in motion by thirty thousand men or women, of which each one lives in a space of six feet square, possesses there a kitchen, a workshop, a bed, children, a garden, does not see very clearly, and should see all. Imperceptibly the limbs begin to creak, the movement spreads, the street speaks. By noon everything is alive, the chimneys smoke, the monster is eating; then he roars, then his thousand claws are in motion. Beautiful spectacle! But, Oh! Paris, he who has not admired thy sombre passages, thy gleams of light, thy gloomy and silent *culs-de-sac;* he who has not heard thy murmurs, between midnight and two o'clock in the morning, still knows nothing of thy true poetry nor of thy great and curious contrasts. There is a small number of amateurs, people who never walk heedlessly, who taste their Paris, who possess so completely her physiognomy that they can perceive on it a wart, a mole, a pimple. For others, Paris is always this marvellous monster, an astonishing assemblage of movements, of machines and thoughts, the city with a hundred thousand romances, the head of the world. But to the first, Paris is sorrowful or gay, ugly or handsome, living or dead; to them, Paris is a creature; each man, each fraction of a house, is a lobe of the cellular tissue of this great wanton, of whom they know perfectly the head, the heart, and the fantastic manners. Thus these are the lovers of Paris: they elevate their noses at such a corner of the street sure of finding there the face of a clock; they say to a friend whose snuff-box is empty, "Take such a passage, you will find in it a tobacco shop, at the left, near to a pastry-cook who has a pretty wife." To ramble through Paris is, for these poets, a costly luxury. How to avoid spending precious minutes before all the dramas, the disasters, the figures, the picturesque accidents, which continually assail you in the midst of this moving queen of cities, clothed with displayed posters and who, nevertheless, has not one clean corner, so complaisant is she to the vices of the French nation! To whom has it not happened to set out in the morning from his lodging to go to the extremity of Paris, and to find himself at dinner time still unable to leave the centre of the city? These, then, will know how to excuse this wandering introduction which, however, may be summed up in an observation eminently useful and novel—as much so as any observation can be new in Paris, where there is nothing new, not even the statue set up yesterday on which a street-boy has already scrawled his name. Yes, then, there are streets, or ends of streets, there are certain houses, unknown for the greater part to people of social distinction, in which a woman belonging to society could not enter without giving rise to the cruelest suspicions concerning herself. If this woman be rich, if she have a carriage, if she go on foot, or disguised, into some of these defiles of the Parisian country, she compromises her reputation as a virtuous woman. But if by chance she should come there at nine o'clock in the evening, the opinion that an observer would permit himself to form might have the most serious consequences. Finally, if this woman be young and pretty, if she enter some house in one of these streets; if this house have a long and dark passage-way, damp and ill-smelling; if at the bottom of this passage-way may be seen trembling the pale light of a lamp, and if under this light may be perceived a horrible visage of an old woman with long and lean fingers,— then in truth, let us say it, in the interests of all young and pretty women, such woman is lost. She is at the mercy of the first man of her acquaintance whom she may encounter in these Parisian morasses. But there are many streets in Paris in which this meeting might become the most frightfully terrible drama, a drama full of blood and of love, a drama of the modern school. Unfortunately, this conviction, this dramatic possibility, will be, like the modern drama, comprehended but by few; and it is a great pity to have to relate a story to a public which does not appreciate all its local merit. But who may flatter himself that he is ever understood? We shall all die unrecognized. It is the plaint of women and authors.

At half-past eight o'clock one evening, in Rue Pagevin, at the period when Rue Pagevin had not one wall that did not echo an infamous word, and in the direction of Rue Soly, the narrowest and the most impassable of all the streets of Paris, not excepting the most frequented corner of the most deserted street; in the early part of the month of February, this adventure came to pass about thirteen years ago.—A young man, by one of those chances which do not present themselves twice in a lifetime, was turning the corner of Rue Pagevin on foot to enter Rue des Vieux-Augustins, on the right, precisely where Rue Soly is. There, this young man, who lived in Rue de Bourbon, thought he recognized in the woman a few feet behind whom he was walking quite carelessly, a vague resemblance to the prettiest woman in Paris, a chaste and delicious being with whom he was secretly and passionately in love, and in love without hope, for she was married. In a moment his heart leaped, an intolerable heat seemed to develop in his diaphragm and to pass into all his veins, he felt a chill in his back and in his head a superficial trembling. He loved, he was young, he knew Paris; and his perspicacity did not permit him to ignore all that there was possible of infamy for a woman, elegant, rich, young and beautiful, walking in this locality, and with a criminally furtive step. *She*, in this mud, at this hour! The love which this young man bore for this lady may well seem romantic, and all the more so that he was an officer in the Garde Royale. If he had been attached to the infantry, the thing might still appear possible; but, a superior officer of cavalry, he belonged to that arm of the service which desires the greatest rapidity in its conquests, which finds food for vanity in its amorous affairs as much as in its uniform. However, the passion of this officer was genuine, and to very many young hearts it will seem noble. He loved this lady because she was virtuous, in her he loved virtue, modest grace, and imposing sanctity, as the dearest treasures of his unavowed passion. She was in truth worthy of inspiring one of those platonic loves which may be met with, in the history of the Middle Ages, like flowers growing in bloody ruins; worthy of being secretly the inspiring principle of all the actions of a young man; a love as high, as pure, as the sky when it is blue; a love without hope, and to which we may attach ourselves because it will never deceive; a love prodigal of unbounded enjoyments, especially at an age when the heart is burning, the imagination keen, and when the eyes of a man see very clearly. There may be met with in Paris very singular night effects, weird and inconceivable. Those only who have amused themselves by observing them can know how fantastic may become through their means a woman in the dusk of evening. At moments the creature whom you are following, accidentally or with design, seems to you light and slender; again the stockings, if they are very white, convince you of the fine and elegant limbs; then the waist, though enveloped in a shawl, as in a pelisse, reveals itself young and voluptuous, in the shadows; then the uncertain lights of a shop or of a street lamp give to the unknown a fleeting illumination, nearly always deceptive, which awakens, lights up the imagination and carries it beyond the limitations of fact. The senses are all excited, everything takes color and animation; the woman assumes an entirely novel aspect; her person becomes beautiful; at certain moments she is no longer a woman, she is a demon, a will-o'-the-wisp, which entices you, by a magnetic attraction, to follow all the way to some respectable house where the poor *bourgeoise*, terrified by your threatening step or the sound of your boots, shuts the door in your face without looking at you. A vacillating gleam, thrown from the shop-window of a shoemaker, suddenly illuminated just below the waist the figure of the woman who was before the young man. Ah! surely, *she* alone had those curves! She alone possessed the secret of that chaste gait which so innocently reveals the beauties of the most attractive forms. That was her shawl and that the velvet bonnet of her morning promenades. On her gray silk stocking not a spot; on her shoe not a splash of mud. The shawl was drawn tightly around the bust, it disclosed vaguely the delicious contours; and the young man had seen the white shoulders at balls,—he knew well what treasures that shawl covered. By the manner in which a Parisian woman wraps herself in her shawl, by the way in which she lifts her feet in the street, a man of quick intelligence can divine the secret of her mysterious course. There is something, I know not what, of quivering, of lightness, in the whole person and in the gait; the woman seems to weigh less, she goes, she goes, or, rather, she glides like a star, and floats carried on by a thought which is betrayed by the folds and by the motion of her dress. The young man quickened his step, passed the woman, and then turned to look at her—Pst! she had disappeared into a passage-way, the grated door of which and its bell still rattled and sounded. The young man turned on his steps and saw this lady mounting, at the end of the passage-way—not without receiving the obsequious salutation of an old portress—a winding staircase, the lower steps of which were strongly illuminated; and Madame ascended buoyantly, quickly, like an eager woman.

"Eager for what?" said the young man to himself, drawing back to flatten himself like a grapevine, against the wall on the other side of the street.

And he watched, unhappy man, all the different stories of the house with the close attention of a police agent searching for his conspirator.

It was one of those houses of which there are thousands in Paris, a house ignoble, vulgar, narrow, yellowish in tone, with four stories and three windows on each floor. The shop and the entresol belonged to the shoemaker. The outer blinds on the first floor were closed. Where was Madame going? The young man thought he heard the tinkle of a bell in the apartment on the second floor. In fact, a light began to move in a room with two windows strongly illuminated, and suddenly lit up the third window, the darkness of which showed that it was that of a first room, evidently either the salon or the dining-room of the apartment. Immediately the silhouette of a woman's bonnet showed itself vaguely, the door closed, the first room became dark again, then the other two windows resumed their ruddy glow. At this moment the young man heard, "Look out there," and received a blow on his shoulder.

"You don't pay attention to anything, then," said a rough voice.

It was the voice of a workman carrying a long plank on his shoulder. And he passed on. This workman was the man sent by Providence, saying to this investigator,—"What are you meddling with? Think of your own duty, and leave the Parisians to their little affairs."

The young man crossed his arms; then, as no one saw him, he suffered tears of rage to roll down his cheeks without drying them. At last, the sight of the shadows playing on the two lighted windows gave him pain, he looked by chance toward the upper part of the Rue des Vieux-Augustins, and he saw a hackney-coach standing before a wall, at a locality where there was neither the door of a house nor the light of a shop.

Is it she? is it not she? Life or death for a lover. And this lover waited. He remained there during a century of twenty minutes. After that, the woman came down, and he then recognized her whom he secretly loved. Nevertheless, he wished still to doubt. She went toward the coach and got into it.

"The house will always be there, I can search it at any time," said the young man following the carriage at a run in order to dissipate his last doubts, and very soon he no longer had any.

The coach stopped in the Rue de Richelieu before the shop of a florist, near the Rue de Ménars. The lady got out, entered the shop, sent out the money to pay the coachman and came out herself after having selected a bunch of marabouts. Marabouts for her black hair! A brunette, she had placed the feathers close to her head to see the effect. The officer fancied he could hear the conversation between her and the florists.

"Madame, nothing is more becoming to brunettes, brunettes have something a little too precise in their contours, and the marabouts lend to their toilet a *softness* which they lack. Madame la Duchesse de Langeais says that they give to a woman something vague, Ossianic, and very *comme il faut.*"

"Very good. Send them to me promptly."

Then the lady turned quickly toward the Rue de Ménars, and entered her own house. When the door of the hôtel in which she lived closed on her, the young lover, having lost all his hopes, and, a double misfortune, his dearest beliefs, walked away through the streets of Paris like a drunken man, and presently found himself in his own room without knowing how he got there. He threw himself into an arm-chair, put his head in his hands and his feet on the andirons, drying his dampened boots until they burned. It was an awful moment, one of those moments in human life when the character is modified, and when the conduct of the best man depends on the good or evil of his first action. Providence or fatality, choose which you will.

This young man belonged to a good family, the nobility of which was not very ancient; but there are so few really old families in these days, that all younger ones pass for ancient without dispute. His grandfather had purchased the office of Counsellor to the Parliament of Paris, of which he afterwards became President. His sons, each provided with a handsome fortune, entered the army and through their matrimonial alliances became attached to the Court. The Revolution swept this family away; but there remained one old dowager, obstinate enough to refuse to emigrate, and who, thrown into prison, threatened with death, and saved on the 9th Thermidor, recovered her property. She recalled to France at the proper time, about 1804, her grandson, Auguste de Maulincour, the only scion of the Carbonnons de Maulincour, who was educated by the good dowager with the triple care of a mother, of a woman of rank, and of an obstinate dowager. Then, when the Restoration arrived, the young man, then eighteen years of age, entered the Maison Rouge, followed the princes to Ghent, was made an officer in the Gardes du Corps, left it to serve in the line, was recalled to the Garde Royale, where at twenty-three years of age he found himself chef d'escadron of a regiment of cavalry, a superb position, and one which he owed to his grandmother, who, notwithstanding her age, knew her own world exceedingly well. This double biography is a compendium of the general and special history, barring variations, of all the noble families who have emigrated, who had debts and property, dowagers and shrewdness. Madame la Baronne de Maulincour had for a friend the old Vidame de Pamiers, formerly a Commander of the Knights of Malta. This was one of those undying friendships founded on sexagenary ties, and which nothing can destroy, because at the bottom of such intimacies there are always to be found certain secrets of the human heart, delightful to divine when we have the time, but insipid to explain in twenty lines and which might furnish the text of a work in four volumes as amusing as *le Doyen de Killerine,* one of those works about which the youth talk, and which they judge but do not read. Auguste de Maulincour belonged therefore to the Faubourg Saint-Germain through his grandmother and through the vidame, and it sufficed him to date back two centuries to assume the airs and the opinions of those who pretended to go back to Clovis. This young man, pale, tall and slender, delicate in appearance, a man of honor and of true courage moreover, who would engage in a duel without hesitating for a yes or for a no, had not yet found himself on any battlefield, and wore at his buttonhole the cross of the Legion of Honor. He was, as you perceive, one of the living errors of the Restoration, perhaps the most pardonable of them. The youth of those days was the youth of no epoch; it came between the memories of the Empire and those of the Emigration, between the old traditions of the Court and the conscientious education of the bourgeoisie, between religion and the masked balls, between two political faiths; between Louis XVIII., who only saw the present, and Charles X., who looked too far into the future; it was, moreover, obliged to accept the will of the king, although royalty deceived it. This youth, uncertain in all things, blind and clear-seeing, was counted as nothing by the old men jealously keeping the reins of State in their palsied hands, while the monarchy might have been saved by their retirement and by the accession of this Young France of which to-day the old doctrinaires, the *émigrés* of the Restoration, still speak slightingly. Auguste de Maulincour was a victim of the ideas which at that time weighed upon this youth, and in this manner. The vidame was still at sixty-seven years of age a very brilliant man, having seen much, lived much, a good talker and man of honor, a gallant man, but who held with regard to women the most detestable opinions; he loved them and he despised them. Their honor, their feelings? Ta-ra-ra-, trifles and nonsense! When he was in their society he believed in them, the *Ci-devant monster;* he never contradicted them and he made them display their brightest qualities. But among his male friends, when they were brought into question, the vidame laid down the principle that to deceive women, to carry on several intrigues at once, should be the sole occupation of young men, who would be wasting their time in occupying themselves with anything else under the government. It is unfortunate to have to sketch so hackneyed a portrait. Has it not figured everywhere? And has it not become literally as threadbare as that of a grenadier of the Empire? But the vidame had upon the destiny of Monsieur de Maulincour an influence which it is necessary to depict; he lectured the young man after his fashion and endeavored to convert him to the doctrines of the great age of gallantry. The dowager, a woman tender-hearted and pious, sitting between her vidame and God, a model of grace and of sweetness, but gifted with that well-bred persistency which triumphs in the long run, had wished to preserve for her grandson the beautiful illusions of life, and had educated him in the highest principles; she gave to him all her own delicacy of feeling and made him a timid man, a coxcomb in appearance. The sensibilities of this young fellow, preserved pure, were not worn by contact without, and he remained so chaste, so scrupulous, that he was keenly offended by actions and maxims to which the world attached not the slightest importance. Ashamed of his susceptibility, the young man concealed it under a false assurance and suffered in silence; but he scoffed with others at things which when alone he reverenced. Thus it happened that he was deceived, because, in accordance with a not uncommon caprice of destiny, he encountered in the object of his first passion, he, a man of gentle melancholy and a spiritualist in love, a woman who held in horror the German sentimentalism. The young man distrusted himself, became contemplative, absorbed in his griefs, complaining of not being understood. Then, as we desire all the more violently the things which we find it most difficult to obtain, he continued to adore women with that ingenious tenderness and those feline delicacies the secret of which belongs to them alone and of which they perhaps prefer to keep the monopoly. In fact, although women complain of the manner in which men love them, they have nevertheless but little liking for those whose souls are half feminine. All their superiority consists in making men believe that they are their inferiors in love; therefore they quit willingly enough a lover when he is sufficiently experienced to rob them of those fears with which they seek to deck themselves, those delightful torments of feigned jealousy, those troubles of hope betrayed, those vain expectations, in short the whole procession of their feminine miseries; they hold in horror the Grandissons. What can be more contrary to their nature than a tranquil and perfect love? They want emotions, and happiness without storms is no longer happiness for them. The feminine souls that are strong enough to bring the infinite into love constitute angelic exceptions, and are among women what noble geniuses are among men. The great passions are as rare as masterpieces. Outside of this love there are only arrangements, irritations passing and contemptible, as are all things that are petty.

Amid the secret disasters of his heart, while he was still searching for the woman by whom he could be comprehended—a search which, let us say in passing, is the great amorous folly of our epoch—Auguste met in the society the farthest from his own, in the secondary sphere of the world of money where banking holds a first place, a perfect creature, one of those women who have about them I know not what that is saintly and sacred, who inspire so much reverence that love has need of all the help of a long familiarity to enable it to declare itself.

Auguste then gave himself up wholly to the delights of the deepest and most moving of passions, to a love that was purely adoring. It was composed of innumerable repressed desires, shades of passion so vague and so profound, so fugitive and so actual, that one knows not what to compare them to; they are like perfumes, like clouds, like rays of the sun, like shadows, like everything which in nature can momentarily shine and disappear, spring to life and die, leaving in the heart long emotions. While the soul is still young enough to nourish melancholy, distant hopes, and to know how to find in woman more than a woman, is it not the greatest happiness that can befall a man to love enough to feel more joy in touching a white glove, or ever so lightly the hair, to listen to a phrase, to cast a single look, than the most rapturous possession can ever give to happy love? Thus it is that rejected persons, the ugly, the unhappy, the unrevealed lovers, women or timid men, they alone know the treasures contained in the voice of the beloved. Taking their source and their principle from the soul itself, the vibrations of the air, charged with fire, bring the hearts so closely into communion, carry so lucidly thought between them, and are so incapable of falsehood, that a single inflection is often a complete revelation. What enchantments can be bestowed upon the heart of a poet by the harmonious intonations of a soft voice! How many ideas they awaken in it! What freshness they shed there! Love is in the voice before the glance avows it. Auguste, poet after the manner of lovers —there are poets who feel, and poets who express, the first are the happier—Auguste had tasted all these first joys, so vast, so fecund. *She* possessed the most pleasing organ that the most artificial women in the world could have desired in order to deceive at her ease; she had that silvery voice which, soft to the ear, is ringing only for the heart which it stirs and troubles, which it caresses in overthrowing. And this woman went by night to Rue Soly, through Rue Pagevin; and her furtive apparition in an infamous house had just destroyed the grandest of passions! The vidame's logic triumphed.

"If she is betraying her husband, we will avenge ourselves," said Auguste.

There was still love shown by that *if*—The philosophic doubt of Descartes is a politeness with which we should always honor virtue. Ten o'clock sounded. The Baron de Maulincour remembered at this moment that this woman was going to a ball that evening at a house to which he had access. He immediately dressed himself, set out, arrived there and searched for her with a gloomy air through all the salons. Madame de Nucingen, seeing him so thoughtful, said to him:

"You do not see Madame Jules, but she has not yet come."

"Good evening, my dear," said a voice.

Auguste and Madame de Nucingen turned round. Madame Jules had arrived, dressed all in white, simple and noble, wearing in her hair the very same marabouts that the young baron had seen her selecting in the flower shop. That voice of love pierced the heart of Auguste. If he had won the slightest right which permitted him to be jealous of this woman, he would have petrified her by saying to her only: "Rue Soly!" But if he, a stranger, had repeated a thousand times this name in the ear of Madame Jules she would have asked him in astonishment what he meant. He looked at her with a stupid air.

For those malicious people who laugh at everything it is perhaps a great amusement to detect the secret of a woman, to know that her chastity is a lie, that her calm face hides some deep thought, that there is some frightful drama hidden under that pure brow. But there are certain souls to whom such a sight is truly saddening, and many of those who laugh, when withdrawn into their inner selves, alone with their consciences, curse the world and despise such a woman. Such was the case with Auguste de Maulincour in the presence of Madame Jules. Singular situation! There was no other relation between them than that which the social world establishes between persons who exchange a few words seven or eight times in the course of a winter, and yet he was calling her to account for a happiness unknown to her, he was judging her without informing her of the accusation.

Many young men have found themselves thus, returning to themselves, in despair at having broken forever with a woman adored in secret; condemned, despised in secret. There are hidden monologues, said to the walls of some solitary lodging, storms roused and calmed without ever having issued from the bottom of hearts, admirable scenes of the moral world, for which a painter is wanted. Madame Jules sat down, leaving her husband who was making the tour of the salon. When she was seated she seemed uneasy, and, while talking with her neighbor, she watched furtively Monsieur Jules Desmarets, her husband, the broker of the Baron de Nucingen. The following is the history of this household:

Monsieur Desmarets was, five years before his marriage, in a broker's office with no other means than the meagre salary of a clerk. But he was one of those men whom misfortune early instructs in the things of this life, and who follow the straight line with the tenacity of an insect making for its nest; one of those dogged young men who slay before obstacles and who wear out all patiences with their own tireless patience. Thus, young as he was, he had all the republican virtues of poor peoples; he was sober, saving of his time, an enemy to pleasure. He waited. Nature had moreover given him the immense advantage of an agreeable exterior. His calm and clear brow; the shape of his placid but expressive face; his simple manners, everything in him revealed a laborious and resigned existence, that lofty personal dignity which is imposing, and that secret nobility of heart which can meet all situations. His modesty inspired a sort of respect in all those who knew him. Solitary moreover in the midst of Paris he saw the world only by glimpses during the brief moments that he spent in his patron's salon on holidays. There were to be found in this young man, as in most of the men who live in this manner, passions of amazing profundity,—passions too vast to permit him ever to compromise himself in petty incidents. His want of fortune compelled him to lead an austere life, and he conquered his fancies by hard work. When he grew pale over his figures, he found his recreation in striving obstinately to acquire that wide and general knowledge which to-day is so necessary to every man who wishes to make his mark in society, in commerce, at the bar, in politics, or in literature. The only peril which these fine souls have to fear is their own uprightness. Should they see some poor girl, and fall in love with her, they marry her, and they wear out their lives in a struggle between poverty and love. The finest ambition is quenched in the book of household expenses. Jules Desmarets fell headlong into his peril. One evening he met at his patron's house a young girl of the rarest beauty. The unfortunates deprived of affection and who consume the fine hours of their youth in long labors, alone know the secret of these rapid ravages which passion makes in their lonely and misunderstood hearts. They are so certain of loving truly, all their forces are concentrated so quickly on the woman who attracts them that, at her side, they receive the most delightful sensation while inspiring frequently none at all. This is the most flattering of all egotisms to a woman who knows how to divine this apparently immovable passion and these emotions so deep that they have required a great length of time to reach the human surface. These poor men, anchorites in the midst of Paris, have all the enjoyments of anchorites and may sometimes succumb to their temptations; but more often deceived, betrayed and misunderstood, it is rarely permitted to them to gather the sweet fruits of this love which to them is like a flower dropped from heaven. One smile from his wife, a single inflection of her voice, sufficed to make Jules Desmarets conceive a passion without bounds. Happily, the concentrated fire of this secret passion revealed itself ingenuously to the one who inspired it. These two beings then loved each other religiously. To express all in a word, they took each other by the hand before all the world like two children, brother and sister, who wished to pass through a crowd where all made way for them admiringly. The young girl was in one of those frightful positions in which human selfishness places some children. She had no civil status, and her name of *Clémence*, her age, were recorded only by a notary public. As for her fortune, it was insignificant. Jules Desmarets was the happiest of men on learning these misfortunes. If Clémence had belonged to some opulent family, he would have despaired of obtaining her; but she was a poor child of love, the fruit of some terrible adulterine passion; they were married. Then began for Jules Desmarets a series of fortunate events. Every one envied his happiness, and his enviers accused him thenceforward of having nothing but good fortune, without recalling either his virtues or his courage. Some days after the marriage of her daughter, the mother of Clémence, who passed in society for her godmother, advised Jules Desmarets to purchase the connection of a broker, promising to procure for him the necessary capital. At that time these connections could still be bought at a moderate price. That evening, in the salon of his broker, a wealthy capitalist, as it happened, on the recommendation of this lady, proposed to Jules Desmarets the most advantageous transaction that it was possible for him to conclude, gave him all the funds that would be required for this purpose, and the next day the happy clerk bought out his patron. In four years Jules Desmarets had become one of the richest members of his profession; many new clients had come to augment the number of those whom his predecessor had left to him. He inspired a boundless confidence, and it was impossible for him not to be conscious, by the manner in which his affairs prospered, of some secret influence due to his mother-in-law, or some hidden protection which he attributed to Providence. At the end of the third year Clémence lost her godmother. By that time Jules, so-called to distinguish him from his elder brother whom he had established as a notary in Paris, possessed an income of about 200,000 francs. There did not exist in all Paris another example of the domestic happiness enjoyed in this household. During five years this exceptional love had only been troubled by one calumny, for which Monsieur Jules exacted signal vengeance. One of his former comrades attributed the fortune of the husband to Madame Jules, explaining that it came from a high protection dearly purchased. The calumniator was killed in a duel. The deep passion of this couple, mutual as it was, and which survived marriage, obtained the greatest success in the social world, though some women were baffled by it. The charming household was respected, everybody fêted it. Monsieur and Madame Jules were sincerely liked, perhaps because there is nothing pleasanter than to see happy people; but they never remained long in any salon, and escaped as if impatient to regain their nest in haste, like two wandering doves. This nest was, moreover, a large and handsome hôtel in the Rue de Ménars, where a feeling for art tempered that luxury which the financial world continues, traditionally, to display, and where they received magnificently, although the obligations of social life suited them but little. Nevertheless, Jules submitted to the demands of the world, knowing that sooner or later a family has need of it; but his wife and he always felt themselves in its midst like greenhouse plants in a tempest. With a delicacy that was very natural, Jules had carefully concealed from his wife the calumny and the death of the calumniator which had well-nigh troubled their felicity. Madame Jules was inclined, by her delicate and artistic nature, to love luxury. Notwithstanding the terrible lesson of the duel, some imprudent women whispered to each other that Madame Jules must frequently be embarrassed for money. The twenty thousand francs which her husband gave her for her dress and for her fancies, could not, according to their calculations, suffice for her expenses. In fact, she was often found more elegantly dressed in her own home than when she went into society. She loved to adorn herself only to please her husband, as though wishing thus to prove to him that to her he was more than all the rest of the world. A true love, a pure love, happy above all, as much so as can be a love which is publicly clandestine. Thus Monsieur Jules, always a lover, and more loving each day, happy to be near his wife, even in her caprices, would have been uneasy if he had not found any in her, as though it would have been the symptom of some illness. Auguste de Maulincour had had the unhappiness of clashing this passion, and of madly falling in love with this woman. Nevertheless, though he carried in his heart a love so sublime, he was not ridiculous. He complied with all the demands of military manners and customs; but he wore constantly, even when drinking a glass of champagne, that dreamy look, that silent disdain for existence, that nebulous expression, which, for various reasons, the *blasés* wear, those dissatisfied with hollow life, and those who believe themselves consumptive, or who please themselves by imagining an affection of the heart. To love without hope, to be disgusted with life, constitute in these days a social position. The enterprise of invading the heart of a sovereign might give, perhaps, more hope than a rashly conceived love for a happy woman. Therefore Maulincour had sufficient reasons for remaining grave and gloomy. A queen retains the vanity of her power, she has against her her lofty elevation; but a pious bourgeoise is like a hedgehog, like an oyster, in their rough envelopes.

At this moment the young officer was beside his nameless mistress, who certainly was not aware that she was doubly faithless. Madame Jules was seated in a naive attitude, like the least artful woman in the world, gentle, full of a majestic serenity. What an abyss is human nature after all? Before beginning the conversation, the baron looked alternately at this lady and at her husband. How many reflections did he not make? He recomposed *Young's Night Thoughts* in a moment. Meanwhile the music was sounding through the apartments, the light was poured from a thousand candles, it was a banker's ball, one of those insolent festivities by which this world of dull gold endeavored to scorn the gilded salons in which laughed the fine company of the Faubourg Saint-Germain, not foreseeing the day when the bank would invade the Luxembourg and take its seat upon the throne. The conspirators were dancing at this moment, as indifferent to the future bankruptcies of power as to future failures of banks. The gilded salons of Monsieur le Baron de Nucingen had that peculiar animation which fashionable Paris, joyous in appearance at least, gives to the festivals of Paris. There, men of talent communicate their wit to fools, and fools communicate that air of happiness which characterizes them. By this exchange everything becomes animated. But a festival in Paris always a little resembles a display of fireworks; wit, coquetry and pleasure all sparkle and all go out like rockets. The next day, every one has forgotten his wit, his coquetries and his pleasure.

"Well, then!" thought Auguste by way of conclusion, "women are, after all, just as the vidame sees them? Certainly, all those dancing here are less irreproachable than Madame Jules appears, and Madame Jules goes to Rue Soly."

Rue Soly was his malady, the very word contracted his heart.

"Madame, you never dance then?" he asked her.

"This is the third time that you have asked me that question since the commencement of the winter," she answered smiling.

"But you have perhaps never answered it."

"That is true."

"I knew very well that you were deceptive, as are all other women—"

And Madame Jules continued to smile.

"Listen, Monsieur, if I told you the real reason, it would seem to you ridiculous. I do not think that it is deceiving not to tell secrets at which the world is in the habit of laughing."

"Every secret demands, in order to be told, a friendship of which I am doubtless unworthy, Madame. But you could not have any but noble secrets, and do you think me then capable of jesting on worthy things?"

"Yes," she said. "You, like all the others, you laugh at our purest feelings; you calumniate them. Besides, I have no secrets. I have the right to love my husband in the face of all the world, I say it, I am proud of it; and if you laugh at me when I tell you that I dance only with him, I shall have the worst opinion of your heart."

"You have never danced, since your marriage, with anyone but your husband?"

"Never, Monsieur. His arm is the only one on which I have leaned, and I have never felt the touch of another man."

"Your physician, has he never felt your pulse?"

"Well, now, you are laughing at me."

"No, Madame, I admire you because I comprehend you. But you let us hear your voice, you let us look at you, but—in fact, you permit our eyes to admire you—"

"Ah! that is one of my griefs," she said, interrupting him. "Yes, I would have had it possible for a married woman to live with her husband as a mistress lives with her lover; for, then—"

"Then why were you a few hours ago on foot, disguised, on Rue Soly?"

"What is Rue Soly?" she asked him.

And her voice so pure betrayed no sign of any emotion, no feature of her face quivered, she did not blush, and she remained calm.

"What! you did not go up to the second floor of a house situated in Rue des Vieux-Augustins, at the corner of Rue Soly? You did not have a hackney-coach waiting ten paces away, and you did not return to Rue de Richelieu, to a flower shop, where you selected the marabout feathers that you are now wearing?"

"I did not leave my house this evening."

In lying thus, she was smiling and imperturbable, she fanned herself; but if someone who enjoyed the right had passed a hand under her girdle, in the middle of her back he would perhaps have found it moist. At that instant Auguste remembered the instructions of the vidame.

"Then it was someone who strangely resembled you," he said with a credulous air.

"Monsieur," she resumed, "if you are capable of following a woman and detecting her secrets, you will permit me to say to you that that is wrong, very wrong, and I do you the honor not to believe you."

The baron turned away, took his stand before the fireplace, and appeared thoughtful. He bent his head; but his look was covertly fixed on Madame Jules, who, not thinking of the reflection in the mirror, cast at him two or three glances that were full of terror. Presently she made a sign to her husband, whose arm she took as she rose to walk about the salon. When she passed close to Monsieur de Maulincour, he, who was speaking with one of his friends, said, raising his voice, as if he were replying to a question:

"There is a woman who certainly will not sleep quietly this night—"

Madame Jules stopped, threw upon him an imposing look full of scorn and continued her walk, without knowing that one look the more, if surprised by her husband, might put in danger her own happiness and the lives of two men. Auguste, the prey of a rage which he smothered in the depths of his soul, presently left the house, swearing to penetrate to the heart of this intrigue. Before leaving, he sought Madame Jules in order to see her once more, but she had disappeared. What a drama cast into that young head so eminently romantic, like all those which have not known love in the wide extent which they ascribe to it! He adored Madame Jules under a new aspect, he loved her with the fury of jealousy, with the frenzied anguish of hope. Unfaithful to her husband, this woman became common. Auguste could now give himself up to the joys of a successful love, and his imagination opened to him the immense career of the pleasures of possession. In fine, if he had lost the angel, he had found the most delicious of demons. He went to bed building a thousand castles in the air, justifying Madame Jules by some romantic fiction in which he did not believe himself. Then he resolved to devote himself wholly, from the morrow, to the search for the causes, the motives of the intrigue which this mystery concealed. It was a romance to read; or, better, a drama to play, and in which he had his part.

M. AND MADAME JULES AND DE MAULINCOUR

Presently she made a sign to her husband, whose arm she took as she rose to walk about the salon. When she passed close to Monsieur de Maulincour, he, who was speaking with one of his friends, said, raising his voice, as if he were replying to a question:

"There is a woman who certainly will not sleep quietly this night—"

Madame Jules stopped, threw upon him an imposing look full of scorn.

Copyright, 1899, by George Barrie & Son.

*

A very fine thing is the trade of a spy, when it is followed for one's own benefit and in the interest of a passion. Is it not to give ourselves the pleasures of a thief while remaining an honest man? But it is necessary to resign one's self to boiling with rage, to roaring with impatience, to freezing the feet in the mud, to be benumbed and to burn, to devour false hopes. It is necessary to go, on the faith of a mere indication, towards an unknown goal, to miss our stroke, to fume, to improvise for ourselves elegies, dithyrambics, to exclaim idiotically before an inoffensive passer-by who stops to admire you; then to knock over old apple-women and their baskets of fruit, to run, to rest, to mount guard beneath a window, to make a thousand suppositions.—But it is the hunt, the hunt in Paris, the hunt with all its chances, less the dogs, the gun and the tally-ho! It is not to be compared with anything but the lives of gamblers. But it needs a heart big with love and with vengeance to ambush itself in Paris, like a tiger waiting to spring on its prey, and to enjoy thus all the possibilities of Paris and of a quarter, in furnishing them one interest the more to those in which they already abound. For this must we not have a multiple soul? Shall we not have to live in a thousand passions, a thousand simultaneous sentiments?

Auguste de Maulincour plunged passionately into this ardent existence, for he felt all its unhappinesses and all its pleasures. He went disguised through Paris, watching at all the corners of Rue Pagevin or of Rue des Vieux-Augustins. He hurried like a hunter from Rue de Ménars to Rue Soly, and from Rue Soly to Rue de Ménars, without obtaining either the vengeance or the reward with which would be punished or recompensed all these cares, these efforts and these ruses! However, he had not yet reached that impatience which wrings our entrails and makes us sweat; he roamed about hopefully, calculating that Madame Jules would not venture during the first few days to return to the locality where she had been detected. So he had devoted these first days to acquiring a knowledge of all the secrets of the street. A novice in this trade, he dared not question either the porter or the shoemaker of the house into which Madame Jules went; but he hoped to be able to establish a post of observation in the house directly opposite to the mysterious apartment. He studied the ground, he endeavored to conciliate prudence and impatience, his love and secrecy.

During the first days of the month of March, in the midst of the plans by which he thought to strike a decisive blow, leaving his post after one of those patient vigils by which he had as yet learned nothing, he was returning about four o'clock in the afternoon to his own house to which he was recalled by a matter relating to his military service, when he was overtaken in Rue Coquillière by one of those heavy showers which instantly flood the gutters, and of which each drop splashes loudly in the puddles of the roadway. A pedestrian in Paris, under these circumstances, is forced to stop short and take refuge in a shop or in a café, if he is rich enough to pay for the forced hospitality or, according to the urgency of the case, under a porte-cochère, that asylum for the poor and the shabby. How is it that none of our painters have ever attempted to reproduce the appearance of a crowd of Parisians grouped during a storm under the dripping portico of a house? Where could they find a richer subject? Is there not, first of all, the musing or philosophical pedestrian, who observes with pleasure all he sees,—whether it be the stripes made by the rain on the gray background of the atmosphere, a species of chasing something like the capricious threads of spun glass; or the whirlwinds of clear water which the wind rolls in luminous dust along the roofs; or the capricious overflowings of the gutter-pipes, crackling and foaming; in short, the thousand other admirable nothings, studied with delight by the idlers, notwithstanding the strokes of the broom with which they are regaled by the occupant of the porter's lodge? Then there is the talkative pedestrian, who complains and converses with the porter's wife while she leans on her broom like a grenadier on his musket; the needy pedestrian, curiously flattened against the wall, without any regard for his rags long accustomed to the contact of the streets; the learned pedestrian, who studies, spells or reads the posters without finishing them; the laughing pedestrian, who amuses himself with those to whom some accident happens in the street, who laughs at the muddy women and makes grimaces to those of either sex who are at the windows; the silent pedestrian, who studies all the windows, all the stories; the laboring pedestrian, armed with a satchel or furnished with a package, who is estimating the rain as so much profit or so much loss; the good-natured pedestrian who arrives like a bomb-shell exclaiming, "Ah! what weather, Messieurs!" and who salutes everybody; and, finally, the true bourgeois of Paris, a man with an umbrella, an expert in showers, who has foreseen this one, has come out in spite of his wife, and who is now seated in the porter's chair. According to his character, each member of this fortuitous society contemplates the sky and finally departs, skipping so as not to splash himself, or because he is in a hurry, or because he sees other citizens marching along in spite of wind and tide, or because, the archway of the house being damp and mortally catarrhal, the bed's edge, as the proverb says, is worse than the sheets. Each one has his own motive. No one is left but the prudent pedestrian, the man who, before he sets out again, waits to spy some bits of blue in the midst of the rifting clouds.

Monsieur de Maulincour took refuge then, with a

whole family of foot passengers, under the porch of an old house, the court-yard of which resembled an immense chimney flue. There were along its plastered, saltpetred and mouldy walls so many lead pipes and so many conduits from all the floors of its four main parts that you would have said it was like the Cascatelles of Saint-Cloud. Water flowed everywhere; it boiled, it leaped, it murmured; it was black, white, blue, green; it cried aloud, it multiplied itself under the broom of the portress, a toothless old woman accustomed to storms, who seemed to bless them as she swept into the street a thousand bits of rubbish of which the curious inventory would have revealed the life and the habits of every dweller in the house. There were scraps of printed cotton, tea-leaves, artificial flower petals faded and worthless, parings of vegetables, papers, fragments of metal. At every stroke of her broom the old woman laid bare the bed of the gutter, that black crevice, cut out in squares, over which the porters are so exercised. The poor lover examined this scene, one of those thousands which agitated Paris presents daily; but he examined it mechanically, like a man absorbed in his thoughts, when, raising his eyes, he found himself face to face with a man who had just entered.

This man was, in appearance at least, a beggar, but not the Parisian beggar, that creation without a name in human language; no, this man formed another type, outside of all the usual ideas suggested by the word "beggar." The unknown was not distinguished in any way by that character, originally Parisian, which strikes us so frequently in the unfortunates whom Charlet has sometimes represented with a rare happiness of observation,—coarse faces rolled in the mud, with hoarse voices, reddened and bulbous noses, mouths deprived of teeth, although menacing; humble and terrible beings, in whom the profound intelligence which shines in their eyes seems like a contradiction. Some of these bold vagabonds have blotched, cracked, veiny skin; the forehead covered with wrinkles; the hair scanty and dirty, like that of a wig thrown into a corner. All of them gay in their degradation, and degraded in their joys, all of them marked with the stamp of debauchery, cast their silence like a reproach; their attitude reveals frightful thoughts. Placed between crime and beggary they no longer have any remorse, and circle prudently around the scaffold without mounting it, innocent in the midst of vice, vicious in the midst of their innocence. They often cause a smile, but they always cause reflection. One represents to you civilization stunted and repressed, he comprehends everything;—the honor of the galleys, country, virtue; then it is the malice of a vulgar crime, and the fine craftiness of elegant wickedness. Another is resigned, a deep mimic but a stupid one. All of them have faint indications of order and of work, but they are pushed back into their mire by a society which does not care to inquire as to what there may be of poets, of great men, of intrepid souls and magnificent organizations among these beggars, these Bohemians of Paris; a people eminently good and eminently wicked, like all the masses who have suffered; accustomed to supporting unheard-of ills, and whom a fatal power always keeps down to the level of the mud. They all have a dream, a hope, a happiness,—cards, lottery or wine. There was nothing of all this strange life in the personage leaning so carelessly against the wall before Monsieur de Maulincour, like some fantastic idea designed by a skilful artist on the back of a canvas turned with its face to the wall in his atelier. This man, long and dry, whose leaden visage betrayed a deep but chilling thought, dried up all pity in the hearts of the curious by his sarcastic aspect and by his black looks which announced an intention of treating every man as his equal. His face was of a dirty white, and his wrinkled skull, denuded of hair, bore a vague resemblance to a block of granite. A few straight and gray locks on each side of his head fell to the collar of his greasy coat which was buttoned to the chin. He resembled at once Voltaire and Don Quixote; he was a scoffer and melancholy, full of disdain, of philosophy, but at least half deranged. He seemed to have no shirt. His beard was long. His rusty black cravat, quite worn out and ragged, exposed a protuberant neck, deeply furrowed, with thick veins like cords. A large brown circle like a bruise was strongly marked beneath each eye. He seemed to be at least sixty years old. His hands were white and clean. His boots were full of holes and trodden down at the heels. His blue pantaloons, mended in several places, were whitened by a species of fluff which made them offensive to the eye. Whether it was that his damp clothes exhaled a fetid odor, or that he had in his normal condition that smell of poverty which belongs to the Parisian dens, just as offices, sacristies and hospitals have their own, a fetid and rancid smell, of which no words can give the least idea, the neighbors of this man moved away from him and left him alone. He cast upon them and then upon the officer his calm and expressionless look, the so celebrated regard of Monsieur de Talleyrand, a dull, cold glance, a species of impenetrable veil beneath which a strong soul conceals profound emotion and the most exact estimation of men, things and events. Not a fold of his face quivered. His mouth and his forehead were impassible; but his eyes lowered themselves with a noble and almost tragic slowness. There was in fact a whole drama in the movement of these withered eye-lids.

The aspect of this stoical figure gave rise in Monsieur de Maulincour to one of those vagabond reveries which begin with a common interrogation and end by comprising a whole world of thought. The storm was past. Monsieur de Maulincour saw no more of the man than the skirt of his coat as it brushed the outside wall; but as he left his place to depart, he saw under his feet a letter which had fallen and which he supposed to have belonged to the unknown, as he had seen him put back in his pocket a handkerchief which he had used. The officer, who picked up the letter to return it to him, read the address involuntarily:

"A Mosieur,
    Mosieur Ferragusse,
Rue des Grands-Augustains, au coing de la rue Soly,
                            PARIS."

The letter bore no postmark and the address served to prevent Monsieur de Maulincour from returning it; there are besides few passions that, in the long run, will not come to be lacking in probity. The baron had a presentiment of the opportunity of this windfall, and determined, by keeping the letter, to give himself the right of entrance into the mysterious house to return it to this man, not doubting that he lived in this suspected dwelling. Already suspicions, vague as the first gleams of daylight, caused him to establish relations between this man and Madame Jules. Jealous lovers suppose everything; and it is by supposing everything and then selecting the most probable of these conjectures that judges, spies, lovers and observers, arrive at the truth which most interests them.

"Is the letter for him? Is it from Madame Jules?"

His unquiet imagination tossed a thousand questions together at him at once; but at the first words he smiled. Here is, textually, in all the splendor of its artless phrases and its ignoble orthography, this letter to which it would be impossible to add anything, just as nothing should be taken away, unless it were the letter itself, but it has been necessary to punctuate it in reproducing it. In the original, there are neither commas nor stops of any kind indicated, not even notes of exclamation,—a fact which tends to demolish the system of points and punctuation by which modern authors have endeavored to depict the great disasters of all the passions:

"HENRY,

"Among the many sacrifisis which I imposed upon myself for your sake was that of no longer giving you any news of myself; but an irresistible voice now tells me to let you know the wrongs you done me. I know beforehand that your soul hardened in vice will not pitty me. Your heart is def to feeling. Is it not so too to the cries of nature? But what matter; I must tell you to what a dredful point your are gilty and the horror of the position in which you have put me. Henry, you knew all what I suffered from my first fault and yet you have plunged me into the same *misery* and then abbandoned me to my despair and my suffering. Yes I will sai it, the belif that I had of being loved and esteamed by you gave me corage to bare my fate. But to-day what have I left? Have you not maid me lose all that I had that was most deer, all that held me to life: parens, frends, 'onor, reputation, I have sacrifised all to you and nothing is left me but oprobrum, shame, and I say it without blushing, poverty. Nothing was wanting to my unhappiness but the sertainty of your contempt and your haite; and now I have them I will find the corage that my project requires. My decision is taken and the honor of my family commands it; I am going then to put an end to my suffering. Do not make any reflecions on my project, Henry. It is awful, I know it, but my condition forses me to it. Without help, without support, without a *friend* to console me, can I live? No. Fate has desided for me So in two days, Henry, in two days, Ida will be no longer worthy of your esteam: but hear the oath that I make you that my conscience is at peace, since I have never seased to be worthy of your friendship. Oh, Henry, my friend, for I can never change to you, promise me that you will forgive me for what I am going to do. My love has given me corage, it will sustane me in virtue. My heart all full of your figger will be for me a preservative against seduction. Do not forget never that my fate is your work, and judge yourself. May Heven not punish you for your crime, it is on my knees that I ask your pardon, for I feel it, nothing will be wanting to my miseries but the sorow of knowing you unhaapy. In spite of the destitution in which I find myself I will refuse all kind of help from you. If you had loved me I would have received it as coming from your friendship, but a benefit given by *pitty, my soul refusis it,* and I would be baser in taking it than he who offered it to me. I have one favor to ask of you. I don't know how long I must stay at Madame Meynardie's, be genrous enough not to come to see me. Your last two visits did me a harm which I shall feel a long time; I do not wish to go into particlars about that conduct of yours. You hate me, that word is written on my 'eart and freeses it with feer. Alas! it is at the moment when I have need of all my corage that all my faccultes abbandon me, Henry, my friend, before I put a barrier between us, give me a last proof of your esteam; write me, answer me, say to me that you respect me still although you no longer love me. Although my eyes are always worthy of meeting yours, I do not ask an intervew; I fear all my weakness and my love. But, for pitty sake, write me a line at once; it will give me the corage I need to meet my troubles. Farewell, orther of all my woes, but the only friend that my heart has chosen and whom it will never forget.

"IDA."

This life of a young girl of which the love betrayed, the fatal joys, the sorrows, the poverty, and the lamentable resignation were summed up in so few words; this poem unknown but essentially Parisian, written in this dirty letter, agitated Monsieur de Maulincour for a moment; he ended by asking himself if this Ida might not be some relation of Madame Jules, and if the evening rendezvous, of which he had been a witness by chance, had not been occasioned by some charitable effort. That the old pauper could have seduced Ida?— This seduction would have been a miracle. Wandering in the labyrinth of his reflections which crossed each other and destroyed one another, the baron arrived at the Rue Pagevin, and saw a hackney-coach standing at the end of the Rue des Vieux-Augustins which is near the Rue Montmartre. All waiting hackney-coaches now had an interest for him.

"Can *she* be there?" thought he.

And his heart beat with a hot and feverish throbbing. He pushed open the little door with the bell, but he lowered his head as he did so in obedience to a sense of shame, for he heard a secret voice which said to him,—"Why do you put your foot into this mystery?"

He went up a few steps, and found himself face to face with the old portress.

"Monsieur Ferragus?"

"Don't know him."

"How? Monsieur Ferragus does not live here?"

"We don't have that man here."

"But my good woman.—"

"I am not a good woman, Monsieur, I am a concierge."

"But Madame," insisted the baron, "I have a letter to give to Monsieur Ferragus."

"Ah! If Monsieur has a letter," said she, changing her tone, "the thing is very different. Will you let me see it, your letter?"

Auguste showed the folded letter. The old woman shook her head with a doubtful air, hesitated, seemed to wish to leave her lodge to go and inform the mysterious Ferragus of this unforeseen incident; finally she said:

"Very well go up, Monsieur, you ought to know where it is—"

Without replying to this remark, by which the wily old woman might have wished to have set a trap for him, the officer went lightly up the stairway and rang loudly at the door of the second floor. His lover's instinct said to him,—"*She* is there."

The beggar of the porch, the Ferragus or the "orther" of Ida's woes, opened the door himself. He appeared in a flowered dressing-gown, pantaloons of white flannel, his feet in pretty embroidered slippers, and his head washed clean. Madame Jules, whose head appeared beyond the casing of the door into the next room, turned pale and fell into a chair.

"What is the matter, Madame?" cried the officer, springing toward her.

But Ferragus stretched forth an arm and threw the officer backward with so strong a movement that Auguste felt as though he had received in the chest a blow from an iron bar.

"Back, Monsieur!" said this man. "What do you want with us? You have been roaming about the quarter for the last five or six days. Are you a spy?"

"Are you Monsieur Ferragus?" said the baron.

"No, Monsieur."

"Nevertheless," continued Auguste, "it is to you that I must return this paper, which you dropped under the doorway of the house beneath which we both took refuge during the rain."

While speaking and in offering the letter to this man, the baron could not refrain from casting an eye around the room in which Ferragus received him. He found it very well arranged, though simply. A fire burned in the chimney-place; near it was a table with a more sumptuous service than seemed consistent with the apparent condition of this man and the humbleness of his lodging. And on a small sofa in the second room, which he could see through the doorway, he perceived a heap of gold, and heard a sound which could be no other than that of a woman weeping.

"This paper belongs to me, I thank you," said the unknown, turning away in such a manner as to make the baron understand that he desired him to leave immediately.

Too curious himself to take notice of the profound examination of which he was the object, Auguste did not see the half magnetic glances by which the unknown seemed to wish to devour him; but if he had encountered that basilisk eye he would have comprehended the danger of his position. Too passionately excited to think of himself, Auguste bowed, went down the stairs and returned home, endeavoring to find a meaning in the connection of these three persons,—Ida, Ferragus and Madame Jules; an occupation which was practically equivalent to that of trying to arrange the outlandish bits of wood of a Chinese puzzle without possessing the key to the game. But Madame Jules had seen him, Madame Jules went there, Madame Jules had lied to him. Maulincour determined to go and pay a visit to this woman the next day, she could not refuse to see him, he was now her accomplice, he had his hands and feet in this mysterious intrigue; he already assumed to himself the power of a sultan, and thought of demanding imperiously from Madame Jules all her secrets.

In those days Paris was seized with the building fever. If Paris is a monster, it is certainly the most maniacal of monsters. It becomes enamored of a thousand fancies; sometimes it falls to building like a great seigneur who loves a trowel; then it drops its trowel and becomes all military, it dresses itself from head to foot as a National Guard, drills and smokes; then all at once it abandons the military manœuvres and throws away its cigar; then it plunges into desolation, falls into bankruptcy, sells its furniture on the Place du Châtelet, stops payment; but a few days later it arranges its affairs, puts itself in festival array and dances. One day it eats barley-sugar by handfuls, by mouthfuls; yesterday it bought *papier Weynen;* to-day, the monster has the tooth-ache and applies an alexipharmic to all its walls; to-morrow it will lay in its provision of pectoral paste. It has its manias for the month, for the season, for the year, like its manias for a day. So at this moment all the world was building and demolishing something, we scarcely know what as yet. There were very few streets in which could not be seen scaffoldings with long poles, furnished with planks set on cross-pieces and fixed from floor to floor in holes cut in the masonry,—a frail construction, shaken by the Limousins, but held together by ropes all white with plaster, scarcely secured from the wheels of carriages by the breastwork of planks, that enclosure required by law which is not built. There is something maritime in all these masts, these ladders, these cordages and the shouts of the masons. So, now at a dozen steps from the Hôtel Maulincour, one of these ephemeral constructions was erected before a house which was being built in cut stone. The next morning, at the moment when the Baron de Maulincour passed in his cabriolet before this scaffolding, on his way to see Madame Jules, a stone, two feet square, which had been elevated to the topmost landing escaped from the ropes which held it by turning on itself, and fell on the baron's servant, whom it crushed behind his carriage. A cry of horror shook both the scaffold and the masons; one of the latter, in danger of death, clung with difficulty to one of the poles and seemed to have been injured by the stone. A crowd collected promptly. All the masons came down, crying, swearing and saying that the cabriolet of Monsieur de Maulincour had caused the jar to their crane. Two inches more and the officer would have had his head crushed by the stone. The valet was dead, the carriage shattered. It was an event for the whole quarter, the newspapers made the most of it. Monsieur de Maulincour, certain that he had not touched the building, protested. Justice intervened, inquest being made, it was proved that a small boy armed with a lath had mounted guard and called to all foot passengers to keep away. The affair ended there. Monsieur de Maulincour obtained nothing for his servant, for his fright, and was obliged to remain in his bed for several days; for the back of the carriage in breaking had bruised him seriously, and the nervous shock of the surprise gave him a fever. He did not go to see Madame Jules. Ten days after this event, and when he first went out, he drove to the Bois de Boulogne in his repaired cabriolet when, as he was descending the Rue de Bourgogne at the locality where the sewer opens directly opposite the Chamber of Deputies, the axle-tree broke sharply in the middle, and the baron was driving so rapidly that this breakage caused the two wheels to come together with force enough to break his head;—but he was preserved from this danger by the resistance of the leathern hood. Nevertheless, he was badly wounded in the side. For the second time in ten days he was carried home, half-dead, to the terrified dowager. This second accident gave him a feeling of distrust and he thought, though vaguely, of Ferragus and of Madame Jules. To clear up his suspicions, he kept the broken axle in his room and sent for his carriage-maker. The carriage-maker came, examined the axle, the fracture, and proved two things to Monsieur de Maulincour. First, the axle was not made in his workshop; he furnished none on which he did not engrave the initials of his name, and he could not explain by what means this axle had been substituted for the other. Secondly, the breakage of this suspicious axle had been caused by a chamber, a species of hollow space, by blow-holes in the metal and by flaws, very skilfully managed.

"Eh! Monsieur le Baron, who ever did that was mighty malicious," said he, "to fix up an axle-tree that way, any one would swear to look at it that the axle was sound—"

Monsieur de Maulincour requested his carriage-maker to say nothing of this affair, and he considered himself duly warned. These two attempts at assassination had been planned with an ability which denoted the enmity of intelligent minds.

"It is war to the death," he said to himself as he turned in his bed, "a war of savages, a war of surprises, of ambuscades, of treachery, declared in the name of Madame Jules. To what sort of man does she then belong? What kind of power does this Ferragus then wield?"

In fact Monsieur de Maulincour, though a soldier and a brave man, could not repress a shudder. In the midst of the many thoughts which now assailed him there was one against which he felt he had neither defense nor courage: would not poison be ere long employed by his secret enemies? Under the influence of these fears, which his momentary weakness, his fever, and the low diet increased still more, he sent for an old woman long attached to the service of his grandmother, a woman who had for him one of those semi-maternal affections, the sublime or the commonplace. Without confiding in her wholly, he charged her to buy secretly and daily in different localities the food he needed, directing her to keep it under lock and key and to bring it to him herself, not allowing anyone, no matter who, to approach her while preparing it. In short, he took the most minute precautions to protect himself against that form of death. He was confined to his bed, alone and ill; he had therefore the leisure to think of his own security, the only necessity sufficiently clear-sighted to enable human egotism to forget nothing. But the unfortunate invalid had poisoned his own life by this dread; and, in spite of himself, suspicion dyed all his hours with its gloomy tints. These two lessons of assassination did, however, instruct him in one of the virtues most necessary to politic men, he understood the wise dissimulation that must be practiced in dealing with the great interests of life. To be silent about our own secrets is nothing; but to be silent from the first, to know how to forget a fact for thirty years, if it is necessary, as did Ali Pacha, in order to be sure of a vengeance meditated for thirty years,—this is a fine study in a country in which there are but few men who know how to keep their own counsel for thirty days. Monsieur de Maulincour no longer lived but through Madame Jules. He was perpetually occupied in examining seriously the means which he could employ in this mysterious struggle to triumph over the mysterious adversaries. His secret passion for that woman grew by reason of all these obstacles. Madame Jules was ever there, erect, in the midst of his thoughts, in the centre of his heart, more attractive now by reason of her presumable vices than by the certain virtues which had constituted her his idol.

The sick man, wishing to reconnoitre the positions of the enemy, thought he might without danger initiate the old vidame into the secrets of his situation. The old commander loved Auguste as a father loves his wife's children; he was shrewd, dexterous; he had a diplomatic intelligence. He listened to the baron, shook his head, and they both held counsel. The worthy vidame did not share his young friend's confidence, when Auguste said to him that in the times in which they now lived the police and the government were able to decipher all mysteries, and that if it were absolutely necessary to have recourse to these powers he would find in them most powerful auxiliaries.

The old man replied:

"The police, my dear boy, is the most incompetent thing in the world, and the government is the most feeble of all in matters concerning individuals. Neither the police nor the government can read hearts. That which might be reasonably asked of them is to search for the causes of an act. Now, the government and the police are eminently unfitted for this task; they lack essentially that personal interest which reveals all to him who has need of knowing all. No human power can prevent an assassin or a poisoner from reaching either the heart of a prince or the stomach of an honest man. The passions make the best police."

The commander strongly advised the baron to set out for Italy, to go from Italy to Greece, from Greece to Syria, from Syria into Asia, and not to return until after he had succeeded in convincing his secret enemies of his repentance, and by so doing make tacitly his peace with them; if not, to remain in his house and even in his own room where he would be safe from the attempts of this Ferragus, and not to leave it until he could crush him in perfect safety. "An enemy should never be touched except to crush his head," said he gravely.

Nevertheless, the old man promised his favorite to employ all the astuteness with which Heaven had provided him in order to, without compromising anyone, reconnoitre the enemy's ground, examine his strength, and pave the way for victory. The commander had in his service an old retired Figaro, the wildest monkey that ever assumed a human form, formerly as clever as a devil, capable bodily as a galley-slave, alert as a thief, sly as a woman, but now fallen into the decadence of genius for want of practice since the new constitution of Parisian society which has reformed even the valets of comedy. This Scapin-Emeritus was attached to his master as to a superior being; but the shrewd old vidame added a good round sum yearly to the wages of his former provost of gallantry, a little attention which strengthened the ties of natural affection by the bonds of self-interest, and procured for the old gentleman a care which the most loving mistress would not have been able to discover for her sick friend. It was this pearl of the old-fashioned comedy valets, relic of the last century, and auxiliary incorruptible from lack of passions to satisfy, in whom the commander and Monsieur de Maulincour now put their trust.

"Monsieur le Baron will spoil all," said this great man in livery when called into counsel. "Let Monsieur eat, drink and sleep in peace. I take the whole matter upon myself."

In fact, eight days after the conference, when Monsieur de Maulincour, perfectly recovered from his indisposition, was breakfasting with his grandmother and the vidame, Justin entered to make his report. As soon as the dowager had returned to her own apartments, he said with that mock modesty which men of talent affect:

"Ferragus is not the name of the enemy who

is pursuing Monsieur le Baron. This man, this devil, is called the Sieur Gratien-Henri-Victor-Jean-Joseph Bourignard. The Sieur Gratien Bourignard is a former master-builder, once very rich and above all one of the handsomest men of his day in Paris, a Lovelace capable of seducing Grandison. My information stops there. He has been a simple workman, and the companions of the Order of the Dévorants at one time elected him for their chief under the title of Ferragus XXIII. The police ought to know that, if the police were instituted to know anything. This man has moved, no longer lives in the Rue des Vieux-Augustins, and roosts now in the Rue Joquelet; Madame Jules Desmarets goes to see him frequently; often enough her husband, on his way to the Bourse, drives her as far as the Rue Vivienne, or she drives her husband to the Bourse. Monsieur le Vidame knows too much about these things to require me to tell him if it is the husband who takes the wife, or the wife who takes her husband; but Madame Jules is so pretty that I will bet on her. All this is positively certain. My Bourignard often plays at Number 129. Saving your presence, Monsieur, he is a rogue who loves the women, and he has his little ways like a man of condition. As for the rest, he often wins, disguises himself like an actor, makes himself as old as he likes, and in short leads the most original life in the world. I don't doubt that he has a good many lodgings, for most of the time he manages to evade what Monsieur le Vidame calls *Parliamentary investigation.* If Monsieur wishes, he could nevertheless be disposed of honorably, seeing what his habits are. It is always easy to get rid of a man who loves women. However this capitalist talks about moving again.—Now, have Monsieur le Vidame and Monsieur le Baron any other commands to give me?"

"Justin, I am satisfied with you, don't go any farther in the matter without orders; but keep a close watch here so that Monsieur le Baron may have nothing to fear.—My dear boy," resumed the vidame, addressing Maulincour, "go back to your old life and forget Madame Jules."

"No, no," said Auguste, "I will not yield to Gratien Bourignard, I will have him bound hand and foot and Madame Jules also."

That evening, the Baron Auguste de Maulincour, recently promoted to a higher rank in a company of the Gardes du Corps, went to a ball at the Elysée-Bourbon, given by Madame la Duchesse de Berri. There, certainly, no danger could lurk for him. The Baron de Maulincour when he came out had, nevertheless, an affair of honor on his hands, an affair which it was impossible to arrange amicably. His adversary, the Marquis de Ronquerolles, had the strongest reasons for being dissatisfied with Auguste, and Auguste had given him cause by his former liaison with the sister of Monsieur de Ronquerolles, the Comtesse de Sérizy. This lady, who did not love German sentimentality, was all the more exacting in the least details of matters of prudery. By one of those inexplicable fatalities, Auguste uttered a harmless jest which Madame de Sérizy took amiss, and which her brother resented. The discussion took place in a corner, with lowered voices. In good society, the two adversaries never make any disturbance. The very next day, the Faubourg Saint-Honoré, the Faubourg Saint-Germain and the Château discussed this affair. Madame de Sérizy was warmly defended, and all the blame was laid on Maulincour. August personages intervened. Seconds of the highest distinction were imposed on Messieurs de Maulincour and de Ronquerolles, and every precaution was taken on the ground that no one should be killed. When Auguste found himself face to face with his adversary, a man of pleasure, to whom no one could possibly deny honorable sentiments, he could not bring himself to see in him the instrument of Ferragus, Chief of the Dévorants, but he was compelled by a secret power to obey an inexplicable presentiment in questioning the Marquis.

"Messieurs," he said to the seconds, "I certainly do not refuse to meet the fire of Monsieur de Ronquerolles; but before doing so I here declare that I was in error, I offer to him whatever excuses he may require of me, publicly even, if he wishes it, because when the matter concerns a woman nothing I think can degrade a man of honor. I therefore appeal to his generosity and his good sense; is there not something rather silly in fighting when the rightful cause may lose?—"

Monsieur de Ronquerolles would not admit that the affair could be finished in this manner, and then the baron, his suspicions strengthened, approached his adversary.

"Well, then, Monsieur le Marquis," he said, "pledge me, before these gentlemen, your word as a gentleman that you do not bring into this meeting any other reason for vengeance than that which is made public?"

"Monsieur, that is no question to ask me."

And Monsieur de Ronquerolles took his place. It was agreed in advance that the two adversaries were to be satisfied with one exchange of shots. Monsieur de Ronquerolles, in spite of the distance determined by the seconds, which seemed to make the death of Monsieur de Maulincour very problematical, not to say impossible, brought down the baron. The ball traversed the latter's body, two fingers' breadth below the heart, but fortunately without fatal injury.

"You aim too well, Monsieur," said the officer of the Guards," to be avenging only dead quarrels."

Monsieur de Ronquerolles believed Auguste to be a dead man, and he could not refrain from smiling sardonically as he heard these words.

"The sister of Julius Cæsar, Monsieur, should not be suspected."

"Always Madame Jules," replied Auguste.

He fainted, without being able to utter a biting jest which expired on his lips; but although he lost a great deal of blood, his wound was not dangerous.

At the end of a fortnight, during which the dowager and the vidame lavished upon him those cares of old age the secret of which can be given only by long experience in life, his grandmother, one morning, dealt him a heavy stroke. She revealed to him the mortal anxieties which were oppressing her old, her last days. She had received a letter, signed "F," in which the history of the secret espionage to which her grandson had lowered himself, was recounted step by step. In this letter, actions unworthy of an honorable man were ascribed to Monsieur de Maulincour. He had, it said, placed an old woman at the stand of hackney-coaches in the Rue de Ménars, an old spy, who pretended to sell water from her cask to the coachmen, but who was really there to watch the actions of Madame Jules Desmarets. He had spied upon the most inoffensive man in the world in order to detect his secrets, when on these secrets depended the life or the death of three persons. He had brought upon himself a relentless struggle, in which, already wounded three times, he would inevitably succumb because his death had been sworn and would be sought by all human means. Monsieur de Maulincour could no longer even avoid his fate by promising to respect the mysterious life of these three persons, because it was impossible to believe in the word of a gentleman capable of descending to the level of a police-spy; and for what reason? to trouble without cause the life of an innocent woman and of a harmless old man. The letter itself was as nothing for Auguste in comparison with the tender reproaches with which the old Baroness de Maulincour overwhelmed him. To betray a want of respect for and confidence in a woman, to spy upon her actions without having any right to do so! And ought a man ever to spy upon the woman by whom he is loved? It was a tirade of excellent reasons which never prove anything, and which, for the first time in his life, threw the young baron into one of those great human furies in which are born, and from which issue, the most important actions of life.

"Since this duel is one to the death," said he in conclusion, "I shall have to kill my enemy by all the means which I may have at my disposal."

The old commander went immediately to interview in the name of Monsieur de Maulincour the chief of the secret police of Paris and, without bringing either the name or the person of Madame Jules into the narrative, although she was in reality the secret spring of it all, he made him aware of the fears which had been inspired in the family of de Maulincour by the unknown person who was bold enough to swear the death of an officer of the Guard, in defiance of the laws and the police. The police official pushed up his green spectacles in amazement, blew his nose several times, offered snuff to the vidame, who for the sake of his dignity pretended not to use snuff, although his own nose was lined with it. Then the chief took notes, and promised, Vidocq and his bloodhounds aiding, that he would render a very good account to the family de Maulincour of this enemy in a few days, saying that there were no mysteries for the police of Paris. A few days after this the chief came to see Monsieur le Vidame at the Hôtel Maulincour, and found the young baron completely recovered from his last wounds. Then he conveyed to them, in bureaucratic style, his thanks for the indications which they had had the goodness to give him and informed them that this Bourignard was a convict, condemned to twenty years' hard labor, but who had miraculously escaped from a gang which was being transported from Bicêtre to Toulon. For thirteen years the police had been vainly endeavoring to recapture him, after having become aware that he had returned with the greatest hardihood to live in Paris, where he had been able to escape the most active search, although he was constantly implicated in many dark intrigues. However, this man, whose life offered the most curious details, would certainly be seized in one or other of his several domiciles and delivered up to justice. The bureaucrat terminated his official report by saying to Monsieur de Maulincour that if he attached enough importance to this affair to wish to witness the capture of Bourignard he might come the next day, at eight o'clock in the morning, to a house in the Rue Sainte-Foi of which he gave him the number. Monsieur de Maulincour dispensed with going in search of this certainty, trusting, with the sacred respect inspired by the police of Paris, to the promptness of the authorities. Three days later, having read nothing in the newspapers concerning this arrest, which, however, should have furnished matter for a curious article, Monsieur de Maulincour was beginning to feel certain anxieties, which were dissipated by the following letter:

"Monsieur le Baron,

"I have the honor to announce to you that you need have no further fear touching the affair in question. The man named Gratien Bourignard, otherwise called Ferragus, died yesterday at his lodgings, Rue Joquelet, No. 7. Those suspicions which we naturally conceived as to his identity have been completely set at rest by the facts. The physician of the Prefecture of Police was detailed by us to assist the physician of the Mayor's office, and the chief of the detective police made all the necessary verifications to obtain absolute certainty. Moreover, the high character of the witnesses who signed the certificate of death, and the affidavits of those who took care of the said Bourignard in his last moments, among others that of the worthy Vicar of the church of the Bonne-Nouvelle, to whom he made his last confession, for he died a Christian, do not permit us to entertain the least doubts.
"Accept, Monsieur le Baron, etc."

Monsieur de Maulincour, the dowager and the vidame breathed again, with an unspeakable pleasure. The good old woman embraced her grandson, shedding a tear and left him to thank God in prayer. The dear old dowager, who was making a novena for Auguste's safety, believed her prayers were answered.

"Well," said the old commander, "now you can go to the ball of which you were speaking to me, I have no longer any objections to offer."

※

Monsieur de Maulincour was all the more eager to go to this ball because Madame Jules would be there. This fête was given by the Prefect of the Seine, in whose salon the two social worlds of Paris met as on neutral ground. Auguste traversed the rooms without seeing the woman who exercised so great an influence on his life. He entered a boudoir as yet deserted, where the card tables were waiting for the players, and he seated himself on a divan, giving himself up to the most contradictory thoughts of Madame Jules. A man suddenly took the young officer by the arm and the baron was stupefied to see the pauper of the Rue Coquillière, the Ferragus of Ida, the lodger in the Rue Soly, the Bourignard of Justin, the convict of the police, the dead man of the day before.

"Monsieur, not a cry, not a word," said Bourignard, whose voice he recognized, although it certainly would have seemed unknown to any other.

He was elegantly dressed, wore the order of the Golden Fleece and a decoration on his coat.

"Monsieur," he resumed in a voice which was sibilant like that of a hyena, "you authorize all my efforts against you by calling the police to your aid. You will perish, Monsieur. It is necessary. Do you love Madame Jules? Are you beloved of her?

By what right do you trouble her peaceful life and blacken her virtue?"

Someone entered the room. Ferragus rose to go.

"Do you know this man?" asked Monsieur de Maulincour, seizing Ferragus by the collar.

But Ferragus quickly disengaged himself, took Monsieur de Maulincour by the hair and shook him scoffingly by the head several times.

"Must you absolutely have lead in it to render it wise?" said he.

"Not personally, Monsieur," replied de Marsay, the witness of this scene; "but I know that he is Monsieur de Funcal, a very rich Portuguese."

Monsieur de Funcal had disappeared. The baron followed in pursuit without being able to overtake him, and when he reached the peristyle he saw Ferragus, who regarded him with a jeering laugh from a brilliant equipage, which was driven away at high speed.

"Monsieur, if you please," said Auguste, re-entering the salon and addressing de Marsay, whom he knew, "where does Monsieur de Funcal live?"

"I do not know, but someone here can no doubt inform you."

The baron, having questioned the Prefect, ascertained that the Comte de Funcal lived at the Portuguese Embassy. At this moment, while he still felt the icy finger of Ferragus in his hair, he saw Madame Jules in all her dazzling beauty, fresh, gracious, artless, resplendent with that womanly sanctity which had won his love. This creature, infernal to him, no longer excited in his soul any emotion but hatred, and this hatred overflowed, bloody, terrible, in his eyes; he watched for the moment when he could speak to her without being overheard by anyone, and then said to her:

"Madame, here are already three times that your *bravi* have missed me—"

"What can you mean, Monsieur?" she replied reddening. "I know that several unfortunate accidents have happened to you, which I have greatly regretted; but how could I have had anything to do with them?"

"You knew then that there were *bravi* sent against me by the man of the Rue Soly?"

"Monsieur!"

"Madame, now I will not be alone in calling you to account, not for my happiness, but for my blood—"

At this moment Jules Desmarets approached.

"What are you saying to my wife, Monsieur?"

"Come to enquire at my house if you are curious, Monsieur."

And Maulincour went out, leaving Madame Jules pale and almost fainting.

There are very few women indeed who have not found themselves, at least once in their lives, apropos of some undeniable fact, confronted with a direct, sharp uncompromising interrogation, one of those questions pitilessly asked by their husbands and of which the apprehension alone gives a chill, of which the very first word enters the heart like the steel of a dagger. Hence this maxim, "All women lie." Officious falsehood, venial falsehood, sublime falsehood, horrible falsehood,—but always the obligation to lie. This obligation once admitted, is it not necessary to know how to lie well? French women do it admirably. Our customs so readily teach them deception! And then, woman is so naïvely impertinent, so pretty, so graceful, so truthful in her lying; she recognizes so fully the utility of it in order to avoid, in social life, the violent shocks which happiness might not be able to resist that it is as necessary to her as the cotton-wool in which she puts away her jewels. Falsehood becomes for women, thus, the foundation of speech, and truth is only an exception; they use it, just as they are virtuous, through caprice or by calculation. Moreover, according to their individual character, some women laugh in lying, some others weep, these become grave, those grow angry. After beginning life by feigning indifference to the homage that flatters them the most, they often end by lying to themselves. Who has not admired their apparent superiority to everything at the very moment when they are trembling for the mysterious treasures of their love? Who has never studied their ease, their facility, their freedom of spirit in the greatest embarrassments of life? With them, nothing is borrowed; deception flows as easily as the snow falls from the sky. Then with what art do they discover the truth in others! With what cleverness do they employ the most direct logic in answer to some passionate question which has revealed to them the secret of the heart of a man who is guileless enough to proceed by questioning them! To question a woman, is not that to deliver one's self up to her? Will she not learn all which we seek to hide from her, and will she not know how to be silent in speaking? And some men have the pretension of being able to struggle with a Parisian woman! With a woman who knows how to hold herself above all dagger-thrusts, saying,— *"You are very inquisitive! What does it matter to you? Why do you wish to know? Ah! you are jealous! And suppose I do not choose to answer you?"*—in short, with a woman who possesses the hundred and thirty-seven thousand manners of saying "NO," and incommensurable variations of the word, "YES." The treatise on the "Yes" and the "No," is it not one of the finest works, diplomatic, philosophic, logographic and moral, which still remains for us to write? But to accomplish this diabolic work, will not an androgynous genius be necessary? For that reason, probably, it will never be attempted. Besides, of all unpublished works, is not that the best known and the best practiced among women? Have you ever studied the behavior, the pose, the *disinvoltura* of a falsehood? Examine it. Madame Desmarets was seated in the right hand corner of her carriage, and her husband in the left corner. Having forced herself to recover from her emotion in coming out of the ball-room, Madame Jules now affected a calm demeanor. Her husband had said nothing to her, and he still said nothing. Jules looked out of the carriage window at the black walls of the silent houses before which he passed; but suddenly, as if driven by a determining thought, in turning the corner of a street he examined his wife who appeared to be cold in spite of the fur-lined pelisse in which she was wrapped; he thought she seemed pensive, and perhaps she really was pensive. Of all those things which are communicable, reflection and gravity are the most contagious.

"What was it, that Monsieur de Maulincour said to you that could affect you so keenly?" said Jules; "and why does he wish me to go to his house and find out?"

"He can tell you nothing in his house that I cannot tell you here," she replied.

Then, with that feminine craft which always slightly degrades virtue, Madame Jules waited for another question. Her husband turned his face to the houses again and continued his study of the porte-cochères. Another question, would it not be a suspicion, a distrust? To suspect a woman is crime in love; Jules had already killed a man without having doubted his wife. Clémence did not know all there was of true passion, of deep reflection, in her husband's silence, just as Jules was ignorant of the wonderful drama that was wringing the heart of his Clémence. And the carriage rolled on through a silent Paris, bearing two lovers who adored each other, and who, softly reclining on the same silken cushions, were nevertheless separated by an abyss. In these elegant coupés returning from a ball between midnight and two o'clock in the morning, how many curious and singular scenes must pass,—restricting ourselves only to those coupés whose lanterns light both the street and the carriage, those with their windows unshaded, in short the coupés of legitimate love, in which the couples can quarrel without fearing to be seen by the passers-by, because the civil code gives the right to provoke, to beat, or to kiss a wife in a carriage or elsewhere, anywhere, everywhere! How many secrets must be thus revealed to nocturnal pedestrians, to those young men who have gone to a ball in a carriage, but are obliged, for whatever cause it may be, to return on foot. It was the first time that Jules and Clémence had found themselves thus, each in a corner. Usually the husband pressed close to his wife.

"It is very cold," said Madame Jules.

But her husband did not hear her. He was studying all the black signs above the shop windows.

"Clémence," he said at last. "Forgive me the question I am about to ask you."

He came closer, took her by the waist and drew her towards him.

"My God! it is coming!" thought the poor woman.

"Well," she said aloud, anticipating the question, "you wish to learn what Monsieur Maulincour said to me. I will tell you Jules, but not without terror. *Mon Dieu*, is it possible that we should have secrets from each other? For the last few moments I have seen you struggling between your conviction of our love and vague fears; but that conviction is clear within us, is it not, and your suspicions, do they not seem to you dark and unnatural? Why not remain in that clear light of confidence which pleases you? When I have told you all, you will still desire to know more; and yet I myself do not know what was hidden beneath the extraordinary words of that man. And what I fear is, that this may lead to some fatal affair between you. I would much prefer that we both forget this unpleasant moment. But in any case, swear to me that you will let this singular adventure explain itself naturally. Monsieur de Maulincour declared to me that the three accidents of which you have heard,—the falling of a stone on his servant, the breaking down of his cabriolet, and his duel about Madame de Sérizy—were the result of some plot I had laid against him. Then he threatened to reveal to you the notion which inclined me to assassinate him. Can you imagine what all this means? My emotion came from the impression produced upon me by the sight of his face expressive of insanity, his haggard eyes and his words broken by some violent inward emotion. I thought him mad. This is all. Now, I should not be a woman if I had not perceived that for more than a year I had become, as they call it, the passion of Monsieur de Maulincour. He has never seen me except at a ball, and our intercourse had always been insignificant, like that which one has at balls. Perhaps he wishes to disunite us, so that he may find me at some future time alone and unprotected. There, see already you are frowning! Oh, how cordially I hate society. We were so happy without him! why take any notice of him? Jules, promise me to forget all this. To-morrow we shall no doubt hear that Monsieur de Maulincour has gone mad."

"What a singular affair!" thought Jules as he descended from the carriage under the peristyle of his stairway.

He gave his arm to his wife, and together they went up to their apartments.

To develop this history in all its truth of detail, and to follow its course through all its windings, it is necessary here to divulge some of love's secrets, to glide beneath the ceilings of a marriage chamber, not shamelessly, but like Trilby, frightening neither Dougal nor Jeannie, alarming no one, being as chaste as our noble French language requires, as bold as was the pencil of Gérard in his painting of *Daphnis and Chloe*. The bedroom of Madame Jules was a sacred spot. Herself, her husband, and her maid alone entered it. Opulence has some noble privileges, and the most enviable are those which permit the development of the sentiments to their fullest extent, fertilizing them by the accomplishment of their thousand caprices, surrounding them with that brilliancy which enlarges them, with those refinements which purify them, with those delicacies which render them still more alluring. If you hate dinners on the grass and meals ill-served, if you experience a pleasure at the sight of a damask cloth of a dazzling whiteness, a silver gilt service, porcelains of exquisite purity, of a table served with gold, rich with chased silverware, lighted by transparent candles, where miracles of the most exquisite cookery are served under covers with armorial bearings,—you must, to be consistent, leave the garrets at the tops of the houses, the grisettes in the streets, abandon the garrets, the grisettes, the umbrellas and pattens to those people who pay for their dinners with tickets; then you will be able to comprehend love as a principle which only develops in all its grace on carpets of the Savonnerie, beneath the opal light of an alabaster lamp, between guarded and discreet walls hung with silk, before a gilded hearth in a chamber deafened to the sounds of the neighbors, street and everything by shades, by shutters, by billowy curtains. You will require mirrors in which to show the play of form, and in which may be repeated infinitely the woman whom we would multiply, and whom love often multiplies; then very low divans; then a bed which, like a secret, is divined without being shown; then, in this coquettish chamber are fur-lined slippers for naked feet, wax candles under glass with muslin draperies, by which to read at all hours of the night, and flowers, not those oppressive to the head, and linen, the fineness of which might have satisfied Anne of Austria. Madame

Jules had realized this delightful programme, but that was nothing. Any woman of taste could have done as much, although, nevertheless, there was in the arrangement of these details a stamp of personality, which gives to this ornament, to that detail, a character that cannot be imitated. To-day more than ever reigns the fanaticism of individuality. The more our laws tend to an impossible equality, the more we get away from it in our manners and customs. Thus, the rich people in France are beginning to become more exclusive in their tastes and in their belongings than they have been for the last thirty years. Madame Jules knew well to what this programme tended, and had arranged everything about her in harmony with a luxury that suits so well with love. The *Quinze Cents Francs et Ma Sophie,* or love in a cottage, are the dreams of starvelings to whom black bread suffices in their present state, but who, become gourmands if they really love, end by carving all the luxuries of gastronomy. Love holds toil and poverty in horror. It would rather die than live from hand to mouth. Most women returning from a ball, impatient for their beds, throw off anywhere their gowns, their faded flowers, their bouquets, the fragrance of which has now departed. They leave their little shoes beneath a chair, walk about in loose slippers, take out their combs and let their hair roll down as it will. Little they care if their husbands see the clasps, the hair pins, the artful props which supported the elegant edifice of the hair and of its dressing. No more mysteries,—everything is let down before the husband, there is no longer any embellishing for the husband. The corset—the most part of the time strictly cared for—lies where it is thrown if the too sleepy maid forgets to take it away with her. Then the whalebone bustle, the oiled silk protections under the sleeves, the pads, the false hair sold by the coiffeur, all the false woman, is there, scattered about in open sight. *Disjecta membra poetæ*, the artificial poetry so much admired by those for whom it has been conceived, elaborated, the fragments of the pretty woman, litter all the corners of the room. To the love of a husband who yawns, the actual woman presents herself, also yawning, in an inelegant disorder and with a tumbled nightcap, that of last night, that of to-morrow night also:

"For, really Monsieur, if you want a pretty nightcap to rumple every night, give me some more pin-money."

There's life as it is! A woman is always old and unpleasing to her husband, but always dainty, elegant and adorned for the other, for that rival of all husbands, for that world which calumniates and tears to shreds her sex. Inspired by a true love, for love has like other beings its instinct of self-preservation, Madame Jules did very differently, and found in the constant benefits of her happy state the necessary impulse to accomplish all those minute personal duties which ought never to be relaxed, because they perpetuate love. These cares, these duties, do they not proceed moreover from a personal dignity which is ravishingly becoming? Are they not subtle flatteries, is this not to respect in one's self the beloved one? So Madame Jules had denied to her husband all access to her dressing-room where she changed her ball dress, and whence she issued dressed for the night, mysteriously adorned for the mysterious fêtes of her heart. In entering the chamber, which was always elegant and graceful, Jules saw there a woman coquettishly enveloped in an elegant peignoir, her hair simply wound in heavy coils around her head; for, not fearing to disarrange them, she guarded them neither from the sight nor the touch of love; a woman always more simple, more beautiful then, than she was before the world; a woman who had found refreshment in her bath, and whose only artifice consisted in being whiter than her muslins, fresher than the freshest perfume, more seductive than the most skilful courtesan, in short, always tender and therefore always loved. This admirable understanding of a wife's business was the great secret of Josephine's charm for Napoleon, as it was in former times that of Cæsonia for Caius Caligula, of Diane de Poitiers for Henri II. But, if it was largely productive for women who have counted seven or eight lustres, what a weapon it is in the hands of young women! A husband gathers with delight the rewards of his fidelity.

So now, on returning home after this conversation which had chilled her with fear and which still gave her the keenest anxiety, Madame Jules took particular pains with her toilet for the night. She wished to make herself, and she did make herself, enchanting. She girdled the batiste of her peignoir slightly opening the corsage, let her black hair fall on her rounded shoulders; her perfumed bath had given her an intoxicating fragrance; her bare feet were in velvet slippers. Strong in her sense of her advantages, she came in, stepping softly, and put her hands over her husband's eyes whom she found standing thoughtfully in his dressing-gown, his elbow on the mantel and one foot on the fender. She said in his ear, warming it with her breath and biting the end of it gently with her teeth:

"What are you thinking about, Monsieur?"

Then, clasping him closely, she enveloped him with her arms to tear him away from his evil thoughts. The woman who loves has a full knowledge of her power; and the more virtuous she is the more effectual is her coquetry.

"About you," he answered.

"Only about me?"

"Yes."

"Oh, that is a very bold 'Yes'"

They went to bed. As she fell asleep Madame Jules said to herself:

"Decidedly, Monsieur de Maulincour will be the cause of some evil. Jules is preoccupied, disturbed, and nursing thoughts he does not tell me."

It was about three o'clock in the morning when she was awakened by a presentiment which had struck her heart as she slept. She had a perception, at once physical and moral, of her husband's absence. She did not longer feel the arm which Jules passed beneath her head, that arm on which she had slept, peaceful and happy for five years, and which she never wearied. A voice had said to her, "Jules suffers, Jules is weeping—" She raised her head and then sat up, felt that her husband's place was cold, and saw him sitting before the fire, his feet on the fender, his head resting on the back of an armchair. He had tears on his cheeks. The poor woman threw herself hastily from her bed and sprang at a bound to her husband's knee.

"Jules, what is it? Are you suffering—speak! tell me! speak to me if you love me."

And in a moment she poured out to him a hundred words expressive of the deepest tenderness.

Jules knelt at the feet of his wife, kissed her knees, her hands, and answered her with fresh tears:

"My dear Clémence, I am most unhappy! It is not loving to distrust your mistress, and you are my mistress. I adore you, and suspect you.—The words which that man said to me this evening have struck to my heart; they stay there in spite of myself, to confound me. There is underneath it all some mystery. In short, and I blush for it, your explanations have not satisfied me. My reason offers me a certain light which my love causes me to reject. It is an awful combat. Could I stay there, holding your head and suspecting thoughts within it, to me unknown?—Oh, I believe in you, I believe in you," cried he, quickly, seeing her smile sadly and open her mouth as if to speak. "Do not say anything to me—reproach me with nothing. From you, the least word would kill me. Besides, could you say a single thing to me which I have not said to myself for the last three hours? Yes, for three hours I have been here, watching you as you slept, so beautiful, admiring your forehead, so pure, so peaceful. Oh! yes, you have always told me all your thoughts, have you not? I alone am in your soul. While I look at you, while my eyes can plunge into yours, I see all plainly. Your life is always as pure as your glance is clear. No, there is no secret behind those transparent eyes."

And he rose and kissed them softly.

"Let me avow to you, my dearest, that for the last five years that which has increased my happiness day by day was the knowledge that you had none of those natural affections which always take away a little from love. You had no sister, nor father, nor mother, nor companion, and I was therefore neither above nor below any one else in your heart; I was there alone. Clémence, repeat to me all those sweet things of the spirit you have so often said to me; do not blame me, console me, I am unhappy. I have certainly an odious suspicion with which to reproach myself, and you—you have nothing in your heart to inflame you. My beloved, tell me, could I rest thus beside you? Could two heads united as ours have been, lie on the same pillow when one was suffering and the other tranquil?—What are you thinking of?" he cried abruptly observing that Clémence was anxious, confused, and could not restrain her tears.

"I am thinking of my mother," she answered in a grave voice. "You will never know, Jules, the sorrow of your Clémence obliged to remember the dying farewells of her mother in hearing your voice, the sweetest of all music; and in thinking of the solemn pressure of the icy hand of a dying one in feeling the caresses of yours, at the moment when you overwhelm me with the assurances of your delightful love."

She raised her husband, took hold of him, strained him to her with a nervous force much greater than that of a man, kissed his hair, and covered it with her tears.

"Ah! I would be hacked to pieces for you! Tell me that I make you happy, that I am to you the most beautiful of women, that I am a thousand women for you. But you are loved as no other man ever will be. I do not know the meaning of the words *duty*, and *virtue*. Jules, I love you for yourself, I am happy in loving you, and I will love you more and more until my last breath. I have pride in my love, I feel that I am destined to have only one sentiment in my whole life. What I am going to say to you is dreadful perhaps,—I am glad to have no child, and I do not wish for any. I feel myself more wife than mother. Well! then, have you fears? Listen to me, my love, promise me to forget, not this hour of mingled tenderness and doubt, but the words of that madman. Jules, I wish it. Promise me not to see him, not to go to him. I have a conviction that if you make one step more into this maze, we shall both roll into an abyss in which I shall perish, but with your name upon my lips and your heart in my heart. Why do you hold me so high in your soul and yet so low in reality? How is it that you, who give credit to so many as to money, cannot give up to me the beggarly gift of a suspicion; and, for the first occasion in your life in which you might prove to me a boundless faith, you dethrone me in your heart! Between a madman and me, it is the madman whom you believe!—Oh Jules—"

She stopped, threw back the hair that fell about her brow and her neck, then in a heart-rending tone she added:

"I have said too much, one word should suffice. If your soul and your forehead still keep this cloud, however light it may be, know well that I shall die of it!"

She could not repress a shudder and turned pale.

"Oh! I will kill that man," thought Jules, as he lifted his wife in his arms and carried her to her bed.—"Let us sleep in peace my angel," he continued. "I have forgotten all, I swear it to you."

Clémence fell asleep to the music of these sweet words, more softly repeated. Jules, as he watched her sleeping, said in his heart:

"She is right, when love is so pure, a suspicion blights it. For that soul so fresh, for that brow so tender, a blemish, yes, that would mean death."

When, between two beings filled with affection for each other and whose lives are in constant communion, a cloud has come, although this cloud may be dissipated, it leaves in these souls some trace of its passage. Either, the mutual tenderness becomes more living, as the earth is rejuvenated after the shower; or, the shock still echoes like distant thunder through a cloudless sky; but it is impossible to recover absolutely the former life, and it will inevitably happen that love will either increase or diminish. At breakfast, Monsieur and Madame Jules showed to each other those particular attentions in which there is always a little affectation. There were glances full of a gaiety which seemed almost forced, and which seemed to be the efforts of persons endeavoring to deceive themselves. Jules had involuntary doubts, and his wife had positive fears. Nevertheless, sure of each other, they had slept. Was this strained condition the effect of a want of faith, or of the memory of their nocturnal scene? They did not know themselves. But they loved each other, they loved each other so purely that the impression at once cruel and beneficent of that scene could not fail to leave its traces in their souls; both of them eager to make those traces disappear, and each wishing to be *the first* to return to the other, they could not yet fail to think of the first cause, of this first discord. For loving souls, this is not grief, pain is still far distant; but it is a sort of mourning which is difficult to depict. If there are indeed relations between colors and the agitation of the soul, if, as Locke's blind man said, scarlet produces on the sight the effects produced on the ear by a fanfare of trumpets, it may perhaps be permissible to compare this reaction of melancholy to soft gray tones. But love saddened, love in which remains a true sentiment of its happiness momentarily troubled, gives voluptuous pleasure which, derived from pain and pleasure both, are all novel. Jules studied his wife's voice, he watched her glances with the freshness of feeling that had inspired him in the earliest moments of his passion for her. The memory of five perfectly happy years, the beauty of Clémence, the candor of her love, promptly effaced in her husband's mind the last vestiges of an intolerable pain.

This next day was Sunday, a day on which there was no Bourse and no business; the two therefore passed the whole day together, getting farther into each others' hearts than they had ever yet done, like two children who in a moment of fear hold each other tightly, pressing together, and clasp each other united by a common instinct. There are in this life of two in one, completely happy days, due to chance, without any connection with yesterday or to-morrow, ephemeral flowers!—Jules and Clémence enjoyed this delicious day as though they had a foreboding that it would be the last of their loving life. What name shall we give to that unknown power which hastens the steps of the traveler before the storm is yet visible, which makes the dying resplendent with life and with beauty a few days before his death and inspires him with the most joyous projects for the future, which tells the midnight student to turn up his lamp while it still shines brightly, which makes a mother to fear the too thoughtful look cast upon her infant by an observing man? We are all affected by this influence in the great catastrophes of our life and we have not yet either named or studied it; it is something more than presentiment and it is not yet sight. All went well until the following day. On Monday, Jules Desmarets, obliged to go to the Bourse at his usual hour, did not depart without asking his wife according to his custom if she wished to be driven anywhere in his carriage.

"No," she said, "the day is too unpleasant to go out."

In fact, it was raining in torrents. It was about half-past two when Monsieur Desmarets reached the Exchange and the Treasury. At four o'clock, in coming out of the Bourse, he found himself face to face with Monsieur de Maulincour, who was waiting for him there with that feverish pertinacity which is the result of hatred and vengeance.

"Monsieur, I have important communications to make to you," said the officer taking the broker by the arm. "Listen to me, I am too loyal a man to have recourse to anonymous letters which would trouble your peace of mind, I prefer to speak to you in person. Moreover, believe that if it were not a question of my life I certainly should not interfere in any manner with the private affairs of a household, even if I thought I had the right to do so."

"If what you have to say to me concerns Madame Desmarets," replied Jules, "I request you, Monsieur, to be silent."

"If I am silent, Monsieur, you may before long see Madame Jules on the prisoners' bench at the Court of Assizes, by the side of a convict. Now do you wish me to be silent?"

Jules turned pale, but his noble countenance instantly resumed a calm which was now false; then, drawing the officer under one of the temporary shelters of the Bourse near which they were standing, he said to him in a voice which concealed his intense inward emotion:

"Monsieur, I will listen to you, but there will be between us a duel to the death, if—"

"Oh! to that I consent," cried Monsieur de Maulincour. "I have the greatest esteem for you. You speak of death, Monsieur? You are doubtless ignorant that your wife perhaps caused me to be poisoned last Saturday evening. Yes, Monsieur, since day before yesterday something extraordinary has developed in me; my hair appears to distill in me through my head a fever and a deadly languor, and I know perfectly well what man touched my hair during the ball."

Monsieur de Maulincour then related, without omitting a single fact, his platonic love for Madame

Jules and the details of the adventure which began this narrative. Any one would have listened to him with as much attention as did the broker. But the husband of Madame Jules had good reason to be more amazed than any other human being. Here, his character displayed itself, he was more amazed than overwhelmed. Made a judge, and the judge of an adored woman, he found in his soul the equity of a judge, as he took the inflexibility of one. A lover still, he thought less of his own shattered life than of that of this woman; he listened not to his own anguish but to the far-off voice that cried to him, "Clémence cannot lie! Why should she betray you?"

"Monsieur," said the officer of the guards in concluding, "being absolutely certain of having recognized Saturday evening in Monsieur de Funcal that Ferragus whom the police declared dead, I have put immediately on his traces an intelligent man. As I returned home I remembered by a fortunate chance the name of Madame Meynardie, mentioned in the letter of that Ida, the presumed mistress of my persecutor. Supplied with this one clue my emissary will soon discover for me the facts of this horrible affair, for he is far more able to discover the truth than the police themselves."

"Monsieur," replied the broker, "I do not know how to thank you for this confidence. You say that you can obtain proof, witnesses, I shall await them. I shall seek courageously the truth of this strange affair, but you will permit me to doubt everything until the evidence of these facts is proven to me. In any case, you shall have satisfaction, as you must know that such is demanded by both."

Jules returned home.

"What is the matter?" said his wife to him. You are so pale you frighten me."

"The day is cold," he answered walking with a slow step into that chamber in which everything spoke of happiness and of love, that chamber so calm in which was gathering a deadly tempest.

"You have not been out to-day?" he asked as though mechanically.

He was impelled to ask this question, doubtless, by the last of a thousand thoughts which had secretly gathered themselves together into a meditation, lucid although it was actively prompted by jealousy.

"No," she answered with a false accent of candor.

At that moment Jules saw in the dressing-room of his wife some drops of rain on the velvet bonnet which she wore in the morning. He was a passionate man, but he was also full of delicacy, and it was repugnant to him to bring his wife face to face with a lie. In such a situation, everything is finished for life between certain beings. And yet these drops of rain were like a flash which tore open his brain.

He left the room, went down to the porter's lodge and said to his concierge, after making sure that they were alone:

"Fouquereau, a hundred crowns of pension if you tell me the truth, dismissal if you deceive me, and nothing at all if, having told me the truth, you ever speak of my question and your answer."

He stopped to examine the concierge's face, leading him to the light of the window, and resumed:

"Did Madame go out this morning?"

"Madame went out at a quarter to three, and I think I saw her come in about half an hour ago."

"That is true, upon your honor?"

"Yes, Monsieur."

"You will have the pension which I promised you; but if you speak of this, remember my promise, you will lose all."

Jules returned to his wife.

"Clémence," he said to her, "I find I must put my household accounts in order, do not be offended at the inquiry I am going to make. Have I not given you forty thousand francs since the beginning of the year?"

"More," she said, "forty-seven."

"Have you found use for them all?"

"Why, yes," she replied. "In the first place, I had to pay several of our last year's bills—"

"I shall never find out anything in this way," thought Jules, "I am not taking the best course."

At this moment his valet de chambre entered and handed him a letter, which he opened indifferently, but which he read eagerly as soon as his eyes had lighted on the signature.

"MONSIEUR,

"For the sake of your peace of mind as well as of our own I have taken the liberty of writing to you without possessing the advantage of being known to you; but my position, my age, and the fear of some misfortune compel me to entreat you to have some indulgence in the unfortunate circumstances in which our afflicted family now finds itself. Monsieur Auguste de Maulincour has for the last few days shown signs of mental derangement, and we fear that he may trouble your happiness by fancies which he has confided to us, Monsieur le Commandeur de Pamiers and myself, during his first attacks of fever. We think it right therefore to warn you of his malady, which is without doubt still curable; but it will have such grave and important effects on the honor of our family and the future of my grandson that I count on your entire discretion. If Monsieur le Commandeur or I, Monsieur, had been able to go to your house we would not have written; but I have no doubt that you will regard the prayer which is here made to you by a mother, to burn this letter.

"Accept the assurance of my distinguished consideration,

BARONNE DE MAULINCOUR, née DE RIEUX."

"How many tortures!" cried Jules.

"But what is passing in your mind?" asked his wife, exhibiting the deepest anxiety.

"I have come," he answered, "to ask myself whether it can be you who have sent me this notice to divert my suspicions," he went on, throwing the letter to her. "Judge therefore what I suffer!"

"Unhappy man," said Madame Jules, letting fall the paper, "I pity him, although he has done me great harm."

"You know that he has spoken to me?"

"Oh, you have been to see him, in spite of your promise?" she cried, struck with terror.

"Clémence, our love is in danger of perishing, and we are outside of all the ordinary rules of life, let us then lay aside all petty considerations in presence of the great perils. Listen, tell me why you went out this morning? Women think they have the right to tell us, sometimes, little falsehoods. Do they not like to amuse themselves often by concealing pleasures which they are preparing for us? Just now you said to me, by mistake no doubt, one word for another, a no for a yes."

He went into the dressing-room and brought out the bonnet.

"See, now! without wishing to play here the part of Bartholo, your bonnet has betrayed you. These spots, are they not rain drops? You must, therefore, have gone out in a street cab, and you must have received these drops of water either in going out to seek one, or entering the house to which you went, or in leaving it. But a woman can leave her own house most innocently, even after she has told her husband that she would not go out. There are so many reasons for changing our plans! To have caprices, is not that one of your rights? You are not obliged to be consistent with yourself. You had forgotten something, a service to render, a visit, or some kind action to do. But nothing hinders a woman from telling her husband what she has done. Does one ever blush on the breast of a friend? Well, it is not the jealous husband who speaks to you, my Clémence, it is the lover, it is the friend, it is the brother."

He flung himself passionately at her feet.

"Speak, not to justify yourself, but to calm my horrible suffering. I know well that you went out. Well, what did you do? Where did you go?"

"Yes, I went out, Jules," she answered in an altered voice, although her face was calm. "But ask me nothing more. Wait with confidence; without which you will lay up for yourself eternal remorse. Jules, my Jules, confidence is the virtue of love. I own to you that in this moment I am too much troubled to answer you; but I am not an artful woman, and I love you, you know it."

"In the midst of all that can shake the faith of a man and rouse his jealousy, for I am not then the first in your heart, I am not then yourself?—Well, Clémence, I still prefer to believe you, to believe your voice, to believe your eyes! If you deceive me, you deserve—"

"Oh! a thousand deaths," she said, interrupting him.

"I hide from you none of my thoughts, and you, —you—"

"Hush!" she said, "our happiness depends upon our mutual silence."

"Ah! I will know all," he cried in a violent access of rage.

At that moment the cries of a woman were heard and the yelping of a shrill little voice came from the ante-chamber to the ears of husband and wife.

"I will enter, I tell you!" it cried. "Yes, I shall enter, I wish to see her, I will see her!"

Jules and Clémence rushed into the salon and they saw the door violently opened. A young woman entered suddenly, followed by two servants who said to their master:

"Monsieur, this woman would come in in spite of us. We told her that Madame was not at home. She answered that she knew very well that Madame had been out but she had seen her come in. She threatened to stay at the door of the house till she could speak to Madame."

"You can go," said Monsieur Desmarets to his domestics.

"What do you want, Mademoiselle?" he added, turning to the unknown.

This *demoiselle* was the type of a woman who is to be met with nowhere but in Paris. She is made in Paris, like the mud, like the pavement of Paris, as the water of the Seine is manufactured in Paris in grand reservoirs through which human industry filters it ten times before delivering it to the cut glass carafes in which it sparkles so clear and pure, from the muddiness that it had. She is therefore a creature truly original. Depicted scores of times by the painter's brush, the pencil of the caricaturist, the plumbago of the designer, she still escapes all analysis because she cannot be caught and rendered in all her moods, like nature, like this fantastic Paris. In fact, she holds to vice by but one spoke and breaks away from it at all the thousand other points of the social circumference. Moreover, she only lets one trait of her character be known, the only one which renders her blamable; her fine virtues are hidden; in her naïve shamelessness she glories. Incompletely rendered in dramas and tales in which she is put upon the scene with all her poesy, she is nowhere really true but in her garret, because she is always calumniated or over-praised elsewhere. Rich, she deteriorates; poor, she is misunderstood. And this could not be otherwise! She has too many vices and too many good qualities; she is too near to a sublime asphyxiation or to a degrading laugh; she is too beautiful and too hideous; she personifies too well Paris, to which she furnishes the toothless portresses, the washwomen, the char-women, beggars, occasionally insolent countesses, admired actresses, applauded singers; she has even given in the olden time two quasi-Queens to the monarchy. Who can grasp such a Proteus? She is all woman, less than woman, more than woman. From this vast portrait the painter of manners can take but certain details, the *ensemble* is the infinite. She was a grisette of Paris, but the grisette in all her splendor; the grisette in a hackney-coach, happy, young, handsome, fresh, but a grisette with claws, with scissors, impudent as a Spanish woman, quarrelsome as a prudish English woman proclaiming her conjugal rights, coquettish as a great lady, moreover frank and ready for everything; a real *lionne* issuing from the little apartment of which she had so often dreamed, with its red calico curtains, its Utrecht velvet-covered furniture, the tea-table, the cabinet of china with painted designs, the sofa, the little moquette carpet, the alabaster clock and candlesticks under glass, the yellow bed-room, the eider-down quilt,—in short all the joys of a grisette's life; the housekeeper, a former grisette herself but a grisette with mustaches and chevrons; the theatre parties, the marrons unlimited, the silk dresses, the bonnets to spoil; in short, all the felicities imagined over the counter of the modiste, except the carriage, which only appears in the dreams of the counter as a marshal's bâton does in those of a soldier. Yes, this grisette had all these things in return for a true affection, or in spite of a true affection, as some others obtain it for an hour a day,—a sort of tax carelessly paid under the claws of an old man. The young woman who was now in the presence of Monsieur and Madame Jules had a foot so uncovered in her shoe that only a slim black line was visible between the carpet and her white stocking. This peculiar footgear, which the Parisian caricature has so well rendered, is a special attribute of the Parisian grisette; but she is still better revealed to the eyes of an observer by the care with which her garments are made to adhere to her form, which they clearly define. Thus the unknown was, not to lose the picturesque expression invented by the French soldier, tied into a greenish dress with a yoke which revealed the beauty of her corsage perfectly visible; for her shawl of Ternaux cashmere, fallen to the floor, was only retained by the two corners which she held twisted around her wrists. She had a delicate face, rosy cheeks, a clear skin, sparkling gray eyes, a round and very prominent forehead, hair carefully smoothed which escaped from under her little bonnet in heavy curls upon her neck.

"My name is Ida, Monsieur. And if that is Madame Jules to whom I have the advantage of speaking, I've come to tell her all I have in my heart against her. It is very wrong when one is set up and when one is in her furniture, as you are here, to wish to take away from a poor girl a man with whom I am as good as married, morally, and who talks of repairing his wrongs by marrying me before the Municipality. There are plenty of handsome young men in the world, ain't there, Monsieur? to please her fancies without wishing to take from me a man of middle-age who makes my happiness. *Quien!* I haven't got a fine hôtel, I— I have my love! I hate handsome men and money, I'm all heart, and—"

Madame Jules turned to her husband:

"You will allow me, Monsieur, not to hear any more of this," she said, re-entering her bedroom.

"If that lady lives with you, I have made a mess of it, I see; but so much the worser," resumed Ida. "Why does she come to see Monsieur Ferragus every day?"

"You deceive yourself, Mademoiselle," said Jules stupefied. "My wife is incapable—"

"Ha, so you are married—you two!" said the

grisette, showing some surprise. "Then it is much worse, Monsieur, isn't it, for a woman who has the happiness of being married in legal marriage to have relations with a man like Henri—"

"But what, Henri?" said Jules, taking Ida and leading her into an adjoining room that his wife might hear no more.

"Why, Monsieur Ferragus—"

"But he is dead," said Jules.

"Nonsense! I went to Franconi's with him yesterday evening and he brought me home, as he should. Besides, your wife can give you news of him. Didn't she go to see him at three o'clock? I know she did; I waited for her in the street, all because that good-natured man, Monsieur Justin, whom you know perhaps, a little old man with seals, who wears corsets, warned me that I had Madame Jules for a rival. That name, Monsieur, is well known among the fictitious ones. Excuse me since it is yours, but if Madame Jules was a Duchess of the Court, Henri is so rich that he could satisfy all her fancies. My business is to protect my property, and I have the right to; for love him, Henri, I do. He's my first inclination, and it concerns my happiness and all my future fate. I fear nothing, Monsieur; I am honest and I have never lied nor stolen the property of any living soul. If it was an Empress who was my rival I'd go straight to her; and if she carried away my future husband I feel capable of killing her, all empress as she was, because all pretty women are equals, Monsieur,—"

"Enough, enough," said Jules. "Where do you live?"

"Rue de la Corderie-du-Temple, No. 14, Monsieur. Ida Gruget, corset-maker at your service, for we make lots of corsets for men."

"And where does he live, the man whom you call Ferragus?"

"But, Monsieur," said she pursing up her lips, "in the first place he's not a man. He's a monsieur, much richer than you are, perhaps. But why do you ask me his address, when your wife knows it? He told me not to give it. Am I obliged to answer you?—I am not, thank God, neither in a confessional nor a police court, and I'm responsible only to myself."

"And if I were to offer you twenty, thirty, forty thousand francs to tell me where Monsieur Ferragus lives?"

"O! no, O *no*, my little friend, and that ends the matter!" she said, emphasizing this singular reply with a popular gesture. "There is no sum that would make me tell that. I have the honor to bid you good day. How does one get out of here?"

Jules, overwhelmed, allowed Ida to depart without thinking further of her. The whole world seemed to crumble beneath his feet; and over his head the heavens were falling in fragments.

"Monsieur is served," said his valet.

The valet and the footman waited in the dining-room a quarter of an hour without seeing their master or mistress.

"Madame will not dine to-day," said the waiting-maid, coming in.

"What's the matter, Joséphine?" asked the valet.

"I don't know," she answered. "Madame is crying, and is going to bed. Monsieur has no doubt some affair on hand in the city, and it has been discovered at a very bad time, do you understand? I wouldn't answer for Madame's life. Men are so clumsy! They're always making scenes without any precaution."

"That's not so," replied the valet in a low voice, "on the contrary it is Madame who,—you understand? What time does Monsieur have to go after pleasure, he who for five years hasn't slept out of Madame's room once; who goes to his office at ten o'clock and only leaves it at noon for déjeuner? His life is all known, it is regular, while Madame goes out nearly every day at three o'clock, no one knows where."

"And Monsieur, too," said the maid taking her mistress's part.

"But Monsieur goes straight to the Bourse. Here's three times that I've told him that dinner was ready," continued the valet after a pause, "and you might as well speak to a post."

Jules entered.

"Where is Madame?" he inquired.

"Madame is going to bed, her head aches," replied the maid, assuming an air of importance.

Jules then said very composedly, addressing his domestics:

"You can take it all away, I shall go and sit with Madame."

And he returned to his wife's room, where he found her weeping but endeavoring to smother her sobs in her handkerchief.

"Why do you weep?" said Jules to her. "You need expect from me neither violence nor reproaches. Why should I avenge myself? If you have not been faithful to my love, it is that you were never worthy of it—"

"Not worthy!"

These words repeated made themselves heard through her sobs, and the accent in which they were said would have moved any other man than Jules.

"To kill you, it would be necessary to love more than perhaps I do," he continued; "but I should never have the courage, I would kill myself rather, leaving you to your—happiness, and to—to whom?"

He did not end his sentence.

"Kill yourself!" cried Clémence, flinging herself at the feet of Jules and clasping them.

But he, wishing to escape this embrace, tried to shake her off, dragging her in so doing toward the bed.

"Let me alone," he said.

"No, no! Jules," she cried. "If you love me no longer I shall die. Do you wish to know all?"

"Yes."

He took her, grasped her violently, and sat down on the edge of the bed holding her between his legs;

then looking with a dry eye at that beautiful face, now red as fire though furrowed with tears:

"Now speak," he said.

Clémence's sobs began again.

"No, it is a secret of life and death. If I tell it, I—No I cannot. Have mercy, Jules!"

"You are still deceiving me—"

"Yes, Jules you may think that I am deceiving you, but soon you will know all."

"But this Ferragus, this convict, whom you go to see, this man enriched by crime, if he does not belong to you, if you do not belong to him—"

"Oh Jules!—"

"Well, is he your mysterious benefactor, the man to whom we owe our fortune, as has already been said?"

"Who said that?"

"A man whom I killed in a duel."

"Oh, God! one death already."

"If he is not your protector, if he does not give you money, if it is you who carry it to him, tell me, is he your brother?"

"What if he were?" she said.

Monsieur Desmarets crossed his arms.

"Why should that have been concealed from me?" he resumed. "Then you have both deceived me, your mother and you? Besides, does a woman go to see her brother every day or nearly every day, eh?"

His wife had fainted at his feet.

"Dead," he said. "And if I were mistaken?"

He sprang to the bell rope, called Joséphine, and lifted Clémence to the bed.

"I shall die of it," said Madame Jules, recovering consciousness.

"Joséphine," cried Monsieur Desmarets, "send for Monsieur Desplein. Then you will go to my brother and ask him to come here as soon as possible."

"Why your brother?" asked Clémence.

Jules had already left the room.

*

For the first time in five years Madame Jules slept alone in her bed, and was compelled to admit a physician into that sacred chamber. These in themselves were two keen pangs. Desplein found Madame Jules very ill, never had a violent emotion been more untimely. He would not say anything definite, and postponed his opinion until the morrow, after leaving a few directions which were not carried out, the emotions of the heart causing all bodily cares to be forgotten. When morning dawned Clémence had not yet slept. She was absorbed in the low murmur of a conversation which lasted several hours between the two brothers; but the thickness of the walls allowed no word which could betray the object of this long conference to reach her ears. Monsieur Desmarets, the notary, went away at last. The stillness of the night and the singular activity of the senses given by strong emotion enabled Clémence to distinguish the scratching of a pen and the involuntary movements of a man engaged in writing. Those who are habitually up at night and who observe the different acoustic effects produced in absolute silence know that often a slight echo can be readily perceived in the same places where equable and continued murmurs are not distinct. At four o'clock the sound ceased. Clémence rose, anxious and trembling. Then, with bare feet and without a wrapper, forgetting her moistened skin and her condition, the poor woman opened softly the door without making any noise. She saw her husband, a pen in his hand, sound asleep in his arm-chair. The candles had burned to the sockets. She slowly advanced and read on an envelope already sealed:

THIS IS MY WILL.

She kneeled down as if before a grave, and kissed the hand of her husband, who woke instantly.

"Jules, my dear, they grant some days to criminals condemned to death," she said looking at him with eyes lit up with fever and with love. "Your innocent wife only asks for two. Leave me free for two days, and—wait! After that I shall die happy,—at least you will regret me."

"Clémence, I grant them."

And then, as she kissed her husband's hand in a touching transport of her heart, Jules, under the spell of this cry of innocence, took her in his arms and kissed her on the forehead, thoroughly ashamed to feel himself still under the power of this noble beauty.

On the morrow, after taking a few hours' rest, Jules entered his wife's room, obeying mechanically his custom of not leaving the house without seeing her. Clémence was asleep. A ray of light passing through a chink in the upper blind of the windows fell on the face of this overburdened woman. Already suffering had impaired her forehead and the fresh redness of her lips. A lover's eye could not mistake the appearance of dark blotches and a sickly pallor which had replaced the uniform tone of the cheeks and the smooth whiteness of the skin, two pure pages on which were revealed so artlessly the sentiments of this beautiful soul.

"She suffers," thought Jules. "Poor Clémence, may God protect us!"

He kissed her very softly on the forehead. She woke, saw her husband and remembered all; but, unable to speak, she took his hand and her eyes filled with tears.

"I am innocent," said she, ending her dream.

"You will not go out to-day?" asked Jules.

"No, I feel too weak to leave my bed."

"If you should change your mind, wait till I return," said Jules.

Then he went down to the porter's lodge.

"Fouquereau, you will watch your door to-day closely, I wish to know exactly who comes to the house and who leaves it."

Then he threw himself into a hackney-coach, caused himself to be driven to the Hotel de Maulincour and there asked for the baron.

"Monsieur is ill," he was told.

Jules insisted on entering, gave his name; and, if he could not see Monsieur de Maulincour, he wished to see the vidame or the dowager. He waited some time in the salon of the old baroness, who came to see him and told him that her grandson was much too ill to receive him.

"I know, Madame," replied Jules, "the nature of his illness from the letter which you did me the honor to write to me, and I beg you to believe—"

"A letter to you, Monsieur! written by me!" cried the dowager, interrupting him; "but I have written no letter. And what was I made to say, Monsieur, in that letter?"

"Madame," replied Jules, "intending to see Monsieur de Maulincour to-day and to return you this letter I thought it best to preserve it in spite of the injunction with which it ends. There it is."

The dowager rang for her spectacles, and the moment she cast her eyes on the paper she exhibited the greatest surprise.

"Monsieur," she said, "my writing is so perfectly imitated that if the matter were not so recent I might be deceived myself. My grandson is ill, it is true, Monsieur; but his reason has never been the least bit in the world affected. We are the puppets of some evil persons; and yet I cannot imagine the object of this impertinence.—You shall see my grandson, Monsieur, and you will at once perceive that he is perfectly sound in his mind."

And she rang the bell again and sent to ask if the baron could receive Monsieur Desmarets. The valet returned with an affirmative answer. Jules ascended to the apartment of Auguste de Maulincour, whom he found seated in an arm-chair near the fire, and who, too feeble to rise, saluted him with a melancholy gesture; the Vidame de Pamiers was sitting with him.

"Monsieur le Baron," said Jules, "I have something to say to you of such a nature as to make it desirable that we should be alone."

"Monsieur," replied Auguste, "Monsieur le Commandeur knows all about this affair and you can speak fearlessly before him."

"Monsieur le Baron," resumed Jules in a grave voice, "you have troubled, well nigh destroyed my happiness, without having any right to do so. Until the moment when we shall be able to see which of us should demand or should grant reparation to the other you are bound to help me in following the dark and mysterious path into which you have flung me. I have now come to ascertain from you the present residence of the mysterious being who exercises such a fearful influence on our destinies and who seems to have at his orders a supernatural power. On my return home yesterday, after hearing your statements, I received this letter."

And Jules handed him the forged letter.

"This Ferragus, this Bourignard, or this Monsieur de Funcal, is a demon!" cried Maulincour after having read it. "Into what a frightful maze have I put my foot? Where am I going?—I did wrong, Monsieur," he added looking at Jules; "but death is certainly the greatest of all expiations, and my death is approaching. You can then ask me whatever you desire, I am at your orders."

"Monsieur, you should know where this unknown lives, I wish positively to penetrate this mystery, even if it should cost me my whole fortune; and in presence of an enemy so cruelly intelligent every moment is precious."

"Justin shall tell you all," replied the baron.

At these words the Commander fidgeted in his chair.

Auguste rang the bell.

"Justin is not in the house," cried the vidame with a hastiness that revealed much.

"Well then," said Auguste excitedly, "the other servants must know where he is, send a man on horseback to find him. Your valet is in Paris, isn't he? He can be found."

The Commander was visibly distressed.

"Justin cannot come, my dear boy," said the old man. "He is dead. I wished to conceal this accident from you, but—"

"Dead!" cried Monsieur de Maulincour, "dead? And when? And how?"

"Last night. He had been supping with some old friends and was doubtless drunk; his friends, as full of wine as he, left him lying in the street. A heavy vehicle ran over him—"

"The convict did not miss him. At the first stroke he killed him," said Auguste. "He has not been so lucky with me, he has been obliged to try four times."

Jules became gloomy and thoughtful.

"I shall not know anything, then," he cried after

a long pause. "Your valet has perhaps been justly punished! Did he not exceed your orders in calumniating Madame Desmarets to a person named Ida, whose jealousy he roused in order to turn her loose upon us."

"Ah! Monsieur in my anger I abandoned Madame Jules to him."

"Monsieur!" cried the husband, keenly irritated.

"Oh! at present, Monsieur," replied the officer claiming silence by a gesture of the hand, "I am ready for all. You cannot make any better that which is already done, and you cannot tell me anything that my own conscience has not already said to me. I am now expecting this morning the most celebrated of professors of toxicology, in order to learn my fate. If I am doomed to intolerable suffering, my resolution is taken, I shall blow out my brains."

"You talk like a child," cried the Commander, horrified by the coolness with which the baron said these words. "Your grandmother would die of grief."

"Then, Monsieur," said Jules, "there is no means of discovering in what part of Paris this extraordinary man resides?"

"I think, Monsieur," replied the old man, "from what I have heard poor Justin say, that Monsieur de Funcal lived at the Portuguese Embassy or at that of Brazil. Monsieur de Funcal is a gentleman who belongs to both those countries. As for the convict, he is dead and buried. Your persecutor, whoever he is, seems to me so powerful that it would be well for you to accept him under his new shape until the moment when you will have the power of confounding and of crushing him; but act with prudence, my dear Monsieur. If Monsieur de Maulincour had followed my advice, nothing of all this would have happened."

Jules retired coldly but with politeness, and now knew of no means to take to reach Ferragus. As he passed into his own house his concierge told him that Madame had gone out to throw a letter into the post box at the head of the Rue de Ménars. Jules felt himself humiliated at this proof of the great intelligence with which his concierge espoused his cause and the cleverness with which he guessed the way to serve him. The zealousness of servants and their peculiar skill in compromising masters who compromise themselves, were known to him, the danger of having them for accomplices, no matter for what purpose, he fully appreciated; but he could not think of his personal dignity until the moment when he found himself thus suddenly degraded. What a triumph for the slave incapable of raising himself to his master, to bring down his master to his own level! Jules was harsh and hard. Another fault. But he suffered so deeply! His life, till this moment so upright, so pure, was becoming crooked, and he was obliged now to scheme and to lie. And Clémence also lied and schemed. It was a moment of immense disgust.

Lost in an abyss of bitter thoughts, Jules stood mechanically motionless at the door of his house. At one moment, yielding to his despair, he thought of fleeing, of leaving France, carrying with his love all the illusions of uncertainty. Then, not doubting that the letter thrown into the post box by Clémence was addressed to Ferragus, he searched for a means of gaining possession of the answer which that mysterious being would send. Then, in analyzing the singular good fortune of his life since his marriage, he asked himself whether the calumny for which he had taken such signal vengeance was not a truth. Finally, reverting to the coming answer from Ferragus, he said to himself:

"But this man so profoundly capable, so logical in his least acts, who sees, who foresees, who calculates and divines our very thoughts, this Ferragus, is he likely to send an answer? Will he not be more likely to employ some other means more in keeping with his power? Will he not send his answer by some skilful rascal, or perhaps in a package brought by some honest man who does not suspect what he brings, or in some parcel of shoes which a shop-girl may innocently deliver to my wife? If Clémence and he have some understanding between them?"

And he distrusted everything, and his mind ran over the immense fields, the shoreless oceans, of conjecture; then, after having floated for a time among a thousand contradictory ideas, he felt he was strongest in his own house, and he resolved to keep watch in it as an ant-lion does at the bottom of his sandy labyrinth.

"Fouquereau," he said to his concierge, "I am not at home to any one who comes to see me. If any one wishes to see Madame or brings anything for her, you will ring twice. And you will bring me all letters that are addressed here, no matter for whom they are intended.—Thus," he thought as he mounted to his study which was in the entresol, "I will foil the schemes of Maître Ferragus. If he sends some messenger clever enough to ask for me, so as to find out if Madame is alone, at least I shall not be tricked like a fool."

He concealed himself in the windows of his study which looked out on the street and then by a final scheme inspired by jealousy he resolved to send his head clerk in his own carriage to the Bourse, in his place, with a letter to another broker, one of his friends, in which he explained his purchases and sales and requested him to attend to them for that day. He postponed his more delicate transactions till the morrow, careless of the fall or rise of stocks and of the debts of all Europe. High privilege of love! it crushes all things, everything pales before it,—the altar, the throne, and the consols. At half-past three o'clock, just at the hour in which the Bourse is in full blast of reports, monthly settlements, premiums, leases, etc., Jules saw Fouquereau enter his study, quite radiant.

"Monsieur, an old woman has just come, but *take care*, I think she's a sly one. She asked for

Monsieur, seemed much annoyed not to find him in, then she gave me a letter for Madame, and here it is."

In a feverish anxiety Jules tore open the letter; then he fell into his chair overcome. The letter was mere nonsense throughout and it would have required a key to read it. It was written in cipher.

"You can go, Fouquereau."

The concierge went out.

"It is a mystery, deeper than the sea where there are no soundings. Ah! it must be love, love only is so sagacious, so ingenious, as this correspondent. My God! I shall kill Clémence."

At this moment a happy idea flashed through his brain with such brilliancy that he felt almost physically illuminated by it. In the days of his toilsome poverty, before his marriage, Jules had made for himself a true friend, a half *Péméja* The extreme delicacy with which he had managed the susceptibilities of a man both poor and modest, the respect with which he had surrounded him, the ingenious address with which he had nobly compelled him to share his own opulence without permitting him to blush at it, increased their friendship. Jacquet continued faithful to Desmarets in spite of his wealth.

Jacquet, an upright man, a toiler, austere in his morals, had slowly made his way in that particular ministry which develops at the same time the greatest knavery and the greatest honesty. Holding a situation in the Ministry of Foreign Affairs, he had charge of the most delicate division of its archives. Jacquet was in this ministry a species of glow-worm, casting his light on the secret correspondence, deciphering and classifying despatches. Placed somewhat higher than the mere bourgeois he found in these diplomatic affairs all that there was of the highest in subaltern ranks, and lived in obscurity, happy in a retirement which sheltered him from reverses, and satisfied to be able to pay in this humble manner his debt to the country. Hereditary associate in his mayoralty, he obtained, as the newspapers express it, all the consideration which was due him. Thanks to Jules, his position had been ameliorated by a worthy marriage. An unrecognized patriot, a ministerial one in fact, he contented himself with groaning in his chimney-corner over the course of the government. For the rest, Jacquet was in his own household an easy-going king, a man with an umbrella, who hired for his wife a carriage which he never entered himself. In short, to complete this sketch of this *philosopher without knowing it*, he had not yet suspected, and never would in all his life suspect all the advantages he might have drawn from his position, having for intimate friend a broker and knowing every morning all the secrets of the State. This man, sublime after the manner of that nameless soldier who died in saving Napoléon by a *qui vive*, lived at the ministry.

In ten minutes Jules was in the office of records, Jacquet offered him a chair, placed methodically on the table his green taffeta eye-shade, rubbed his hands, took up his snuff-box, stretched himself till his shoulder blades cracked, swelled out his chest, and said:

"What chance brings you here, *Mosieur* Desmarets? What do you want with me?"

"Jacquet, I have need of you to decipher a secret, a secret of life and death."

"It doesn't concern politics?"

"If it did, I shouldn't come to you for information," said Jules. "No, it is a family matter, concerning which I require of you the most profound silence."

"Claude-Joseph Jacquet, dumb by profession. You are not acquainted with me, then?" he said laughing. "Discretion is my lot."

Jules showed him the letter saying to him:

"You must read me this letter addressed to my wife—"

"The devil, the devil, a bad business," said Jacquet, examining the letter as a usurer examines a note to be negotiated. "Ah! that's a *gridiron* letter. Wait a minute."

He left Jules alone in the office, but returned almost immediately.

"This is silliness, my friend! it is written with an old *gridiron* used by the Portuguese ambassador, under Monsieur de Choiseul, at the time of the dismissal of the Jesuits." Here, see.

Jacquet placed upon the writing a piece of paper, cut out in regular squares like one of those paper-laces which the confectioners wrap around their sugar-plums, and Jules could then read with perfect ease the words that were visible in the interstices:

Have no more anxieties, my dear Clémence, our happiness will not be troubled any more by any one, and your husband will lay aside his suspicions. I cannot come to see you. However ill you may be, you must have the courage to come; make the effort, search for strength; you will find it in your love. My affection for you has induced me to submit to the most cruel of operations, and I cannot leave my bed. I had several moxas applied yesterday evening to the back of my neck, from one shoulder to the other, and it was necessary to let them burn a long time. You understand me? But I thought of you, and I did not suffer too much. To baffle all the investigations of de Maulincour, who will not persecute us much longer, I have left the protecting roof of the Embassy and am now safe from all pursuit in the Rue des Enfants-Rouges, No. 12, with an old woman named Madame Étienne Gruget, mother of that Ida who will pay dearly for her silly prank. Come here to-morrow at nine in the morning. I am in a room which is reached only by an interior staircase. Ask for M. Camuset. Adieu till to morrow. I kiss your forehead my darling.

Jacquet looked at Jules with a sort of honest terror which covered a true compassion and uttered his favorite exclamation in two separate and distinct tones:

"The devil, the devil."

"That seems clear to you, does it not?" said Jules. "Well, there is in the depth of my heart a voice which pleads for my wife, and which makes itself heard above all the pangs of jealousy. I shall endure until to-morrow the most horrible of tortures; but at least to-morrow between nine and ten o'clock I shall know all, and I shall be unhappy or happy for the rest of my life. Think of me then, Jacquet."

"I shall be at your house to-morrow at eight o'clock. We will go there together, and I will wait for you, if you like, in the street. You may run some danger, and you ought to have near you some devoted person who will understand a mere sign and whom you can safely trust. Count on me."

"Even to help me to kill someone?"

"The devil, the devil!" said Jacquet, quickly, repeating, as it were, the same musical note, "I have two children and a wife—"

Jules pressed the hand of Claude-Jacquet and went away. But he returned precipitately.

"I forgot the letter," he said, "but that's not all, it must be resealed."

"The devil, the devil! you opened it without saving the seal, but the impression is luckily deep enough. There, leave it with me, and I will bring it to you *secundum scripturam.*"

"At what time?"

"At half-past five—"

"If I am not yet in, just give it to the concierge and tell him to send it up to Madame."

"Do you want me to-morrow?"

"No, adieu."

Jules arrived promptly at the Place de la Rotonde-du-Temple, he left his cabriolet there and went on foot to Rue des Enfants-Rouges, where he examined the house of Madame Étienne Gruget. There would be cleared up the mystery on which depended the fate of so many persons; Ferragus was there, and to Ferragus led all the threads of this strange intrigue. The coming together of Madame Jules, of her husband and of this man, would it not be the Gordian knot of this already bloody drama, and for which the blade would not be wanting that should cut the most intricate ties?

This house was one of those which belonged to the class called *cabajoutis*. This very significant name is given by the populace of Paris to those houses which are built, as it were, piecemeal. They are nearly always buildings originally separate but afterwards brought together according to the fancy of the various proprietors who have successively enlarged them; or they are houses begun, left unfinished, again built upon, and finally completed; unhappy houses, which have passed, like certain peoples, under several dynasties of capricious masters. Neither the floors nor the windows form an *ensemble*, to borrow from the art of painting one of its most picturesque terms; everything is in discord, even the external decorations. The cabajoutis is to Parisian architecture what the *capharnaüm* is to the apartments, a general receptacle in which all sorts of things are thrown higgledy-piggledy.

"Madame Étienne?" asked Jules of the portress.

This portress had her lodge under the main entrance, in one of those species of chicken coops, a little wooden house on rollers, and sufficiently like those sentry boxes which the police have set up by all the stands of hackney-coaches.

"*Hein?*" said the portress, laying down the stocking she was knitting.

In Paris, the various component parts which make up the physiognomy of any given portion of this monstrous city are admirably in keeping with its general character. Thus, porter, concierge or suisse, whichever name may be given to that essential muscle of the Parisian monster, is always in conformity with the neighborhood of which he is a part, and of which he is often an epitome. Lazy, and with lace on every seam of his coat, the concierge dabbles in stocks on the Faubourg-Saint-Germain; the porter takes his ease in the Chaussée-d'Antin; he reads his newspapers in the Bourse quarter; he has a business of his own in the Faubourg Montmartre. The portress is a former prostitute in the quarter of prostitutes; in the Marais she has morals, is ill-natured and full of whims.

On seeing Jules this portress took a knife to stir the almost extinguished peat in her foot-warmer; then she said to him:

"You want Madame Étienne, is it Madame Étienne Gruget?"

"Yes," said Jules Desmarets, assuming a vexed air.

"Who makes passementerie?"

"Yes."

"Well, then, Monsieur," said she, issuing from

her cage, laying her hand on Jules's arm and leading him to the end of the long dark passage-way vaulted like a cellar, "you will go up the second staircase at the end of the courtyard. Do you see the windows where there are the pots of pinks? That's where Madame Étienne lives."

"Thank you, Madame. Do you think she is alone?"

"But why shouldn't she be alone, that woman? She is a widow."

Jules hastened up a very dark stairway, the steps of which were lumpy with hardened mud left by the feet of those who came and went. On the second floor he saw three doors, but no sign of pinks. Fortunately, on one of the doors the oiliest and the darkest of the three, he read these words written in chalk:

"Ida will come at nine o'clock to-night."

"This is the place," thought Jules.

He pulled an old bell-cord, black with age, with a handle, and heard the smothered sound of a cracked bell and the barking of an asthmatic little dog. The way in which the sounds manifested themselves in the interior announced an apartment encumbered with articles which left no space for the least echo,—a characteristic feature of the lodgings occupied by work-people, by the humble households, in which space and air are always lacking. Jules looked about mechanically for the pinks and finally found them on the outer sill of a sliding window, between two filthy drain-pipes. Here were flowers; here, a garden two feet long and six inches wide; here, a wheat-ear; here, all life epitomized, but here, also, all the miseries of that life. A ray of light, falling from heaven as if by special favor on these shabby flowers and this superb stalk of wheat, brought out in full distinctness the dust, the grease, and that nameless color peculiar to Parisian dens, a thousand uncleanlinesses which enclosed, spotted and made old, the damp walls, the worm-eaten baluster of the stairway, the disjointed window casings and the doors originally painted red. Presently an old woman's cough and the heavy step of a woman shuffling painfully along in list slippers announced the mother of Ida Gruget. This old woman opened the door, came out on the landing, raised her head and said:

"Ah! it's Monsieur Bocquillon. Why no. For sure! how much you are like Monsieur Bocquillon. You are his brother, perhaps. What can I do for you? Come in, Monsieur."

Jules followed this woman into the first room where he saw huddled together cages, household utensils, ovens, furniture, little earthenware dishes full of food or of water for the dog and the cats, a wooden clock, bed-quilts, engravings of Eisen, heaps of old iron, all these things mixed and tumbled together in such a manner as to produce a most grotesque effect, the true capharnaüm of Paris, to which were not lacking even a few old numbers of the *Constitutionnel.*

Jules, instigated by a sense of prudence, paid

no attention to the widow Gruget, who said to him:

"Come in here, Monsieur, and warm yourself."

Fearing to be overheard by Ferragus, Jules asked himself whether it would not be wiser to conclude in this first apartment the arrangement he had come to propose to the old woman. A hen which descended cackling from a loft roused him from his inward meditation. He came to a resolution; he therefore followed Ida's mother into the room with the fireplace, where they were accompanied by the wheezy little pug, a dumb personage, who jumped upon an old stool. Madame Gruget had displayed all the foolishness of semi-pauperism when she invited her visitor to warm himself. Her fire-pot concealed completely two brands sufficiently far apart. The skimmer lay on the ground, the handle in the ashes. The mantel-shelf, adorned with a little wax Jesus under a square glass-case bordered with bluish paper, was piled with wools, bobbins and utensils used in the making of trimmings. Jules examined all the furniture in the room with a curiosity full of interest, and showed in spite of himself a secret satisfaction.

"Well, Monsieur, tell me, do you want to make an arrangement for any of my things?" said the widow seating herself in a yellow cane arm-chair which seemed to be her headquarters.

In it she kept altogether her handkerchief, her snuff-box, her knitting, half-peeled vegetables, spectacles, a calendar, a bit of livery fringe just commenced, a greasy pack of cards, and two volumes of novels, all stuck into the hollow of the back. This article of furniture, in which this old creature *was floating down the river of life,* resembled the encyclopædic bag which a woman carries with her when she travels and in which may be found a compendium of her household belongings, from the portrait of her husband to *eau de Mélisse* for faintness, sugar-plums for the children, and English court-plaster in case of cuts.

Jules studied everything. He looked attentively at the yellow visage of Madame Gruget, at her gray eyes without eyebrows, deprived of lashes, her toothless mouth, her wrinkles black-shaded, her cap of rusty tulle with ruffles still more rusty, her cotton petticoats full of holes, her worn-out slippers, her broken fire-pot, her table heaped with plates and with silks and with unfinished work in cotton and in wool, in the midst of which appeared a bottle of wine. Then he said to himself:

"This woman has some passion, some hidden vice,—she is mine.—Madame," said he aloud, making a sign of intelligence to her, "I have come to order some trimmings of you—"

Then he lowered his voice.

"I know," he continued, "that you have with you an unknown who takes the name of Camuset."

The old woman looked at him suddenly, but without giving the least sign of astonishment.

"Tell me, can he overhear us? Consider that this is a question of a fortune for you."

"Monsieur," she replied, "speak without fear, I have no one here. But if I had anyone up there, it would be impossible for him to hear you."

"Ah! the sly old creature, she knows how to answer like a Norman," thought Jules. "We shall be able to come to an agreement.—Do not give yourself the trouble to lie, Madame," he resumed. "In the first place, you must know that I mean no harm to you, nor to your lodger ill with his moxas, nor to your daughter Ida, the corset-maker, and friend of Ferragus. You see, I know all about it. Reassure yourself, I am not of the police, nor do I desire anything that can hurt your conscience. A young lady will come here to-morrow between nine and ten o'clock, to talk with the friend of your daughter. I want to be where I can see all and hear all, without being seen or heard by them. You will furnish me the means of doing so, and I will reward this service by a sum of two thousand francs paid down, and a yearly annuity of six hundred. My notary shall prepare the deed before you this evening; I will put in his hands your money, he will pay it to you to-morrow after the conference at which I desire to be present and during which I shall acquire proofs of your good faith."

"Will that injure my daughter, my dear Monsieur?" she asked, throwing a suspicious and cat-like glance upon him.

"In no way, Madame. But, moreover, it seems to me that your daughter treats you pretty badly. A girl who is loved by a man as rich and as powerful as Ferragus should find it easy to make you more comfortable than you seem to be."

"Ah! my dear Monsieur, not so much as one poor theatre ticket for the Ambigu or the Gaieté, where she can go as much as she likes. It's shameful! A girl for whom I sold my silver forks and spoons, and I now eat, at my age, with German metal, and all to pay her apprenticeship and give her a trade where she could coin money if she chose. For, as to that, she takes after me, she's as clever as a witch, I must do her that justice. At least she might give over to me her old silk dresses, I who am so fond of wearing silk. No, Monsieur; she goes to the *Cadran Bleu*, dinner at fifty francs a head, rolls in her carriage like a princess, and mocks at her mother as though she were just nothing at all. *Dieu de Dieu!* what heedless young ones we have brought into the world, it is the finest thing that can be said about us. A mother, Monsieur, that is a good mother! for I have hidden her foolishness, and I have always kept her in my bosom, to take the bread out of my mouth and cram everything into her own. Ah! well now, she comes, she wheedles you, she says to you, 'how do you do, Mother.' And there's all her duty paid toward the author of her days. Go along, as I tell you. But she'll have children one of these days, and she'll find out what it is to have such bad baggages, which one can't help loving all the same."

"What! she does nothing for you?"

"Ah, nothing? No, Monsieur, I don't say that;

if she did nothing that would be a little too much. She pays my rent, gives me fire-wood and thirty-six francs a month.—But Monsieur what's that at my age, fifty-two years old, with eyes that ache at night, ought I to be still working? Besides, why won't she have me with her? I should shame her there? Then let her say so. In truth, ought one to be buried out of the way for such dogs of children who have forgotten you even before they've shut the door?"

She pulled her handkerchief out of her pocket and with it a lottery ticket that dropped on the floor; but she hastily picked it up saying:

"Hi! That's the receipt for my taxes."

Jules at once perceived the reason of the sagacious parsimony of which the mother complained, and he was only the more certain that the widow Gruget would agree to the proposed bargain.

"Well, then, Madame," he said, "accept what I offer you."

"You said, Monsieur, two thousand francs in ready money and six hundred annuity?"

"Madame, I've changed my mind and I will promise you only three hundred annuity. This way seems to me more to my interest. But I will give you five thousand francs in ready money. Wouldn't you like that better?"

"Bless me, yes, Monsieur."

"You will have more comfort, and you can go to the Ambigu-Comique, to Franconi's, everywhere, at your ease, in a hackney-coach."

"Ah, I don't like Franconi, for they don't talk there. But, Monsieur, if I accept, it is because it will be very advantageous to my child. At least I shall no longer be an expense to her. Poor little thing, after all, I shouldn't want to take her pleasures from her. Monsieur, youth must amuse itself! and so, if you assure me that I will do no harm to anyone—"

"To no one," repeated Jules. "But now, how will you manage it?"

"Well, Monsieur, by giving to Monsieur Ferragus this evening a little tea made of poppy-heads he'll sleep sound, the dear man! And he has good need of it because of his sufferings, for he does suffer, so that it is a pity. But, too, I should like to know what kind of invention it is for a healthy man to burn his back just to get rid of a tic-douloureux which only torments him once in two years! To get back to our affair, I have my neighbor's key, and her lodging is just above mine and there is a room adjoining the one in which Monsieur Ferragus is lying, with only a partition between them. She is away in the country for ten days. Well, then, in making a hole during the night in the partition-wall you will be able to see them and to hear them at your ease. I am on good terms with a locksmith, a very friendly man, who talks like an angel, and he will do that for me, and no one will know anything about it."

"Here's a hundred francs for him; come this evening to Monsieur Desmarets, a notary, here's his address. At nine o'clock the deed will be ready, but—*motus!*"

"Enough, as you say—*momus! Au revoir,* Monsieur."

Jules returned home almost calmed by the certainty of knowing everything on the morrow. As he entered the house he found in the porter's lodge the letter, perfectly resealed.

"How do you feel now?" he said to his wife, in spite of the coldness which separated them.

The loving habits are so difficult to quit.

"Pretty well, Jules," she replied in a coquettish voice; "will you come and dine beside me?"

"Yes—" he replied, giving her the letter; "here is something that Fouquereau handed me for you."

Clémence, who was pale, colored high when she saw the letter, and this sudden redness caused the keenest pain to her husband.

"Is that joy?" he said laughing, "or the effect of expectation?"

"Oh! of many things," she said, examining the seal.

"I will leave you, Madame."

And he went down to his study, where he wrote to his brother, giving him directions about the annual payment to the widow Gruget. When he returned he found his dinner served on a little table near the bed of Clémence, and Joséphine ready to wait on him.

"If I were up, how I should like to serve you myself!" she said when Joséphine had left them.

"Oh! even on my knees," she added, passing her white hand through her husband's hair. "Dear noble heart, you have been very kind and gracious to me just now. You have done me more good by showing me such confidence than all the doctors on earth could do me with their prescriptions. Your womanly delicacy, for you know how to love like a woman,—well, it has shed I know not what balm in my soul and which has almost cured me. There is a truce between us. Jules, move your head this way, that I may kiss it."

Jules could not deny himself the pleasure of embracing his wife. But it was not without a sort of remorse in his heart; he felt himself small before this woman whom he was still tempted to believe innocent. She displayed a sort of melancholy joy. A tender hope shone on her features through the expression of her grief. They seemed equally unhappy to be obliged to deceive each other; another caress, and they would have been unable longer to resist their suffering and they would have avowed all to each other.

"To-morrow evening, Clémence?"

"No, Monsieur—to-morrow at noon you will know all, and you will kneel down before your wife. Oh no, you shall not be humiliated, no, everything is pardoned; no, you have not been wrong. Listen; yesterday you did cruelly hurt me; but my life perhaps would not have been complete without that agony, it shall be a shadow that shall make brighter our celestial days."

"You bewitch me," cried Jules, "and you will fill me with remorse."

"Poor friend, destiny is stronger than we, and I am not the accomplice of my destiny. I shall go out to-morrow."

"At what hour?" asked Jules.

"At half-past nine."

"Clémence," he said, "take every precaution, consult Doctor Desplein and old Haudry."

"I will consult only my heart and my courage."

"I shall leave you free, and will not come to see you till noon."

"Will you not keep me company a little this evening? I am no longer in pain—"

After having finished his business, Jules returned to his wife, recalled to her by an invincible attraction. His passion was stronger than all his sufferings.

*

The next day, towards nine o'clock, Jules escaped from his own house, hurried to Rue des Enfants-Rouges, went up-stairs and rang the bell of the widow Gruget.

"Ah, you've kept your word, as true as the dawn. Come in, Monsieur," said the old passementerie maker as she recognized him. "I have made you a cup of coffee with cream in case that—" she resumed when the door was closed. "Oh! real cream, a little pot of it that I saw milked myself at the dairy we have in the market des Enfants-Rouges."

"Thank you, Madame, no, not anything. Show me—"

"Well, well, my dear Monsieur. Come this way."

The widow conducted Jules into a room above her own where she showed him triumphantly an opening of the size of a two-franc piece, made during the night in a place corresponding with one of the highest and darkest rosettes in the wall paper of Ferragus's chamber. This opening in both rooms was above a wardrobe, the slight traces of his work left by the locksmith had therefore left no evidence on either side of the wall, and it was very difficult to perceive in the shadow this species of loop-hole. Thus Jules was obliged, in order to look through it, to maintain himself in a rather fatiguing attitude by standing on a tall stool which the widow Gruget had been careful to bring.

"There's a gentleman with him," said the old woman as she retired.

Jules perceived, in fact, a man occupied in dressing a string of wounds produced by a certain number of burnings on the shoulders of Ferragus, whose head he recognized from the description given him by Monsieur de Maulincour.

"When do you think I shall be cured?" he asked.

"I do not know," replied the unknown; "but according to the doctors it will require seven or eight more dressings."

"Well then, good-bye until to-night," said Ferragus, holding out his hand to the man who had just replaced the last bandage.

"Till to-night," replied the other, pressing his hand cordially. "I wish I could see you through with your sufferings."

"Well, the papers of Monsieur de Funcal will be delivered to us to-morrow, and Henri Bourignard is certainly dead," said Ferragus. "The two fatal letters which have cost us so dear no longer exist. I shall become then once more a social being, a man among men, and I shall certainly be worth the sailor whom the fishes have eaten. God knows if it is for my own sake that I have made myself a Count!"

"Poor Gratien, you, our wisest head, our beloved brother, you are the Benjamin of the band, as you know."

"Adieu, watch well my Maulincour."

"You can rest easy on that score."

"Ho! stay, Marquis," cried the old convict.

"What is it?"

"Ida is capable of everything after the scene of last night. If she has thrown herself into the river, I certainly would not fish her out. She will keep better the secret of my name, the only one she possesses; but still look after her; for, after all, she is a good girl."

"Very well."

The stranger departed. Ten minutes later Jules heard, not without a feverish shiver, the peculiar rustle of a silk gown and almost recognized the sound of his wife's footsteps.

"Well, father," said Clémence, "poor father, how do you find yourself? What courage!"

"Come, my child," replied Ferragus, extending his hand to her.

And Clémence presented her forehead which he kissed.

"Come now, what is the matter my poor little girl? What new troubles?—"

"Troubles, father! but it is the death of your daughter, whom you love so much. As I wrote you yesterday, it is absolutely necessary that you should find in your head, so fertile in ideas, a way to see my poor Jules, to-day even. If you knew how good he has been to me, in spite of all suspicions, apparently so legitimate! Father, my love is my very life. Would you wish to see me die?

Ah! I have already suffered so much! and I feel it, my life is in danger."

"Lose you, my daughter," said Ferragus. "Lose you through the curiosity of a miserable Parisian? I will burn Paris! Ah! you may know what a lover is, but you do not know what a father is."

"Father, you frighten me when you look at me that way. Do not weigh in the balance two so different feelings. I had a husband before I knew that my father was living—"

"If your husband was the first to lay kisses on your forehead," replied Ferragus, "I was the first to drop tears upon it.—Reassure yourself, Clémence, speak to me frankly. I love you enough to be happy in knowing that you are happy, although your father may have little place in your heart, while you fill the whole of his.

Mon Dieu! How such words do me good! You make yourself loved all the more, and it seems to me that it is stealing something from Jules. But, my good father, think, he is in despair. What shall I say to him in two hours?"

"Child, do you think I waited for your letter to save you from this evil which threatens you? And what will become of those who have ventured to touch your happiness, or to come between us? Have you then never recognized the second providence which watches over you? You do not know that twelve men full of strength and of intellect form a rank around your love and your life, ready to do all things to protect you? Is it a father who risked death in going to meet you in the public promenades, or in coming to admire you in your little bed in your mother's house during the night time? Is it the father to whom the remembrance of your childish caresses alone gave strength to live when a man of honor ought to have killed himself to escape infamy? is it *I* in short, I who only breathe by your mouth, who only see through your eyes, who only feel through your heart, is it I who would not know how to defend with the claws of a lion, with the soul of a father, my one blessing, my life, my daughter?—But since the death of that angel who was your mother I have dreamed of but one thing, of the happiness of publicly avowing you as my daughter, of clasping you in my arms in the face of heaven and earth, of killing the *convict*—There was a momentary pause—. Of giving you a father, of being able to press without shame your husband's hand, of living without fear in your hearts, of being able to say to all the world before you, 'this is my daughter,' in short to be a father openly!"

"O my father, my father!"

"After a great deal of trouble, after searching the whole globe," continued Ferragus, "my friends have found for me the skin of a man to put on. A few days hence I shall be Monsieur de Funcal, a Portuguese count. Ah! my dear daughter there are few men who would have had at my age the patience to learn Portuguese and English which that devil of a sailor spoke fluently."

"My dear father!"

"Everything has been foreseen, and in a few days his Majesty, John VI., King of Portugal, will be my accomplice. It will only be necessary for you to have a little patience where your father has had a great deal. But for me, it is very simple. What would I not do to reward your devotion for these last three years! To come so religiously to console your old father, to risk your own happiness!"

"My father!" And Clémence took the hands of Ferragus and kissed them.

"Come now, a little more courage, my Clémence, keep the fatal secret till the end. He is not an ordinary man, Jules; however, are we sure that his lofty character and his great love would not prevent him from entertaining a sort of disrespect for the daughter of a —"

"Oh!" cried Clémence, "you have read the heart of your child, I have no other fear," she added in a heart-rending tone. "It is a thought that turns me to ice. But, father, think that I have promised him the truth in two hours."

"Well, then, my daughter tell him to go to the Portuguese Embassy and see the Comte de Funcal, your father, I will be there."

"And Monsieur de Maulincour who has told him of Ferragus? My God! father, to deceive, to deceive, what torture!"

"To whom do you say this? But only a few days more and there will not exist a man who can expose me. Besides, Monsieur de Maulincour should be beyond the faculty of remembering.— Come, silly child, dry your eyes, and think—"

At this instant a terrible cry rang from the room in which was Monsieur Desmarets:

"My daughter, my poor daughter!"

This clamor came through the small opening in the wall over the wardrobe, and struck with terror Ferragus and Madame Jules.

"Go and see what it is, Clémence."

Clémence ran rapidly down the little staircase, found wide open the door into Madame Gruget's apartment, heard the cries which echoed through the upper floor, mounted the stairway quickly, guided by the noise of the sobs into the fatal chamber whence, before entering, these words came to her ear:

"It is you, Monsieur, with your inventions, who are the cause of her death."

"Will you be quiet, miserable woman," said Jules, putting his handkerchief over the mouth of the widow Gruget, who cried:

"Murder! Help!"

At this instant Clémence entered, saw her husband, uttered a cry and fled.

"Who will save my daughter?" asked the widow Gruget after a long pause, "you have assassinated her!"

"How?" asked Jules mechanically, stupefied at having been recognized by his wife.

"Read, Monsieur," cried the old woman dissolving

into tears. "Are there any annuities that can console for that!"

"Farewell, mother: I bequeeth you all that I hav. I beg your pardon for my forlts, and the last gref which I give you in puttin an end to my days. Henry, who I love more than myself, has told me that I made his misfortunes and since he has driven me away from him and I have lost all my hopes of beings estableeched I am going to droun myself. I shall go below Neuilly so they can't put me in the Morgue. If Henry does not hate me any more after I have punished myself by deth ask him to bury a poor girl whus heart beat for him alon and to forgif me for I was wrong to medle in what didn't concern me. Take good care of his moqca. How he has suffered, that poor fellow. But I shall have the same curage to destroy myself that he had to burn himself. Send home the corsets I have finished to my customers. And pray God for your daughter.

"IDA."

"Take this letter to Monsieur de Funcal, he who is upstairs. If there is still time, he alone can save your daughter."

And Jules disappeared, running like a man who has committed a crime. His legs trembled. His swelling heart received torrents of blood, hotter and more copious than at any moment of his life, and sent them out again with a most unusual violence. The most contradictory thoughts struggled in his mind, and yet one thought dominated all others. He had not been loyal to the being whom he loved the most. And it was impossible for him to argue with his conscience, whose voice growing louder because of his fault, came like an echo of those

THE WIDOW GRUGET AND M. DES-MARETS

Clémence ran rapidly down the little staircase, found wide open the door into Madame Gruget's apartment, heard the cries which echoed through the upper floor, mounted the stairway quickly, guided by the noise of the sobs into the fatal chamber whence, before entering, these words came to her ear:

"It is you, Monsieur, with your inventions, who are the cause of her death."

Copyright, 1900, by George Barrie & Son.

inward cries of his love during the cruelest hours of doubt which had lately agitated him. He spent the greater part of the day wandering around Paris, and not daring to return home. This man of integrity trembled to meet the spotless brow of the woman he had misjudged. The quality of crimes varies according to the purity of our consciences, and the deed which for some hearts is scarcely a fault takes the proportion of a sin in certain purer souls. The word purity, is it not, in fact, of a heavenly comprehensiveness? And the slightest stain on the white robe of a virgin, does it not make something ignoble, as much so as are the rags of a beggar. Between these two, the only difference is that between a misfortune and a fault. God never measures repentance, He does not divide it, and He requires as much to efface a spot as to make Him forget a lifetime. These reflections fell with all their weight on Jules, for passions, like human laws, do not pardon, and they reason more justly; are they not based on a conscience of their own as infallible as an instinct? Jules finally came home despairing, pale, crushed beneath a sense of his wrong doing, and yet expressing in spite of himself the joy which his wife's innocence gave him. He entered her room throbbing with emotion, he saw her in bed, she had a high fever. He seated himself by the side of the bed, took her hand, kissed it and covered it with his tears.

"Dear angel," he said when they were alone, "it is repentance."

"And for what?" she answered.

As she said this she laid her head back upon the pillow, closed her eyes and remained motionless, keeping the secret of her sufferings that she might not frighten her husband,—the delicacy of a mother is the delicacy of an angel. It was the sum of all womanliness. The silence lasted long. Jules, thinking Clémence asleep, went to question Joséphine as to her mistress's condition.

"Madame came home half-dead, Monsieur. We sent at once for Monsieur Haudry."

"Did he come? what did he say?"

"He said nothing, Monsieur. He did not seem satisfied, gave orders that no one should go near Madame except the nurse, and said he would come back this evening."

Jules returned softly to his wife's room, sat down in an arm-chair and remained there by the side of the bed, motionless, with his eyes fixed on those of Clémence; when she raised her eyelids she saw him at once, and a glance escaped her tear-dimmed eyes, tender, full of passion, free from reproach and bitterness, a glance which fell like a flame of fire upon the heart of that husband nobly absolved and forever loved by this being whom he had killed. The presentiment of death struck both their minds with equal force. Their looks were blended in one anguish, as their hearts had long been blended in one love, felt equally by both, shared equally. There were no questions, but a horrible certainty. In the wife, a complete generosity; in the husband, an awful remorse; and in both souls, the same vision of the end, the same conviction of fatality.

There was a moment when, thinking his wife asleep, Jules kissed her softly on the forehead and said, after having long contemplated her:

"My God! leave me this angel still long enough for me to absolve myself of my wrongs by a long adoration:—A daughter she is sublime; a wife, what word can express her?"

Clémence raised her eyes, they were full of tears.

"You pain me," she said in a feeble voice.

It was getting late, Dr. Haudry came and requested the husband to withdraw during his visit. When he came out, Jules did not ask him one question; one gesture was enough.

"Call in consultation any other physician in whom you have the greatest confidence; I may be wrong."

"Doctor, tell me the truth. I am a man, I shall know how to hear it; and I have moreover the deepest interest in knowing it, as I have certain affairs to settle—"

"Madame Jules is fatally ill," replied the physician. "There is some moral malady which has made great progress and which complicates her physical condition, which was already so dangerous and rendered still graver by her imprudences,—to leave her bed, bare-footed at night; to go out when I forbade it, yesterday on foot, to-day in a carriage. She has wished to kill herself. However, my judgment is not final, she has youth and an astonishing nervous strength.—It might be well to risk all to gain all by employing some violent reactive; but I will not take upon myself to order it, I will not even advise it; and in consultation I shall oppose its use."

Jules returned to his wife. During eleven days and eleven nights he remained beside her bed, taking no sleep except during the day when he laid his head upon the foot of this bed. Never did any man push to a greater extreme the jealousy of care and the craving for devotion. He could not endure that the slightest service should be done by others for his wife; he continually held her hand and seemed thus to wish to communicate his life to her. There were days of uncertainty, of false hopes, good days, an amelioration, then a crisis,—in short, all the horrible vacillations of death as it hesitates, wavers, and finally strikes. Madame Jules always found strength to smile on her husband; she pitied him, knowing that soon he would be alone. It was a double agony, that of life, that of love; but life grew feebler and love grew mightier. There was a frightful night, that in which Clémence passed through that delirium which always precedes the death of the young. She talked of her happy love, she talked of her father, she related her mother's revelations on her death-bed and the obligations which she had laid upon her. She struggled, not for life but for her love which she could not leave.

"Grant, oh! God," she said, "that he may not know that I would wish him to die with me."

Jules, unable to bear this scene, was at that moment in the adjoining room and did not hear the prayer, which he doubtless would have fulfilled.

When the crisis had passed Madame Jules recovered some strength. The next day she was again beautiful and tranquil; she talked, hope came to her, she adorned herself as the sick often do. Then she asked to be alone all day and sent her husband away with one of those entreaties made so earnestly that they are granted as we grant the prayer of a little child. Moreover, Jules had need of this day. He went to call on Monsieur de Maulincour in order to demand from him the duel to the death formerly arranged between them. It was not without great difficulty that he succeeded in reaching the presence of the author of his misfortunes; but the vidame, when he learned that the visit related to an affair of honor, followed the precepts which had always governed his life and introduced Jules into the baron's chamber. Monsieur Desmarets looked about him for the Baron de Maulincour.

"Oh! that is really he," said the Commander, motioning to a man who was sitting in an arm-chair beside the fire.

"Who, Jules?" said the dying man in a broken voice.

Auguste had lost the only faculty that makes us live—memory. At his aspect Monsieur Desmarets recoiled in horror. He could not recognize the elegant young man in that thing without a name in any language, according to Bossuet's expression.

It was in truth a corpse with whitened hair; bones scarcely covered by a wrinkled, blighted, withered skin; white eyes without movement; a mouth hideously gaping like those of idiots or debauchees killed by their excesses. No trace of intelligence remained upon that brow nor in any feature; nor was there in that flabby skin either color or any appearance of circulating blood. In short, here was a man shrunken, almost dissolved, brought to the state of those monsters we see preserved in museums in glass bottles, floating in alcohol. Jules fancied that he saw above this face the terrible head of Ferragus, and this complete vengeance terrified his own hatred. The husband found pity in his heart for the doubtful debris of what had been, so recently, a young man.

"The duel has taken place," said the Commander.

"He has killed many," cried Jules sorrowfully.

"And many dear ones," added the old man. "His grandmother is dying of grief, and I shall follow her, perhaps, into the tomb."

The day after this visit Madame Jules grew worse from hour to hour. She profited by a moment's strength to take a letter from under her pillow, presented it eagerly to Jules and made him a sign which was easy to understand,—she wished to give him in a kiss her last breath of life, he took it and she died. Jules fell half-dead himself, and was taken to his brother's house. There, as in his tears and his delirium he deplored his absence of the day before, his brother informed him that this separation was eagerly desired by Clémence, who wished to spare him the sight of the religious paraphernalia, so terrible to tender imaginations, which the Church displays when conferring the last sacraments upon the dying.

"You could not have borne it," said his brother. "I could not sustain the sight myself, and all the servants wept. Clémence was like a saint. She gathered strength to bid us all good-bye, and that voice, heard for the last time, rent our hearts. When she asked pardon for the pain she might have involuntarily caused those who served her, there was a cry mixed with sobs, a cry—"

"Enough, enough," said Jules.

He wished to be alone that he might read the last thoughts of this woman whom all the world had admired, and who had passed away like a flower:

"My beloved, this is my last will. Why should we not make wills for the treasures of the heart as for other riches? Was not my love my whole property? I wish here to consider only my love; it was the only fortune of your Clémence, and it is all that she can leave you in dying. Jules, I am still loved, I die happy. The doctors explain my death in their own manner, I alone know the true cause. I shall tell it to you, whatever pain it may cause you. I do not want to carry away with me in a heart all yours a secret which you do not share, although I die the victim of an enforced silence.

"Jules, I was nurtured and brought up in the deepest solitude, far from the vices and the falsehoods of the world, by the loving woman whom you knew. Society did justice to those conventional qualities by which a woman pleases in society, but I knew secretly this celestial soul, and I could cherish the mother who made my childhood a joy without bitterness, in knowing well why I cherished her. Was that not to love doubly? Yes, I loved her, I feared her, I respected her, and yet nothing weighed on my heart, neither respect nor fear. I was everything to her, she was everything to me. For nineteen years, full of happiness, without a care, my soul, solitary in the midst of the world which muttered around me, reflected only the purest image, that of my mother, and my heart beat only through her and for her. I was scrupulously pious, and I found pleasure in remaining pure before God. My mother cultivated in me all the noble and self-respecting sentiments. Ah! it gives me pleasure to avow it to you, Jules; I know now that I was indeed a young girl, and that I came to you virgin in heart. When I left the absolute solitude, when for the first time I braided my hair and crowned it with almond blossoms, when I had with complacency added a few satin bows to my white dress, thinking of the world I was going to see and which I was curious to see,—ah, Jules, that innocent and modest coquetry was all for you: for as I entered the world it was you whom I saw first of all. Your face, I remarked it, it stood out from the throng of others; your person pleased me; your voice and your manners inspired me with favorable presentiments; and when you came up, when you spoke to me, the color on your forehead, when your voice trembled,—that moment gave me memories with which I still throb in writing to you to-day when I think of them for the last time. Our love was at first the keenest of sympathies, but it was soon mutually discovered and then as speedily shared, just as in after times we have mutually experienced its innumerable pleasures. From that moment my mother was only second in my heart. I told her so and she smiled, the adorable woman! Next I was yours, all yours. There is my life, and all my life, my dear husband. And here is what remains for me to tell you. One evening, a few days before her death, my mother revealed to me the secret of her life, not without shedding burning tears. I have loved you better since I learned, before the priest who was charged to absolve my mother, that there are passions condemned by the world and by the Church. But, surely, God will not be severe when they are the sins of souls as tender as was that of my mother; only, that angel could never bring herself to repent. She loved much, Jules, she was all love. So I have prayed for her daily, without ever having judged her. Then I learned the cause of her deep maternal tenderness; then I learned that there was in Paris a man whose life and whose love centered on me; that your fortune was his work and that he loved you; that he was exiled from society; that he bore a tarnished name, for which he was more unhappy on my account, on ours, than on his own. My mother was his only consolation, and when my mother died, I promised to take her place. With all the ardor of a soul whose feelings had never been perverted I saw only the happiness of softening the bitterness which poisoned the last moments of my mother, and I pledged myself to continue her work of secret charity, the charity of the heart. The first time that I saw my father was beside the bed where my mother had just expired; when he raised his eyes full of tears it was to find in me a revival of all his dead hopes. I had sworn, not to lie but to keep silent, and that silence, what woman would have broken it? There is my fault, Jules, a fault which I expiate by death. I doubted you. But fear is so natural to a woman, and above all to a woman who knows all that she may lose! I trembled for my love. My father's secret appeared to me to mean the death of my happiness, and the more I loved the more I feared. I dared not avow this feeling to my father; it would have wounded him, and in his situation any wound was agony. But without letting me know it, he shared my fears. That heart so fatherly trembled for my happiness as much as I trembled myself, and did not dare to speak, obeying the same delicacy which kept me mute. Yes, Jules, I believed that you could not love some day the daughter of Gratien as much as you loved your Clémence. Without this profound terror could I have kept back anything from you, from you who live in the innermost fibres of my heart? The day when that odious, that unfortunate, officer spoke to you I was forced to lie. That day, for the second time in my life, I knew what pain was, and that pain has been growing until this moment, when I speak with you for the last time. What matters now my father's position? You know all. I might have, by the help of my love, conquered my illness, borne all its sufferings, but I could not stifle the voice of doubt. It is not possible that my origin would affect the purity of your love, weaken it, diminish it? This fear nothing has been able to destroy in me. This is, Jules, the cause of my death. I could not live fearing a word, a look; a word which perhaps you would never say, a look you would never give; but I cannot help it, I fear them. I die beloved, there is my consolation. I have learned that in the last four years my father and his friends have well-nigh moved the world, to deceive the world. In order to give me a station in life, they have bought a dead man, a reputation, a fortune, all this that a living man might live again; all this for you, for us. We were to have known nothing of it. Well, my death will without doubt save my father from that falsehood; he will die of my death. Farewell, Jules, my heart is all here. To show you my love in the innocence of its terror, is not that to bequeath to you all my soul? I could not have had the strength to speak to you; I have had enough to write to you. I have confessed to God the sins of my life; I have indeed promised to think only of the King of Heaven; but I have not been able to resist the pleasure of making my confession also to him who is for me the whole of earth. Alas! shall I not be pardoned for it, this last sigh, between the life that was and the life which is to be! Farewell, then, my beloved Jules; I go to God, before whom love is without a cloud, before whom you will come one day. There, under His throne, reunited forever, we can love each other through the ages. This hope alone consoles me. If I am worthy of being there before you, from there I will follow you through life, my soul will accompany you; it will envelope you, for you will still remain here below. Lead then a holy life, that you may the more surely come to me. You may do such good upon this earth! It is not an angel's mission for the suffering soul, to shed happiness around him, to give to others that which he has not? I bequeath you to the unhappy. It is only their smiles and their tears of which I shall not be jealous. We shall find a great charm in the sweet beneficences. Can we not still live together, if you would join my name, that of your Clémence, to these good works? After having loved as we loved, there is naught but God, Jules. God does not lie, God does not deceive. Adore Him only, I wish it. Nourish the good in all those who suffer, comfort the sorrowing members of His church. Farewell, dear soul that I have filled, I know you; you will never love twice. I shall then expire happy in the thought that makes all women happy. Yes, my grave will be your heart. After this childhood which I have related to you has not my life flowed on within your heart? Dead, you will never drive me forth. I am proud of this rare life! You will have only known me in the flower of my youth; I leave you regrets without disillusions. Jules, it is a very happy death.

"You who have so fully understood me, permit me to ask one thing of you, a superfluous thing, doubtless, the fulfilment of a woman's fancy, the prayer of a jealousy we all must feel. I pray you to burn all that especially belonged to us, to destroy our chamber, to annihilate all that might be a souvenir of our love.

"Once more farewell, the last farewell, full of love, as will be my last thought and my last breath."

※

When Jules had read this letter there came into his heart one of those frenzies of which it is impossible to describe the frightful crises. All sorrows are individual, their effects are not subjected to any fixed rule! Some men will stop their ears that they may hear nothing; some women close their eyes that they may see nothing; there are great and splendid souls who fling themselves into sorrow as into an abyss. In the matter of despair, everything is true. Jules escaped from his brother's house and returned to his own, wishing to pass the night beside his wife and see that celestial creature to the last moment. As he walked along, with that indifference to life known only to those who have reached the last degree of wretchedness, he remembered that in Asia the laws forbade the married to survive each other. He wished to die. He was not yet crushed, he was still in the fever of his grief. He reached his home without obstacle and went up into the sacred chamber; he saw his Clémence on the bed of death, beautiful as a saint, her hair carefully arranged, her hands joined, already wrapped in her shroud. Tapers lighted a priest in prayer, Joséphine weeping in a corner, kneeling, and two men standing near the bed. One of them was Ferragus. He stood erect, motionless, gazing at his daughter with a dry eye; his head you might have taken for bronze. He did not see Jules. The other was Jacquet, Jacquet to whom Madame Jules had ever been kind. He had felt for her one of those respectful friendships which rejoice the heart without troubling it, which are a gentle passion, love without its desires and its storms; and he had come religiously to pay his debt of tears, to bid a long adieu to the wife of his friend, to kiss for the first time the icy brow of the woman he had tacitly made his sister. All was silence. Here, death was neither terrible as it is in the church, nor pompous as it is when it traverses the streets; it was death under the domestic roof, touching death; here was the mourning of the heart, tears drawn from every eye. Jules sat down near Jacquet and pressed his hand and without uttering a word all these persons remained as they were till morning. When daylight paled the tapers, Jacquet, foreseeing the painful scenes which would then take place, drew Jules into the adjoining room. At this moment the husband looked at the father and Ferragus looked at Jules. These two sorrows arraigned each other, measured each other, and comprehended each other in that look. A flash of fury shone for an instant in the eyes of Ferragus.

"It is you who killed her," thought he.

"Why was I distrusted?" seemed to answer the husband.

This scene was one that might have passed between two tigers, recognizing the futility of a struggle, after having examined each other during a moment of hesitation, without even a growl.

"Jacquet," said Jules, "have you attended to everything?"

"Yes, to everything," replied the bureau chief, "but everywhere a man had forestalled me, who had ordered and paid for all."

"He tears his daughter from me!" cried the husband in a violent accession of his despair.

He rushed back into his wife's room; but the father was no longer there. Clémence had been placed in a leaden coffin, and workmen were preparing to solder on the lid. Jules returned, horrified at this sight, and at the sound of the hammer used by these men he involuntarily burst into tears.

"Jacquet," he said, "there has come to me out of this terrible night an idea, one only, but an idea I must realize at any price. I do not want Clémence to rest in any cemetery in Paris. I wish to burn her body, to gather her ashes and to keep her with me. Say nothing to me about this, but make arrangements to have it carried out. I am going to shut myself up in *her* chamber, and I shall remain there until the moment of my departure. You alone shall come in to give me an account of your proceedings.—Go, and spare nothing."

During this morning, Madame Jules, after lying in a mortuary chapel at the door of her house, was taken to Saint-Roch. The church was entirely draped in black. The species of luxury displayed for this service had drawn a crowd; for in Paris all things are sights, even the most genuine grief.

There are persons who stand at their windows to see how a son weeps when following the body of his mother, as there are those who wish to be commodiously placed to see how a head falls on the scaffold. No people in the world have ever had more voracious eyes. But the curious were on this occasion particularly surprised to perceive that the six lateral chapels of Saint-Roch were also draped in black. Two men in black attended a mortuary mass said in each of these chapels. In the chancel, no other persons were seen but Monsieur Desmarets, the notary, and Jacquet; and outside the screen, the servants. There was, for the church loungers, something inexplicable in so much pomp and so few mourners. Jules had determined that no indifferent person should be present at this ceremony. High mass was celebrated with all the sombre magnificence of funeral services. In addition to the ordinary service of Saint-Roch, thirteen priests from other parishes were present. Thus it was, perhaps, that the *Dies iræ* had never produced upon Christians, assembled by chance, by curiosity, but thirsting for emotions, an effect more profound, more nervously glacial, than the impression now produced by this hymn at the moment when the eight voices of the choristers, accompanied by those of the priests and the voices of the choir-boys, intoned it alternately. From the six lateral chapels, twelve other childish voices rose shrill from grief, and mingled with it mournfully. Dread was manifested in all parts of the church;

everywhere cries of anguish responded to cries of terror. This terrible music spoke of sorrows unknown to the world, and of secret friendships which wept for the dead. Never in any human religion have the terrors of the soul, violently torn from the body and stormily shaken in presence of the fulminating majesty of God, been rendered with such force. Before that clamor of clamors must bow, humiliated, all artists and their most passionate compositions. No, nothing can compare with that hymn, which sums up all human passions and gives to them a galvanic life beyond the coffin, in bringing them, still palpitating, before the living and avenging God. These cries of childhood, mingling with the sounds of deep voices, and thus comprehending in this canticle of death the human life in all its developments, recalling the sufferings of the cradle, swelling to the griefs of other ages, with the strong accents of the men, with the quavering of the old men and the priests,—all this strident harmony, full of lightning and thunder, does it not speak to the most daring imagination, to the coldest heart, to the Philosophers themselves! In hearing it, it seems that God thunders. The vaulted arches of no human church are cold; they tremble, they speak, they scatter fear by all the might of their echoes. You think you see the unnumbered dead rising and stretching out their hands. It is no longer a father, nor a wife, nor a child, who is under the black pall, it is humanity rising from its dust. It is impossible to judge the Catholic, Apostolic and Roman faith unless the soul has known the deepest grief of mourning, in weeping for the adored one who lies under the tomb; unless it has felt all the emotions which then fill the heart, translated by this hymn of despair, by those cries which crush the soul, by that sacred terror which increases from strophe to strophe, which turns toward heaven, and which terrifies, which shrivels, which elevates the soul, and which leaves within our mind, as the last verse finishes, a consciousness of eternity. You have been brought very close to the vast idea of the Infinite; and then all is silent in the church. No word is said; the scoffers themselves *do not know what they feel.* The Spanish genius alone was able to invent these untold majesties for the most unheard-of sorrows. When the supreme ceremony was over, twelve men in black issued from the six chapels and came to hear around the coffin, the song of hope which the church makes known to the Christian soul before the human form is buried. Then each of these men entered a mourning coach; Jacquet and Monsieur Desmarets took the thirteenth; the servants followed on foot. An hour later, the twelve unknown men were at the summit of that cemetery popularly called Père-Lachaise, standing in a circle around an open grave into which the coffin had been lowered, in the presence of a curious crowd gathered from all parts of this public garden. Then, after a few short prayers, the priest threw a handful of earth on the remains of this woman; and the grave-diggers, having asked for their fee, made haste to fill the grave in order to go to another.—

Here this history seems to end; but perhaps it would be incomplete if after having given a rapid sketch of Parisian life, if after having followed its capricious undulations, the effects of death there were forgotten. Death in Paris is unlike death in any other capital, and but few persons know the trials of true grief when brought into conflict with the civilization, with the administration, of Paris. Perhaps, also, Jules and Ferragus XXIII. may have proved sufficiently interesting to make the ending of their lives not entirely tedious. Besides, many people like to be told all, and wish, as one of the most ingenious of our critics has said, to know by what chemical process the oil burned in Aladdin's lamp. Jacquet, being a Government employé, naturally applied to the authorities for permission to exhume the body of Madame Jules and to burn it. He went to see the Prefect of Police, under whose protection the dead sleep. That functionary demanded a petition. It was necessary to buy a sheet of stamped paper, to give to sorrow its proper administrative form; it was necessary to employ the bureaucratic jargon to express the wishes of a crushed man to whom words were lacking; it was necessary to translate coldly and repeat on the margin the nature of the request:

The petitioner
requests the incineration
of his wife.

When he saw this, the chief charged with the duty of making a report to the Councilor of State, the Prefect of Police, said in reading this marginal note in which the *object* of the demand was clearly stated, as he had recommended:

"That is a serious matter! my report cannot be ready under a week."

Jules, to whom Jacquet was obliged to speak of this delay, comprehended the words that he had heard Ferragus utter, "I'll burn Paris." Nothing seemed to him now more natural than to annihilate this receptacle of monstrosities.

"But," he said to Jacquet, "you must go to the Minister of the Interior, and get your minister to speak to him."

Jacquet went to the Minister of the Interior and asked for an audience which was granted him, but at the end of two weeks. Jacquet was a persistent man. He traveled from bureau to bureau, and finally reached the private secretary of the minister, to whom he had made the private secretary of the Minister of Foreign Affairs say a word in his behalf. These high protectors aiding, he obtained for the morrow a brief interview in which, being armed with a line from the Autocrat of Foreign Affairs written to the Pasha of the Interior, Jacquet hoped to carry the matter by assault. He prepared all his reasons, answers to peremptory questions, his replies to the *but in case of;* but everything failed.

"The matter does not concern me," said the minister. "It is an affair for the Prefect of Police.

Moreover, there is no law which gives to husbands any legal right to the bodies of their wives, nor to fathers to those of their children. The matter is serious! Then there are questions of public utility involved, which require that this should be examined. The interests of the city of Paris might suffer. In short, if the matter depended entirely upon me I could not decide *hic et nunc*, I should require a report."

A *report* is to the present system of administration what Limbo is in the Christian religion. Jacquet knew very well the mania for reports, and he had not waited until this occasion to groan over that bureaucratic absurdity. He knew that since the invasion of public business by the reports, an administrative revolution consummated in 1804, there was never known a single minister who would take upon himself to have an opinion, to decide the slightest matter, unless that opinion, that matter, had been winnowed, sifted and plucked to pieces by the paper-spoilers, the quill-drivers and the splendid intelligences of his bureaus. Jacquet —he was one of those men worthy of having Plutarch for his biographer—saw that he had made a mistake in his management of this affair, and that he had rendered it impossible, by trying to proceed legally. He should simply have taken Madame Jules to one of Desmarets' estates in the country; and there, under the good-natured authority of some village mayor, to have gratified the sorrowful longing of his friend. Constitutional and administrative legality begets nothing; it is a barren monster, for peoples, for kings, and for private interests; but the people decipher only those principles which are written in blood; the evils of legality being only pacific it flattens a nation down, that is all. Jacquet, a lover of liberty, returned home reflecting on the benefits of arbitrary power, for man judges the laws only by the light of his own passions. When he found himself in the presence of Jules he was obliged to deceive him, for the unhappy man, a prey to a violent fever, had been confined to his bed for two days. The minister happened to speak that very evening at a ministerial dinner of the singular fancy of a Parisian wishing to burn his wife, after the manner of the Romans. The clubs of Paris took up the subject, and discussed for a while the antique funeral ceremonies. Ancient things were then becoming the fashion, and some persons declared that it would be a fine thing to reestablish for high personages the funeral pyre. This opinion had its defenders and its detractors. Some said that there were too many great men, and that this custom would greatly increase the price of firewood, that among a people as fickle in their whims as are the French it would be ridiculous to see at every turn a Longchamp of ancestors promenading in their urns; and if the urns were valuable they were likely some day to be sold at auction, or to be seized, full of respectable ashes, by creditors, who are accustomed to respect nothing. Others made answer that there would be much more safety for our ancestors thus enclosed than at Père-Lachaise, for, before very long, the city of Paris would be compelled to order a Saint Bartholomew against its dead, who were invading the neighboring country and threatening to take possession one day of the territory of Brie. It was, in short, one of those futile and witty Parisian discussions which frequently cause deep and painful wounds. Happily for Jules, he knew nothing of the conversations, the *bon mots,* the arguments, which his sorrow had furnished to the tongues of Paris. The Prefect of Police was indignant that Monsieur Jacquet had appealed to the minister to avoid the delays, the wisdom, of the Commissioners of Public Highways. The exhumation of Madame Jules was a question of highways. Therefore, the Police Bureau was doing its best to reply promptly to the petition, for one appeal was quite sufficient to set the office in motion, and once in motion the subject would be thoroughly investigated. The administration might carry all cases up to the Council of State, another machine very difficult to set in motion. The second day, Jacquet was obliged to tell his friend that he must renounce his desire; that in a city in which the number of tears embroidered on black draperies is tariffed, where the laws recognize seven classes of funerals, where the ground for the dead is sold for its weight in silver, where grief is exploited, kept by double entry, where the prayers of the Church are paid for dearly, where the vestry intervenes to claim payment for two or three slender voices added to the *Dies iræ,*—all attempt to get out of the administrative rut prescribed for grief is impossible.

"It would have been," said Jules, "a comfort in my misery, I had meant to die far away from here, and I hoped to hold Clémence in my arms in the tomb! I did not know that the bureaucracy could extend its claws into our very coffins."

He now wished to see if room had been left for him beside his wife. The two friends went to the cemetery. When they reached it, they found, as at the doors of the theatres or the entrance to museums, as in the court yards of the diligences, *ciceroni* who offered to guide them through the labyrinth of Père-Lachaise. It would have been impossible for either of them to find the spot where Clémence lay. Ah! frightful anguish! They went to consult the porter of the cemetery. The dead have a concierge, and there are hours when the dead are not to be seen. It would be necessary to upset all the regulations of the upper and lower police to obtain permission to come and weep in the night in silence and solitude, over the tomb where a loved one lies. There is a regulation for winter, a regulation for summer. Certainly, of all the porters in Paris he of Père-Lachaise is the luckiest. In the first place, he has no gate-cord to pull; then, instead of a lodge he has a house, an establishment, which is not quite ministerial although there are a very great number of administrators and several employés, and this governor of the dead has an income and is endowed with immense powers, of which none can complain; he plays the despot at his ease. His lodge is not a commercial establishment, although it has offices, a system of accounts, receipts, expenses and profits. This man is not a *suisse,* nor a concierge, nor a porter; the gate which admits the dead stands always wide open, and although there are monuments to be cared for he is not a care-taker; in short, he is an indefinable anomaly, an authority which participates in all and yet is nothing, an authority placed—like death by which it lives— outside of all. Nevertheless, this exceptional man grows out of the city of Paris, a chimerical creation like the ship which serves as its emblem, a creature of reason, moved by a thousand paws which are seldom unanimous in their motion, so that its employés are almost irremovable. This guardian of the cemetery is, then, the concierge arrived at the condition of a functionary, not soluble by dissolution. His place is by no means a sinecure; he does not allow anyone to be buried without a permit, he must count his dead, he points out to you in this vast field the six square feet where you will one day put all you love or all you hate, a mistress or a cousin. Yes, know this well, all the feelings and emotions of Paris come to end at this porter's lodge, and there are administrationized. This man has registers for his dead, they are in their tombs and in his books. He has under him keepers, gardeners, grave-diggers, assistants. He is a personage. The mourners in tears do not speak to him at first. He only appears in serious cases, — one corpse mistaken for another, a murdered body, an exhumation, a dead man who comes to life. The bust of the reigning king is in his hall, and he perhaps preserves the ancient royal, imperial, and quasi-royal busts in some cupboard, a sort of little Père-Lachaise all ready for revolutions. In short, he is a public man, an excellent man, good father and good husband, — epitaph apart. But so many diverse sentiments have passed before him on biers, he has seen so many tears, true and false; he has seen sorrow under so many countenances and on so many countenances, he has seen six millions of eternal woes! For him, a grief is no longer anything but a stone, eleven lines in thickness and four feet in height, twenty-two inches wide. As for *regrets*, they are the annoyances of his office, — he neither breakfasts nor dines without first wiping off the rain of an inconsolable affliction. He is kind and tender to all other feelings; he will weep over some hero of the drama, over Monsieur Germeuil in the *Auberge des Adrets*, the man with the butter-colored breeches assassinated by Robert Macaire; but his heart is ossified in the matter of real dead men. The dead are only numbers to him; it is his business to organize death. Then, finally, he does meet, three times in a century, a situation in which his rôle becomes sublime, and then he is sublime every hour, — in times of pestilence.

When Jacquet accosted him, this absolute monarch was in a sufficiently-bad humor.

"I told you," he cried, "to water the flowers from Rue Masséna to the Place Regnaud-de-Saint-Jean-d'Angély! You paid no attention to me—you there. *Sac à papier!* if the relations should take it into their heads to come to-day because the weather is fine they would all get at me,—they would shriek as if they were burned, they would say horrid things of us and calumniate us—"

"Monsieur," said Jacquet to him, "we wish to know where Madame Jules is buried."

"Madame Jules *who?*" he asked. "Within the last week we have had three Madame Jules.—Ah," he said, interrupting himself, "here comes the funeral of Colonel de Maulincour, go and get the permit.—A fine procession that!" he resumed. "He has soon followed his grandmother. Some families, when they begin to go, rattle down as if for a wager. There is plenty of bad blood in these Parisians."

"Monsieur," said Jacquet, touching him on the arm, "the person of whom I speak is Madame Jules Desmarets, the wife of the broker of that name."

"Ah! I know," he replied, looking at Jacquet. "Was not that the funeral in which there were thirteen mourning coaches and only one mourner in each of the first twelve? That was so droll that it struck us all—"

"Monsieur, take care, Monsieur Jules is with me, he might hear you, and what you say is not seemly."

"I beg pardon, Monsieur—you are right. Excuse

me, I took you for the heirs.—Monsieur," he continued, consulting a plan of the cemetery, "Madame Jules is in the Rue Maréchal-Lefebvre, Alley No. 4, between Mademoiselle Raucourt of the Comédie-Française and Monsieur Moreau-Malvin, a distinguished butcher, for whom a handsome tomb in white marble has been ordered, which will certainly be one of the finest in our cemetery."

"Monsieur," said Jacquet, interrupting him, "that does not help us."

"That's true," he replied looking around him.

"Jean," he cried to a man whom he saw at a little distance, "conduct these gentlemen to the grave of Madame Jules, the wife of the broker. You know it, near to Mademoiselle Raucourt, the tomb where there is a bust."

And the two friends followed one of the keepers; but they did not reach the steep path which leads to the upper alley of the cemetery without having to pass through more than a score of propositions offered to them with a honeyed softness by the agents of marble-workers, iron-founders and monumental sculptors.

"If Monsieur would like to order *something*, we could arrange it for him on the most reasonable terms.—"

Jacquet was fortunate enough to be able to spare his friend the hearing of these proposals, so fearful for still bleeding hearts, and they finally reached the resting-place. When he saw this earth so recently turned, and in which the masons had stuck stakes to mark the places for the stone posts required to support the iron railing, Jules leaned on the shoulder of Jacquet, raising himelf at intervals to cast long glances at the clay mould where he was forced to leave the remains of the being by whom he still lived.

"How miserably she lies there," he said.

"But she is not there," replied Jacquet, "she is in your memory. Come, let us go, let us leave this odious cemetery, where the dead are adorned like women for a ball."

"Suppose we take her away from there?"

"Can it be done?"

"All things can be done," cried Jules.—"So I shall lie there," he added after a pause. "There is room enough."

Jacquet finally succeeded in getting him to leave this great enclosure, divided like a chess-board by bronze railings, by elegant compartments, in which were enclosed the tombs decorated with palms, with inscriptions, with tears as cold as the stones on which sorrowing hearts had caused to be carved their regrets and their coats of arms. Many clever phrases are there engraved in black letters, epigrams reproving the curious, *concetti*, wittily turned farewells, rendezvous given at which only one side ever appears, pretentious biographies, glitter, rubbish and tinsel. Here, may be seen the thyrsus; there, lance heads; farther on, Egyptian urns, now and then a few cannons, on all sides the emblems of a thousand professions; in short all styles,—Moorish,

Greek, Gothic, friezes, ovules, paintings, urns, Genii, temples, a great many faded immortelles and dead rosebushes. It is a forlorn comedy! it is another Paris, with its streets, its signs, its industries, its lodgings; but seen through the diminishing end of an opera-glass, a microscopic Paris, reduced to the littleness of shadows, of the larvæ of the dead, a human race which has no longer anything great about it except its vanity. Then Jules saw at his feet, in the long valley of the Seine, between the slopes of Vaugirard and Meudon, between those of Belleville and Montmartre, the real Paris, enveloped in a bluish veil produced by its smoke and which the sunlight rendered at this moment diaphanous. He embraced in his furtive glance these forty thousand houses, and said, pointing to the space comprised between the column of the Place Vendôme and the gilded cupola of the Invalides:

"She was carried away from me there by the fatal curiosity of that world which excites itself and interferes for the purpose of interfering and exciting itself."

At a distance of four leagues, on the banks of the Seine, in a modest village lying on the slope of one of the hills of that long hilly enclosure in the middle of which great Paris stirs like a child in its cradle, a scene of death and of sorrow was taking place, far indeed removed from all the Parisian pomps, with no accompaniment of torches, or of tapers, or mourning coaches, without the prayers of the Church, death in all its simplicity. Here are the facts: The body of a young girl was found early in the morning, stranded on the river bank, in the slime and reeds of the Seine. Some men employed in dredging sand saw it as they were getting into their frail boat, on their way to their work.

"Look there! Fifty francs earned," said one of them.

"That is true," said the other.

And they approached the body.

"It is a very pretty girl."

"Let us go and make our statement."

And the two sand-dredgers, after covering the body with their jackets, went to the village mayor, who was much embarrassed at having to make out the legal papers necessitated by this discovery.

The news of this event spread with that telegraphic rapidity peculiar to regions where social communications have no interruption, where the scandal, the gossip, the calumnies, the social tale on which the world regales itself, have no break of continuity from one boundary to another. Before long, some persons arriving at the mayor's office relieved him from all embarrassment. They were able to convert the *procès-verbal* into a simple certificate of death. Through them the body of the young girl was recognized as that of the demoiselle Ida Gruget, corset maker, living at Rue de la Corderie-du-Temple, No. 14. The judiciary police intervened, the widow Gruget, mother of the defunct, arrived, bringing with her the last letter of her daughter. Amidst the mother's lamentations a doctor certified to death by asphyxia, through the injection of black blood into the pulmonary system, and everything was said. The inquest over, the certificate signed, by six o'clock the same evening authority was given to bury the grisette. The curé of the place refused to receive her into the church and to pray for her. Ida Gruget was therefore wrapped in a shroud by an old peasant woman, put into a common coffin made of pine planks, and carried to the village cemetery by four men, followed by a few curious peasant women who discussed this death, commenting upon it with wonder mingled with some commiseration. The widow Gruget was charitably taken in by an old lady who prevented her from following in the sad procession of her daughter's funeral. A man of triple functions, the bell-ringer, beadle and grave-digger of the parish, had dug a grave in the village cemetery, a cemetery half an acre in extent behind the church,—a church well known, a classic church, furnished with a square tower with a pointed roof covered with slate, supported on the outside by angular buttresses. Behind the circular back of the chancel lay the cemetery, enclosed with a dilapidated wall,—a little field full of hillocks; no marbles, no visitors, but surely in every furrow tears and true regrets which were lacking for Ida Gruget. She was cast into a corner among the brambles and the tall grass. When the coffin had been laid in this field, so poetic in its simplicity, the grave digger found himself alone, with the night falling. While filling the grave he stopped now and then to gaze over the wall along the road; at one moment with his hand on his spade he was looking at the Seine which had brought him this body.

"Poor girl!" cried a man who suddenly appeared.

"How you frightened me, Monsieur," said the grave-digger.

"Was there any service held over the body you are burying?"

"No, Monsieur. Monsieur le curé was not willing. This is the first person buried here who didn't belong to the parish. Here, everybody knows everybody else. Does Monsieur—why, he's gone!"

Some days had elapsed when a man dressed in black called at the house of Jules, and without asking to see him deposited in his wife's chamber a great porphyry vase on which he read these words:

INVITA LEGE,

CONJUGI MOERENTI

FILIOLÆ CINERES

RESTITUIT,

AMICIS XII. JUVANTIBUS,

MORIBUNDUS PATER.

"What a man!" cried Jules, bursting into tears.

Eight days sufficed the husband to carry out all the wishes of his wife and to arrange his own affairs; he sold his practice to a brother of Martin Faleix, and left Paris while the authorities were still discussing whether it was lawful for a citizen to dispose of the body of his wife.

Who has not encountered on the Boulevards of Paris, at the turn of the street, or beneath the arcades of the Palais-Royal, or in fact in any part of the world where chance may offer him the sight, a being, man or woman, at whose aspect a thousand confused thoughts spring into his mind? At the appearance of this being we are suddenly interested, either by features whose fantastic conformation reveals an agitated life, or by the curious general effect produced by the gestures, the air, the gait, and the garments, or by some profound look, or by other inexpressible signs which impress us forcibly and suddenly, without our being able to exactly explain to ourselves the cause of our emotion. The next day, other thoughts, other Parisian images, carry away this passing dream. But if we meet the same personage again, either passing at some fixed hour like an employé of the mayor's office who belongs to the marriage-bureau during eight hours, or wandering about the public promenades, like those individuals who seem to be a sort of furniture belonging to the Parisian streets and who are always to be found in the public places, at first representations, or in the noted restaurants of which they are the finest ornament,—then this being enfeoffs himself in your memory and remains there, like the first volume of a novel, the end of which is lost. We are tempted to question this unknown and say to him, "Who are you? Why are you lounging here? By what right do you wear that plaited ruffle, why do you carry a cane with an ivory top, why that faded waistcoat? Why those blue spectacles with double glasses?" Or, "Why do you still wear the cravat of the *Muscadins?*" Among these wandering creatures there are some that belong to the species of the ancient terminal statues; they say nothing to the soul; they are there, and that is all: Why? No one knows; they are figures, like those which serve as a type to the sculptors for the four Seasons, for Commerce, for Plenty. Some others, former lawyers, old merchants, antique generals, go about, walk, and yet seem always stationary. Like those trees which hang, half-uprooted, over the banks of a stream, they seem never to take part in the torrent of Paris nor in its youthful, active crowd. It is impossible to know if it has been forgotten to bury them, or if they have escaped from their coffins; they have reached a quasi-fossil condition. One of these Parisian *Melmoths* had come within a few days to mingle with the sober and quiet population which, when the weather is fine, invariably furnishes the space which lies between the south entrance of the Luxembourg and the north entrance of the Observatoire, a space without a class, the neutral space of Paris. In fact, Paris is no longer there; and there Paris still lingers. This spot partakes at once of the street, the place, the boulevard, the fortification, the garden, the avenue, the highroad, of the province and of the capital; certainly all that is to be found there, and yet the place is nothing of all that,—it is a desert. Around this spot without a name stand the hospital of the Enfants Trouvés, the Bourbe, the Cochin Hospital, the Capucins, the hospital La Rochefoucauld, the Deaf and Dumb Asylum, the hospital of the Val-de-Grâce; in short, all the vices and all the misfortunes of Paris find there their asylum; and that nothing may be lacking to this philanthropic enclosure, science there studies the tides and the longitudes; Monsieur de Chateaubriand has erected there the Marie-Thérèse Infirmary, and the Carmelites have founded a convent there. The great events of life are represented by bells which ring incessantly through this desert, for the mother giving birth, and for the babe that is born, and for the vice that succumbs, and for the workman who dies, for the virgin who prays, for the old man who is cold, for genius which deludes itself. Then, at a distance of two steps, is the cemetery of Mont-Parnasse, which draws hour after hour to itself the sorry funerals of the Faubourg Saint-Marceau. This esplanade, which commands a view of Paris, has been taken possession of by the players of bowls, old gray figures, full of kindliness, worthy men who continue our ancestors, and whose physiognomies can only be compared with those of their public, the moving gallery which follows them. The man who had become during the last few days an inhabitant of this desert region assisted assiduously at these games of bowls, and would certainly be considered the most striking creature of these various groups who—if it be permissible to liken the Parisians to the different orders of zoölogy—belong to the genus mollusk. This new-comer kept sympathetic step with the *cochonnet*, the little bowl which serves as the point aimed at and on which the interest of the game centres; he leaned against a tree when the cochonnet stopped; then, with the same attention that a dog gives to his master's gestures, he watched the bowls flying through the air or rolling along the ground. You would have taken him for the fantastic genius of the cochonnet. He said nothing, and the bowl-players, the most fanatic men that can be encountered among the sectarians of any religion whatever, had never asked him the reason of this obstinate silence; only some very great minds thought him deaf and dumb. On those occasions on which it became necessary to determine the different distances between the bowls and the cochonnet, the cane of the unknown served as the infallible measure, the players coming up and taking it from the icy hands of this old man, without asking him for the loan of it, without even making him a sign of friendliness. The loan of his cane was like a servitude to which he had negatively consented. When a shower came up, he remained near the cochonnet, the slave of the bowls, the guardian of the unfinished game. Rain affected him no more than the fine weather did, and he was like the players themselves, an intermediary species between the Parisian who has the least intelligence of his kind and the animal which has the highest. In other respects, pallid and shrunken, indifferent to his own person, vacant in mind, he often came bare-headed, showing his white hair and his square, yellow, bald skull, not unlike the knee which pierces the pantaloon of a beggar. He was open-mouthed, without intelligence in his glance, without any steadiness in his walk; he never smiled, never lifted his eyes to heaven, and kept them habitually on the ground, where he seemed to be always looking for something. At four o'clock an old woman arrived to take him away, no one knows where, towing him along by the arm as a young girl drags a wilful goat which still wants to browse by the wayside when it should go to the stable. This old man was a horrible thing to see.

In the afternoon, Jules Desmarets, alone in his traveling carriage, passed rapidly through Rue de l'Est, and came upon the esplanade of the Observatoire at the moment when this old man, leaning against a tree had allowed his cane to be taken from his hand amid the noisy vociferations of the players pacifically irritated. Jules, thinking he recognized that face, wished to stop, and in fact his carriage came to a standstill. The postilion, hemmed in by some carts, did not ask for a passage-way through the insurgent bowl-players; he had too much respect for uprisings, the postilion.

"It is he!" said Jules, beholding in that human wreck Ferragus XXIII., Chief of the Dévorants.— "How he loved her!" he added after a pause.— "Go on postilion!" he cried.

Paris, February, 1833.

HISTORY OF THE THIRTEEN

LA DUCHESSE DE LANGEAIS

TO

FRANTZ LISTZ

LA DUCHESSE DE LANGEAIS

*

In a Spanish town on an island of the Mediterranean there is a convent of the Bare-footed Carmelites in which the rule of the Order instituted by Saint Theresa is still maintained with the primitive rigor of the reformation brought about by that illustrious woman. This fact is true, extraordinary as it may seem. Although the religious establishments of the Peninsula and those of the Continent were nearly all destroyed or subverted by the explosions of the French Revolution and the Napoleonic wars, this island having been constantly protected by the British navy, the wealthy convent and its peaceful inmates were sheltered from the general disasters and spoliation. The storms of every kind which disturbed the first fifteen years of the nineteenth century broke idly on this rock, not far from the coast of Andalusia. If the name of the Emperor was carried even to this shore, it may be doubted whether the fantastic train of his glory and the flaming majesty of his meteoric life were ever realized by the saintly women kneeling in this cloister. A conventual rigor which nothing relaxed recommended this haven to the Catholic world. Moreover, the purity of its rule drew to it from the most distant parts of Europe sorrowful women, whose souls, deprived of all human ties, sighed for this slow suicide accomplished in the bosom of God. No other convent moreover was better adapted to that complete separation from the things of this world which the religious life demands. Nevertheless, there may be found on the Continent a great number of these houses, magnificently built in view of their purpose. Some are ensconced in the depths of the most solitary valleys; others overhang the steepest mountains, or crown the brinks of precipices; everywhere man has sought the poetry of the infinite, the solemn horror of silence; everywhere he has desired to draw closest to God; he has sought him on the summits, in the depths of abysses, on the edges of cliffs, and has found him everywhere. Yet nowhere as on this rock, half European, half African, could be found so many differing harmonies all blending to so elevate the soul, to remove the most dolorous impressions, to assuage the keenest, to give from the sorrows of life a profound rest. This monastery was built at the extremity of the island, on the highest point of the rock which, by some great convulsion of nature, has been broken off sharply on the side of the sea, where at all points it presents the sharp angles of its surfaces, slightly worn away at the water line, but inaccessible. This rock is protected from all attack by dangerous reefs which extend far out into the sea, and among which play the sparkling waves of the Mediterranean. It is only from the sea that one can perceive the four principal parts of this square structure, whose form, height, and doorways, have all been minutely prescribed by monastic laws. On the side towards the town, the church completely hides the massive building of the cloister, with its roof covered with large tiles which render it invulnerable to squalls, storms, and the fierce heat of the sun. The church, the generous gift of a Spanish family, crowns the town. The façade, bold and elegant, gives a noble aspect to this little maritime town. Is not the view of a city with its crowded roofs, nearly all of them disposed like an amphitheatre before a beautiful harbor, and rising above all a magnificent portal with Gothic triglyph, with campaniles, slender towers and pierced spires, a spectacle full of terrestrial grandeur? Religion dominating life, in offering to men unceasingly both the end and the way of life, an image moreover altogether Spanish! Transplant this scene to the middle of the Mediterranean beneath an ardent sky; add to it palms, and dwarfed perennial trees, which mingle their waving green fronds with the sculptured leafage of the immobile architecture; look at the white fringes of the sea breaking over the reefs and contrasting with the sapphire blue of the water; admire the galleries, the terraces built upon the roof of each house where the inhabitants come to breathe the evening air among the flowers, between the tops of the trees of their little gardens. Then, in the harbor some white sails. And lastly, in the serenity of the early evening, listen to the music of the organ, the chant of the vespers, the sweet chimes of the bells on the open sea. Everywhere, sound and calm; but oftenest, the calm everywhere. Within, the church was divided into three naves, dark and mysterious. Doubtless the fury of the winds forbade the architect to construct those lateral arched buttresses which adorn almost all other cathedrals, and between which are constructed the chapels, hence the walls which flanked the two small naves and sustained this structure, admitted no light into it. Exteriorly, these strong walls presented the aspect of their gray masses supported at intervals by enormous buttresses. The great nave and its two small lateral galleries were therefore lighted only by a rose-window of stained glass, placed with miraculous art over the portal, whose favorable exposure had permitted a wealth of stone lacework and the beauty peculiar to the order miscalled Gothic. The greater part of these three naves was given up to the townsfolk, who came to hear Mass and the services. In front of the choir was a railing, behind which hung a brown curtain with ample folds, slightly parted in the middle so as to allow only the officiating priest and the altar to be seen. This railing was divided at equal intervals by pillars which supported an interior gallery and the organs. This work in carved wood, in harmony with the decoration of the church, formed externally the small columns of the galleries supported by the pillars of the great nave. It was thus impossible for any curious person who might be bold enough to mount upon the narrow balustrade of these galleries to see within the choir anything but the long octagonal stained-glass windows which pierced the wall at equal distances around the high-altar.

At the time of the French expedition into Spain for the purpose of reëstablishing the authority of King Ferdinand VII., and after the fall of Cadiz, a French general, sent to this island to obtain its recognition of the Royal Government, prolonged his stay that he might reconnoitre this convent, if possible, and gain admittance. The enterprise was, certainly, a delicate one. But a man of passion, a man whose life had been—so to speak—a series of poems in action, and who had always lived romances instead of writing them, above all, a man of deeds, might well be tempted by a project apparently impossible. To open the gates of a convent for himself, legally! the Pope or the metropolitan Archbishop himself would scarcely have sanctioned it. To employ artifice or force, in case of failure, was he not certain to lose his station, all his military future, and miss his aim in addition? The Duc d'Angoulême was still in Spain, and of all the indiscretions which a man in favor with the commander-in-chief could commit, this alone would be punished without pity. This general had solicited his present mission for the purpose of satisfying his secret curiosity, although never was curiosity more desperate. But this last effort was a matter of conscience. The house of these Carmelites was the only Spanish convent which had escaped his search. While crossing from the mainland, a voyage which took less than an hour, a presentiment favorable to his hopes had arisen in his heart. Since then although he had seen nothing of the convent but its walls, and of the nuns not so much as their robes, and though he had heard nothing but the chants of their liturgies, yet he had gathered under these walls and from these chants faint indications that seemed to justify his slender hope. And, slight as were the auguries thus capriciously awakened, never was human passion more violently aroused than was the curiosity of the general. But the heart knows no insignificant events; it magnifies all things; it puts in the same balance the fall of an empire of fourteen years' duration and the fall of a woman's glove, and nearly always the glove outweighs the empire. Here, then, are the facts in all their actual simplicity. After the facts will come the emotions.

An hour after the general had landed on this island the royal authority was reëstablished. A few constitutional Spaniards, who had taken refuge there by night after the fall of Cadiz, embarked on a vessel which the general permitted them to charter for a voyage to London. There was thus neither resistance nor reaction. This little insular restoration could not, however, be accomplished without a Mass, at which must necessarily be present the two companies of troops of the expedition. Not being aware of the rigor of the cloister among the Barefooted Carmelites, the general had hoped to be able to obtain in the church some information concerning the nuns immured in the convent, one of whom might be a being dearer to him than life, and more precious than honor. His hopes were at first cruelly disappointed. Mass was indeed celebrated with pomp. In honor of this solemn occasion, the curtains which habitually hid the choir were drawn aside and gave to view the rich ornaments, the priceless paintings and the shrines encrusted with precious stones whose brilliancy effaced that of the numerous votive offerings in gold and in silver hung by the mariners of the port on the pillars of the great nave. The nuns had all retired to the seclusion of the organ-gallery. Yet in spite of this first check, and during the Mass of thanksgiving, there suddenly developed a drama endowed with more secret interests than had ever moved the heart of man. The sister who played the organ aroused an enthusiasm so vivid that not one of the military contingent present regretted the order which had brought him to the ceremony. The common soldiers even listened with pleasure, and all the officers were ravished by it. As to the general, he remained calm and cold in appearance. The sensations which were aroused in him by the different selections played by the nun rank with the small number of things whose expression words can not convey, rendering it impotent, but which, like death, like God, like eternity, can be perceived only at their slender point of contact with man. By a strange chance, the music of the organ seemed to belong to the school of Rossini, the composer who has carried more human passion than any other into the art of music, and whose works will some day, by their number and their extent, inspire Homeric respect. Of the scores of this fine genius the nun seemed to have more particularly studied that of *Moses in Egypt*, doubtless because the sentiments of sacred music are there carried to the highest degree. Perhaps these two spirits, the one so gloriously European, the other unknown, had met together in some intuitive perception of the same poetry. This opinion was that of two officers, true *dilettanti*, who no doubt regretted in Spain the theatre Favart. At last, in the *Te Deum* it was impossible not to recognize a French soul in the character which the music suddenly took on. The triumph of His Most Christian Majesty evidently roused the keenest joy in the bottom of the heart of this nun. Surely, she was a French woman. Presently the patriotic spirit burst forth, sparkling like a jet of light to the repeats of the organ, in which the sister introduced *motifs* which breathed all the delicacy of Parisian taste, and with which were vaguely blended sentiments of our finest national anthems.

Spanish hands could never have put into this graceful homage to victorious arms the fire that thus betrayed the origin of the musician.

"There is, then, France everywhere?" said a soldier.

The general left the church during the *Te Deum*, it was impossible for him to listen to it. The notes of the musician revealed to him at last the woman madly loved, and who had buried herself so deeply in the heart of religion and had so carefully hidden herself away from the sight of the world that she had escaped up to this time the most persistent search skilfully set on foot by men armed not only with great power but with superior intelligence. The suspicion awakened in the general's heart was almost justified by the vague echo of an air of sweet melancholy, *Fleuve du Tage*, a French ballad, of which he had often heard the prelude in the Parisian boudoir of the woman he loved, and which this nun now used to express amid the joy of the conquerors the regrets of an exile. A terrible sensation! To hope for the resurrection of a lost love, to find it again still lost, to have a mysterious glimpse of it after five years during which passion had been exasperated by the void and intensified by the inutility of the efforts made to satisfy it!

Who has not, once at least, in his life, overturned everything about him, his papers, his house, ransacked his memory impatiently, in searching for some precious object and then felt the ineffable pleasure of finding it after a day or two consumed in the vain search; after having hoped and despaired of its recovery; after having expended the liveliest irritations of the soul for this important nothing which has caused almost a passion? Well, extend this kind of fury through five years; put a woman, a heart, a love, in the place of this nothing; lift the passion into the highest realms of feelings; and then picture to yourself an ardent man, a man with the heart and the face of a lion, one of those men with a mane, who are imposing and who communicate to all those about them a respectful terror. Perhaps you will then understand the abrupt departure of the general during the *Te Deum*, at the moment when the prelude of an air once heard with delight under gilded ceilings, vibrated through the nave of this church by the sea.

He descended the steep street which led up to the church, and did not stop until the deep tones of the organ no longer reached his ear. Unable to think of anything but the love whose volcanic eruption fired his heart, he only perceived that the *Te Deum* was ended when the Spanish congregation poured from the church. He felt that his conduct and appearance might appear ridiculous, and he returned to take his place at the head of the procession, explaining to the alcade and to the governor of the town that a sudden indisposition had obliged him to come out into the air. Then it suddenly occurred to him to use this pretext at first carelessly given as a means of prolonging his stay on the island. Excusing himself because of the aggravation of his discomfort, he declined to preside at the banquet offered by the authorities of the island to the French officers; he took to his bed after writing to the major-general that a passing illness compelled him to turn over his command to the colonel. This artifice, so commonplace but so natural, left him free from all duties during the time necessary for the accomplishment of his projects. In his character of a man essentially catholic and monarchical he acquainted himself with the hours of the various services and affected the utmost interest in the duties of religion,—a piety which in Spain would excite no surprise.

The very next day, while his soldiers were embarking, the general went up to the convent to be present at vespers. He found the church deserted by the townspeople who, in spite of their devotion, had all gone to the port to see the embarkation of the troops. The Frenchman, glad to find himself alone in the church, took care to make the clink of his spurs resound under the vaulted roof. He walked noisily, he coughed, he spoke aloud to himself, in order to inform the nuns, and above all the organist, that if the French were departing, one, at least, remained behind. Was this singular method of communication heard, understood?—the general believed it was. In the *Magnificat,* the organ seemed to send him a response which was brought him by the vibrations of the air. The soul of the nun floated towards him on the wings of her notes, quivering in the movements of the sounds. The music burst forth in all its power; it inspired the church. This hymn of joy, consecrated by the sublime liturgy of Roman

Christianity to the uplifting of the soul in presence of the splendors of the ever-living God, became the expression of a heart almost terrified at its own happiness in the presence of the splendors of a perishable love which still lived and came to move it once more beyond the religious tomb in which women are buried to rise again, brides of Christ.

*

The organ is beyond all question the grandest, the most daring, the most magnificent of all the instruments created by human genius. It is an orchestra in itself, from which a skilful hand may demand all things, it can express all things. Is it not in some sort an elevation on which the soul may poise itself ere it launches itself into space, endeavoring to perceive in its flight a thousand scenes, to depict life, to traverse the infinite which separates heaven from earth? The longer a poet listens to its gigantic harmonies the more will he be inclined to believe that between kneeling humanity and the God hidden by the dazzling rays of the sanctuary, the hundred voices of this terrestrial choir can alone fill the vast distance and serve as the only interpreter strong enough to transmit to heaven human prayers in the omnipotence of their desires, in the diversity of their melancholy, with the tints of their meditative ecstasies, with the impetuous spring of their repentance and the thousand imaginations of their beliefs. Yes, beneath these long vaults, the harmonies born of the genius of sacred things find grandeurs yet unheard of with which they adorn, with which they strengthen themselves. There, the dim light, the profound silence, the chants alternating with the thunder of the organ, seem to make for God a veil through which His luminous attributes radiate. All these sacred riches now seemed flung like a grain of incense on the frail altar of an earthly love, before the eternal throne of a jealous and avenging God. In fact, the joy of the nun had not that character of grandeur and of gravity which is in harmony with the solemnity of the *Magnificat;* she gave to the music richness, graceful developments, the different rhythms of which seemed to breathe of human gayety. Her motifs had the brilliancy of the roulades of a cantatrice striving to express love, and the notes rose buoyantly like those of a bird by the side of its mate. Then, at moments, she darted back into the past, to sport there or to weep there alternately. Her changing moods had something disordered about them, like the agitation of a woman happy at the return of her lover. Then, after the flexible fugues of delirium and the marvelous effects of this fantastic recognition, the soul that spoke thus returned upon itself. The musician, passing from the major to the minor key, revealed to her auditor the story of her present situation. Suddenly, unexpectedly, she recounted to him her long melancholy and depicted for him her lingering moral malady. She had abolished every day a feeling, cut off every night some thought, reduced gradually her heart to ashes. After soft modulations the music took on slowly, tint by tint, the hue of profound sadness. Soon the echoes poured forth in torrents the well-springs of grief. Then, all at once, the higher notes struck a concert of angelic voices, as if to announce to her lost lover, lost but not forgotten, that the reunion of two souls could only take place in heaven: hope most precious! Then came the *Amen*. There, no longer any joy nor any tears, neither melancholy nor regrets. The *Amen* was a return to God; this last chord was grave, solemn, terrible. The musician revealed the veil which covered the nun, and after the last thunder of the basses which made the hearers tremble even to their hair she seemed to sink again into that tomb from which she had for a moment issued. When the echoes had by degrees ceased their long vibration it seemed that the church, until then luminous, had again been plunged into profound obscurity.

The general had been completely carried away by the course of this powerful genius, and had followed her through all the regions which she had traversed. He comprehended in their full meaning all the images that crowded that burning symphony, and for him these chords echoed far. For him, as for the sister, this poem was the future, the present, and the past. Music, even that of the theatre, is it not for tender and poetic souls, for wounded and suffering hearts, a text which they interpret at the will of their memories? If it requires the heart of a poet to make a musician, are not poetry and love required to hear, to comprehend, the great works of music? Religion, love, and music, are they not the triple expression of the same fact, the need of expansion which agitates every noble soul? These three forms of poetry all lead to God, who alone can unravel all terrestrial emotions. Thus this holy human trinity participates in the infinite grandeurs of God, whom we never figure to ourselves without surrounding Him by the fires of love, the golden timbrels of music, of light and of harmony. Is it not the principle and the end of all our works?

The French general divined that in this desert, on this rock surrounded by the sea, the nun had taken possession of music to pour into it the excess of passion that consumed her. Was it a homage made to God of her love? was it the triumph of love over God? questions difficult to answer. But, certainly, the general could not doubt that he had found in this heart dead to the world, a passion as burning as his own. When vespers were ended, he returned to the alcade's house, where he lodged. Giving himself over at first to the thousand delights lavished by a satisfaction long waited for, painfully sought, he could see nothing beyond. He was still loved. Solitude had nourished love in that heart, as much as love had grown in his own by the barriers, successively surmounted, which this woman had placed between herself and him. This expansion of the soul had its natural duration. Then came the desire to see this woman again, to reclaim her from God, to ravish her from Him,—a bold project, welcome to this bold man. After the repast he retired to his bed to escape questions, to be alone, to be able to think without interruption, and he remained plunged in the deepest meditation until the morning broke. He only rose to go to

Mass. He went to the church, placed himself close to the screen; his brow touched the curtain; he longed to tear it away, but he was not alone,—his host had accompanied him through politeness and the least imprudence might compromise the future of his passion and ruin his new hopes. The sound of the organ again filled the church but not under the touch of the same hand; the musician of the last two days was absent from the keyboard. All was chill and pale to the general. Was his mistress overcome by the same emotions under which had well nigh succumbed his own vigorous man's heart? Had she so truly shared, comprehended, a faithful and eager love that she now lay dying on her bed in her cell? At the moment when a thousand thoughts like these were rising in the Frenchman's mind he heard beside him the voice of the beloved, he recognized the clearness of its tones. This voice, slightly modified by a tremor which gave it all the grace lent to young girls by their chaste timidity, detached itself from the volume of song of the chant like that of a prima donna over the harmonies of a finale. It gave to the soul an impression like that produced on the eyes by a fillet of silver or of gold threading a dark frieze. It was indeed she! Still Parisian, she had not lost her gracious charm though she had quitted the adornments of the world for the headband and the coarse serge of a Carmelite. After having revealed her love the night before in the midst of the praises addressed to the Lord she now seemed to say to her lover: "Yes it is I, I am here, I love forever; yet I am sheltered from love. Thou wilt hear me, my soul shall enfold thee, and I shall remain beneath the brown shroud of this choir from which no power can tear me. Thou canst not see me."

"It is indeed she!" said the general to himself, lifting his head from his hands on which he had been leaning; for he had not been able at first to sustain the crushing emotion which rose like a whirlwind in his heart when that well-known voice vibrated under the arches, to the accompaniment of the murmur of the waves.

The storm raged without and calm was within the sanctuary. This voice, so rich, continued to display all its charming cajoleries, it fell like balm upon the parched heart of this lover, it flowered in the air about him, which he well might desire to breathe so as to receive the emanations of a soul exhaled with love in the words of the prayer. The alcade came to rejoin his guest, he found him in tears at the elevation of the Host, which was chanted by the nun, and carried him away to his house. Surprised to find such devotion in a French soldier, the alcade invited the confessor of the convent to join them at supper, and informed the general, to whom no news had ever given such pleasure. During the supper, the confessor was the object of such respectful attention on the part of the Frenchman that the Spaniards were confirmed in the high opinion they had formed of his piety. He inquired with great interest the number of the nuns, asked for details about the revenues of the convent and its wealth, with the air of a man who wished politely to entertain the good old priest with the matters in which he was most interested. Then he inquired about the life led by these holy sisters. Could they go out? Could they be seen?

"Señor," said the venerable priest, "the rule is severe. If the permission of our Holy Father must be obtained before a woman can enter a house of Saint-Bruno, here is the same rigor. It is impossible for any man to enter a convent of the Bare-footed Carmelites unless he is a priest and delegated by the Archbishop for duty in the house. No nun can go out. It is true, however, that THE GREAT SAINT—Mother Thérèse—did frequently leave her cell. The Visitor, or the Mothers Superior, can alone, with the authorization of the Archbishop, permit a nun to see strangers, especially in case of illness. Now, ours is one of the chief Houses of the Order and we have consequently a Mother Superior residing in the convent. We have among other foreigners a French woman, Sister Thérèse, the one who directs the music of the chapel."

"Ah!" said the general, feigning surprise. "She must have been gratified by the triumph of the Arms of the House of Bourbon?"

"I told them the object of the Mass, they are always a little curious."

"Perhaps Sister Thérèse has some interest in France; she might perhaps be glad to receive some news from there, or to ask some questions?"

"I think not or she would have spoken to me about it."

"As a compatriot," said the general, "I should be curious to see her.—If that were possible, if the Mother Superior would consent, if—"

"At the grating, even in presence of the reverend mother, an interview would be impossible for anyone, no matter whom; but in favor of a liberator of the Catholic throne and of our holy religion, in spite of the strictness of our Mother, the rule might perhaps be relaxed a moment," said the confessor, slightly winking his eyes. "I will speak about it."

"How old is Sister Thérèse?" asked the lover, who dared not question the priest about the beauty of the nun.

"She is no longer of any age," replied the good old man with a simplicity which made the general shudder.

*

The next morning, before the siesta, the confessor came to announce to the Frenchman that Sister Thérèse and the Mother Superior consented to receive him at the grating of the convent parlor before the hour of Vespers. After the siesta, during which the general had whiled away the time by walking around the port in the noonday heat, the priest came to seek him and introduced him into the convent; he guided him under a gallery which ran the length of the cemetery and in which fountains, several green trees and numerous arcades maintained a cooling freshness in harmony with the silence of the place. When they reached the end of this long gallery the priest caused his companion to enter a parlor divided in the middle by a grating covered with a brown curtain. On the side, to a degree public, in which the confessor left the general, there was a wooden bench along one side of the wall; some chairs, also of wood, were near the grating. The ceiling was crossed by projecting beams of evergreen oak without ornament. The daylight only entered this apartment through two windows in the division set apart for the nuns, so that this feeble light, mostly absorbed by the brown tones of the woodwork, scarcely sufficed to reveal the great black Christ, the portrait of Saint Thérèse and a picture of the Virgin which hung on the gray panels of the wall. The feelings of the general were subdued, in spite of their violence, to a tone of melancholy. He became calm in this domestic calm. Something mighty as the grave seized him beneath these chilling rafters. Was this not its eternal silence, its profound peace, its suggestions of the infinite? Then the stillness and the fixed thought of the cloister, this thought which fills the air, in the half-light, in all things, and which, nowhere traced, is yet magnified by the imagination, this great word, *Peace in the Lord,* enters there with living power into the least religious soul.

Convents of men are not easily conceivable; man seems feeble and unworthy in them,—he is born to act, to fulfil a life of toil, which he evades in his cell. But in a monastery of women, what virile strength and yet what touching weakness! A man may be pushed by a thousand sentiments into the depths of an abbey, he flings himself into them as from a precipice; but a woman enters there drawn only by one sentiment,—she does not unsex herself, she becomes the bride of God. You may say to the man, "Why did you not struggle?" But the seclusion of the woman, is it not always a sublime struggle? The general found this silent parlor and this convent lost in the midst of the sea full of memories of Him. Love seldom reaches upward to solemnity; but love still faithful in the bosom of God, is there not something solemn in it, and more than a man has the right to hope for in this nineteenth century, and with our manners and customs? The general's soul was one that might readily be impressed by the infinite grandeurs of this situation, he was one of those sufficiently elevated to forget political interests, worldly honors, Spain, the world of Paris, and rise to the heights of this sublime termination. Moreover, what could be more truly tragic? How many emotions might be found in the situation of these two lovers, reunited alone in the middle of the sea, on a granite ledge, yet separated by an idea, by an impassable barrier! Look at this man saying to himself, "Can I triumph over God in that heart?" A slight sound made this man quiver, the brown curtain was drawn back; then he saw in the half-light a woman standing whose face was hidden from him by a prolongation of the veil folded on her head; according to the rule of the order she was clothed in that garb, the color of which has become proverbial. The general could not see the naked feet of the nun, which would have revealed to him a frightful emaciation; yet through the numerous folds of the coarse robe which covered and did not adorn this woman he divined that tears, prayer, passion, solitude, had already wasted her away.

The cold hand of a woman, doubtless that of the Mother Superior, held back the curtain; and the general, examining the necessary witness of this interview, encountered the black and thoughtful eyes of an old nun, almost a centenarian, a clear and youthful look, which belied the numberless wrinkles which furrowed her pale face.

"Madame la Duchesse," he said in a voice shaken by emotion to the nun who bowed her head, "Does your companion understand French?"

"There is no duchesse here," replied the nun. "You are in presence of Sister Thérèse. The woman whom you call my companion is my mother in God, my superior here below."

These words, so humbly uttered by the voice that once harmonized with the luxury and elegance in which this woman had lived, queen of the world of Paris, by lips whose language had formerly been so gay, so mocking, struck the general as if with lightning.

"My holy Mother speaks only Latin and Spanish," she added.

"I understand neither. Dear Antoinette, make my excuses to her."

As she heard her name softly uttered by a man once so hard to her, the nun was shaken by an inward emotion which betrayed itself by the slight trembling of her veil on which the light fell directly.

"My brother," she said passing her sleeve beneath her veil, perhaps to wipe her eyes, "my name is Sister Thérèse."

Then she turned to the mother and said to her in Spanish these words which the general plainly heard; he knew enough of the language to understand them, perhaps also to speak them:

"My dear Mother, this cavalier presents his respects to you and begs you to excuse him for not laying them himself at your feet; but he knows neither of the two languages which you speak—"

The old woman bowed her head slowly, her countenance took an expression of angelic softness, heightened nevertheless by the consciousness of her power and her dignity.

"You know this cavalier?" she asked with a penetrating glance at the sister.

"Yes, my Mother."

"Retire to your cell, my daughter!" said the Mother Superior in a tone of authority.

The general hastily withdrew behind the curtain, so that his face might not reveal the terrible emotion which agitated him; and in the shadow he seemed to see still the piercing eyes of the Mother Superior. This woman, arbiter of the frail and fleeting joy he had won at such a cost, made him afraid and he trembled, he whom a triple range of cannon had never terrified. The duchess walked towards the door, but she turned:

"My Mother," she said in a voice of horrible calmness, "this Frenchman is one of my brothers."

"Remain then, my daughter," replied the old woman after a pause.

This admirable jesuitism revealed so much love and such regret that a man of a weaker organization than the general would have given way in experiencing so lively a pleasure in the midst of an immense peril, for him so novel. Of what value were words, looks, gestures, in a scene in which love must be hidden from the eyes of the lynx, the claws of a tiger! The Sister Thérèse came back.

"You see, my brother, what I dared to do that I might speak to you, for one moment, of your salvation, and of the prayers which my soul addresses to heaven every day for you. I have committed a mortal sin. I have lied. How many days of penitence to efface that lie! but it will be to suffer for you. You do not know, my brother, what happiness it is to love in heaven, to be able to avow our feelings now that religion has purified them, has transported them into the highest regions, and that it is permitted us to no longer consider anything but the soul. If the doctrines, if the spirit of the saint to whom we owe this refuge had not lifted me far above terrestrial miseries to a sphere, far indeed from that where she is, but certainly above the world, I could not have seen you. But I can see you, hear you, and remain calm—"

"Antoinette," cried the general, interrupting her at these words, "let me see you, you whom I love now passionately, to distraction, as you once wished me to love you."

"Do not call me Antoinette, I implore you. The memories of the past do me harm. See in me only Sister Thérèse, a creature trusting to the divine pity. And—" she added after a pause, "calm yourself, my brother. Our Mother would separate us pitilessly if your face betrayed earthly passions, or if your eyes shed tears."

The general bowed his head as if to collect

himself. When he again lifted his eyes to the grating he saw between two bars the pale, emaciated, yet still ardent face of the nun. Her complexion, where once had bloomed all the loveliness of youth, where once there shone the happy contrast of a creamy whiteness with the color of the rose of Bengal, had now taken the warm translucent tone of a porcelain cup through which a feeble light shines faintly. The beautiful hair of which this woman was once so proud had been shorn. A band bound her forehead and enveloped her face. Her eyes surrounded with dark circles, due to the austerities of her life, launched, at moments, feverish rays and their habitual calm was but a veil. In a word, of this woman only the soul remained.

"Ah! you will leave this tomb, you who have become my life! You belonged to me, and you were not free to give yourself, even to God. Did you not promise me to sacrifice all to the least of my commands? Now, perhaps, you will think me worthy of this promise when you know what I have done for you. I have sought you through the whole world. For five years you have been the thought of every instant, the occupation of my life. My friends, very powerful friends as you know, have helped me with all their ability to search the convents of France, of Italy, of Spain, of Sicily, of America. My love was rekindled with every fruitless search; I have made many a long journey on a false hope, I have expended my life and the strongest beatings of my heart around the black walls of cloisters. I do not speak to you of a fidelity unlimited, what is it? nothing in comparison with the infinite desires of my love. If in other days your remorse was real you cannot now hesitate to follow me."

"You forget that I am not free."

"The duke is dead," he said hastily.

Sister Thérèse reddened.

"May Heaven receive him!" she said with quick emotion; "he was generous to me. But I was not speaking of those ties, one of my faults was my willingness to break them all without scruple for you."

"You speak of your vows," cried the general, frowning. "I did not believe that anything would weigh in your heart against your love. But do not doubt, Antoinette, I will obtain from the Holy Father a brief which will cancel your vows. I will surely go to Rome, I will petition every earthly power; and if God could descend, I—"

"Do not blaspheme."

"Do not fear how God would see it! Ah! I would much more gladly know that you would escape from these walls for me; that this very night you would throw yourself into some bark, at the foot of these rocks. We would depart to be happy anywhere, to the end of the world! And with me, you would come back to life, to health in the shelter of love."

"Do not say such things," returned Sister Thérèse, "you do not know what you have become to me. I love you much better than I have ever loved you. I pray to God for you daily, and I see you no longer with the eyes of my body. If you but knew, Armand, the joy of being able without shame to deliver yourself to a pure affection which God protects! You do not know how happy I am to call down the blessings of Heaven upon your head. I never pray for myself: God will do with me according to His will. But you, I would wish at the price of my eternity to have some assurance that you are happy in this world, and that you will be happy in the other, throughout the ages. My life eternal is all that misfortune has left me to offer you. Now, I have grown old in tears, I am no longer either young or beautiful; moreover, you would despise a nun who again became a woman, whom no sentiment, not even maternal love, could absolve.—What could you say to me that would outweigh the unnumbered reflections which have accumulated in my heart during five years, and which have changed it, hollowed it, withered it? I should have given it less sorrowfully to God!"

"What I would say to you, dear Antoinette! I would say to you that I love you, that affection, love, true love, the happiness of living in a heart wholly one's own, and without one reservation, is so rare and so difficult to find that I have doubted you, that I have put you to cruel tests; but to-day I love you with all the powers of my soul,—if you will follow me into some retreat I will no longer listen to any other voice than yours, I will no longer look on any other face than yours—"

"Silence, Armand! You are shortening the single

moment in which we are permitted to see each other here below."

"Antoinette, will you follow me?"

"But I never leave you. I live in your heart, but otherwise than by the interest of worldly pleasure, of vanity, of selfish joy; I live here for you, pale and faded, in the bosom of God! If He is just you will be happy—"

"Phrases all! But if I wish to have you pale and faded? But if I cannot be happy without possessing you? You will still be thinking of duties in the presence of your lover? He is never, then, above all things else in your heart? In other days you preferred to him society, yourself, I know not what; now it is God, it is my salvation. In Sister Thérèse I recognize still the duchess, ignorant of the joys of love, and still unfeeling beneath a pretence of tenderness. You do not love me, you have never loved—"

"Ah! my brother—"

"You will not leave this tomb; you love my soul, you say? Well then, you shall lose forever this soul, I will kill myself—"

"My Mother," cried Sister Thérèse in Spanish, "I have lied to you, this man is my lover!"

Immediately the curtain fell. The general, standing stupefied, scarcely heard the interior doors closing violently.

"Ah! she loves me still!" he cried, comprehending all that there was of sublimity in the cry of the nun. "She shall be carried away from here—"

THE INTERVIEW IN THE CONVENT

"My Mother," cried Sister Thérèse in Spanish, "I have lied to you, this man is my lover!"

Copyright, 1899, by George Barrie & Son

He left the island immediately, returned to headquarters, reported himself still ill, asked for a leave of absence and returned immediately to France.

The following adventure will explain the situation in which we found the two persons of this history.

*

What is called in France the Faubourg Saint-Germain is not a quarter of Paris, nor a sect, nor an institution, nor indeed anything that can be definitely expressed. The Place Royale, the Faubourg Saint-Honoré, the Chaussée-d'Antin, all contain mansions in which may be found the atmosphere of the Faubourg Saint-Germain. Thus to begin with, all the Faubourg is not in the Faubourg. Persons born far from its influence may feel it and affiliate with this world, whilst others born in its midst may be forever banished from it. The manners, the forms of speech, in a word the traditions, of the Faubourg Saint-Germain have been to Paris for the last forty years what the Court was to it in former days, what the Hôtel Saint-Paul was in the fourteenth century, the Louvre in the fifteenth, the Palais, the Hôtel Rambouillet, the Place Royale, in the sixteenth, and, finally, Versailles in the seventeenth and eighteenth centuries. Through all phases of history the Paris of the upper class and of the nobility has had its centre, just as the Paris of the people will always have its own. This recurring singularity offers ample matter for reflection to those who wish to observe or to paint the different social strata; and perhaps its causes should be investigated, not only to explain the character of this story but also to serve important interests,—

more important to the future than to the present, if the teachings of experience were not always as profitless for political parties as for youth. The great seigneurs and the men of wealth, who always imitate the great seigneurs, have at all epochs withdrawn their houses from much frequented places. If the Duc d'Uzès built for himself, during the reign of Louis XIV., the handsome hôtel at the gate of which he placed the fountain of Rue Montmartre, a beneficent act which rendered him, in addition to his virtues, an object of such popular veneration that all the people of the quarter followed him to his grave, it was because this quarter of Paris was then deserted. But no sooner were the fortifications leveled, the marshes beyond the boulevards covered with houses, than the d'Uzès family abandoned their fine hôtel which is occupied in our days by a banker. Then the nobility, compromised by the surrounding shops, abandoned the Place Royale, the neighborhood of the Parisian centre, and crossed the river in order to be able to breathe at its ease in the Faubourg Saint-Germain, where palaces had already arisen around the hôtel built by Louis XIV. for the Duc du Maine, the Benjamin of his legitimatized sons. For those accustomed to the splendors of life is there, in fact, anything more ignoble than the tumult, the mud, the cries, the offensive smells, the narrowness of populous streets? Are not the habits of a shop-keeping or manufacturing quarter in constant discord with the habits of the great world? Commerce and labor are going to bed just when aristocracy is going to dine; the one is in noisy activity while the other is in need of repose; their computations are never on the same basis, one is the receipt and the other the expenditure. Thus arise manners and customs diametrically opposed. This observation has in it nothing of disdain. An aristocracy is in some sort the thought of a society, as the bourgeoisie and the proletariat are its organism and its action. From this comes the need of different seats and localities for these differing forces; and from their antagonism grows an apparent antipathy which produces the diversity of movements all operating, however, towards a common end. These social discords result so logically from every constitutional code that the liberal, the most disposed to complain of it —as of an attack upon the sublime ideas under which the ambitious of the lower classes hide their designs—would find it prodigiously absurd if Monsieur le Prince Montmorency lived in Rue Saint-Martin, on the corner of the street which bears his name, or if Monsieur le Duc de Fitz-James, descendant of the royal Scottish race, had his hôtel in Rue Marie-Stuart at the corner of Rue Montorgueil. *Sint ut sunt, aut non sint,*—this fine pontifical saying might serve as a motto for the great world of every nation. This fact, obvious to every epoch and accepted always by the people, bears within it reasons of State; it is at once an effect and a cause, a principle and a law. The masses have a sound common sense which only deserts them at the moment when the evil-disposed excite their passions. This common sense rests on the essential truths of a common order, as true at Moscow as in London, as true in Geneva as in Calcutta. Everywhere, whenever you assemble families of unequal fortunes within a given space you will see them dividing into superior circles, those of patricians, of the first, second, and third classes of society. Equality may perhaps be a *right*, but no human power can convert it into a *fact*. It would be well for the happiness of France if this truth could be popularized. The least intelligent classes may still feel the benefits of political harmony. This harmony is the poetry of order, and the people are conscious of a lively need of order. The co-operation of things among themselves,—unity, to express all in one word,—is it not the simplest expression of the principle of order? Architecture, music, poetry, all rest in France, more than in any other country, upon this principle which moreover is written in the depths of its clear and pure language,—and language will always be the most infallible formula of a nation. Thus you may see the people here adopting the most poetical airs, the best modulated; attaching themselves to the most simple ideas; choosing incisive formula which are most closely packed with thought. France is the only country in which a little phrase may bring about a great revolution. The masses here have never revolted except to endeavor to bring into unison men, things, and principles. Thus no other nation has ever so well understood the idea of unity which should exist in the aristocratic life, perhaps because no other has so well comprehended political necessities; history has never found it lagging behind. France is often deceived, but as a woman is deceived,—by generous ideas, by ardent sentiments whose extent at first escapes calculation.

Thus to begin with, for its first characteristic trait the Faubourg Saint-Germain has the splendor of its mansions, its large gardens, their stillness formerly in keeping with the magnificence of its territorial fortunes. Is not this space intervening between a class and the whole capital a material expression of the moral distance which should separate them? In all created things the head has its indicated place. If, by chance, a nation causes its head to fall at its feet it perceives, sooner or later, that it has committed suicide. As the nations do not wish to die, they, therefore, apply themselves to the reconstruction of a head. When a nation has no longer the strength to do this, it perishes, as perished Rome, Venice and so many others. The distinction introduced by the difference in habits and manners between the other spheres of social activity and the superior sphere implies, necessarily, an actual and commanding worth at the aristocratic summits. Whenever in any state, under any form which the *government* may assume, the patricians fail in their conditions of complete superiority, they become powerless, and the people soon overthrow them. The people desire always to see in their hands, in their hearts, and in their heads fortune, power and the initiative,—speech, intelligence and glory. Without this triple strength all their privileges vanish. The people, like women, love strength in those who govern them and their love is not given where they do not respect; they will not yield obedience to those who do not command their homage. A despised aristocracy is like a sluggard king, a husband in petticoats; it is naught before it becomes nothing. Thus the separation of the great, their distinct habits, in a word the general customs of the patrician castes, is both the symbol of a real power and the cause of their destruction when they have lost power. The Faubourg Saint-Germain has allowed itself to be temporarily cast aside because it has not chosen to recognize the conditions of its existence, which existence could easily have been perpetuated. It should have had the good faith to see in time, as the English aristocracy saw, that institutions have their climacteric years in which the same words have no longer the same signification, in which ideas clothe themselves in new garments, and in which the conditions of political life change entirely their form without any essential change in their being. These thoughts have natural developments which are essentially relevant to this tale, into which they enter both in definition of its causes and in explanation of its facts.

The grandeur of châteaux and of aristocratic palaces, the luxury of their details, the constant sumptuousness of their appointments, the orbit in which the fortunate proprietor, rich before he was born, moves without constraint and without disagreeable contacts; the habit of never descending to the petty daily calculations of life, the leisure at his disposal, the superior instruction which he early acquires,—in short, all those patrician traditions which give him social powers which his adversaries can scarcely acquire by study, by a force of will, by tenacious clinging to some vocation,—all these things should elevate the soul of a man who from his youth possesses such privileges, should fill him with that high respect for himself the least consequence of which is a nobility of the heart in keeping with the nobility of the name. This is true of certain families. Here and there in the Faubourg Saint-Germain may be met noble characters, exceptions which weigh against the widespread egotism which has been the ruin of that exclusive world. These advantages pertain to the French aristocracy, as they do to all the patrician flowering which nations produce on their surface as long as their existence rests on *domain*,—domain of the soil like the domain of wealth, the only solid basis of regular society; but these advantages remain with patricians of all kinds only so long as they fulfill the condition upon which the people leave them in possession. They hold them as a kind of moral fief, the *tenure* of which has its obligations to the sovereign, and here the sovereign is certainly to-day the people. Times have changed, and so have arms.

The knight to whom formerly it sufficed to wear the coat of mail, the hauberk, to know how to wield his lance and to display his pennon, must to-day give proof of the qualities of his mind; and where there was formerly required only a brave heart, there must be to-day a strong brain. Art, science and wealth are the social triangle on which the arms of power are now blazoned and from which modern aristocracy proceeds. A noble theorem is the equal of a great name. The Rothschilds, those modern Fuggers, are princes *de facto*. A great artist is really an oligarchy, he represents an entire century and becomes almost always a law. Thus, the gift of language, the motor power at high pressure of the writer, the genius of the poet, the perseverance of the merchant, the will of a statesman who concentrates in himself a thousand dazzling qualities, the sword of the general, these personal conquests made by an individual which give him authority over society,—the aristocratic class should seek to acquire to-day the monopoly of all these, as formerly it had that of material strength. To remain at the head of a nation, is it not always necessary to remain worthy of conducting it; of being for it the soul and the mind, in order to guide the hands? How can a people be led without the qualities of command? What would be the marshal's baton without the intrinsic strength of the captain who holds it in his hand? The Faubourg Saint-Germain has played with batons, thinking them the power itself. It has reversed the terms of the proposition which justify its existence. Instead of throwing aside the symbols which offended the people and holding fast secretly the essentials of power, it has let the bourgeoisie seize the power whilst it clung with fatal persistency to its symbols, and has constantly forgotten the laws imposed upon it by its numerical weakness. An aristocracy which personally constitutes scarcely the thousandth part of society must, to-day as heretofore, multiply its means of action in a society in order to oppose in the great crisis a weight equal to that of the masses. In our day, means of action should be real forces, and not historical traditions. Unhappily, in France, the nobility, still swelling with a sense of its ancient and banished power, excites a sort of prejudice against which it is difficult for it to defend itself. Perhaps this is a national defect. The Frenchman, more than any other man, never finishes on a lower level; he mounts from the step on which he finds himself to that next higher; he seldom pities the unfortunates over whose heads he lifts himself, he sighs only to see so many happy ones above him. Although he has a good deal of heart, he only too often prefers to listen to his intelligence. This national instinct which always sends the French in advance, this vanity which eats into their fortunes and rules them as rigidly as the principle of economy rules the Hollanders, has for three centuries absolutely dominated our nobility, which in this respect has been eminently French. The man of the Faubourg Saint-Germain has always convinced himself of his intellectual superiority because of his material superiority. Everything in France has convinced him of this because since the establishment of the Faubourg Saint-Germain—an aristocratic revolution which began on the day the monarchy left Versailles—the Faubourg Saint-Germain has, allowing for a few lapses, always leaned upon power, which will always be in France more or less Faubourg Saint-Germain. Hence its defeat in 1830. At that epoch it was like an army operating without a base. It had not profited by the peace to plant itself in the heart of the nation. It sinned from a defect of instruction, and from a total inability to survey the whole field of its interests. It killed a certain future in favor of a doubtful present. This, perhaps, was the reason of this false policy: the physical and moral distance which this superior class endeavored to maintain between itself and the rest of the nation has fatally had for its only result, in the last forty years, the development in the upper class of a personal sentiment at the expense of the patriotism of caste. Formerly, when the French nobility were great, rich and powerful, the gentlemen knew how in moments of danger to choose their leaders and to obey them. As they became less eminent they showed themselves less capable of discipline; and, as in the Later Empire, each one wished to be Emperor; perceiving their equality in weakness each fancied himself individually superior. Every family ruined by the Revolution and by the equal division of property thought only of itself instead of considering the whole great family of the aristocracy, and fancied that if each were enriched the whole body would be strong. An error. Wealth is but a sign of power. These families, composed of persons who preserved the lofty traditions of courtesy, of true elegance, of pure language, of reserve and of a noble pride, as became their state—qualities which become petty when made the chief occupation of an existence to which they should only be accessory,—all these families had a certain intrinsic worth which, judged superficially, left them in appearance only a nominal value. Not one of these families has had the courage to ask itself, "Are we strong enough to hold supreme power?" They flung themselves down as the lawyers did in 1830. Instead of showing itself as a protector like a grandee, the Faubourg Saint-Germain was grasping like a parvenu. The day on which it was demonstrated to the most intelligent nation in the world that the restored nobility had organized power and the budget for its own profit, that day the nobility received a mortal wound. It wished to be an aristocracy when it was no longer capable of being anything but an oligarchy,—two widely different systems, as will be comprehended by any man clever enough to read intelligently the patronymic names of the lords of the Upper Chamber. Undoubtedly the royal government was well intentioned; but it constantly forgot that it was necessary to make everything for the best for the people, even their own happiness, and that France, that capricious female, will be made happy or beaten in her own way. Had there been many dukes like the Duc de Laval, whose modesty made him worthy of his name, the throne of the eldest branch would have become as firm as that of the House of Hanover. In 1814, and above all in 1820, the French nobility had to rule the best informed epoch, the most aristocratic middle-class, and the most feminine nation in the world. The Faubourg Saint-Germain could have easily led and amused a middle-class intoxicated with worldly distinctions, enamored of art and science. But the petty leaders of this great epoch of intelligence hated all the art and the sciences. They did not even know how to present religion, of which they stood greatly in need, under the poetic colors which would have made it beloved. While Lamartine, Lamennais, Montalembert and other writers whose talents were lit with poetry renewed or uplifted religious ideas, all those who were bungling the government made the bitterness of religion to be felt. Never was a nation more amenable, it was at that time like a woman who weary of resisting becomes complacent; never was power more awkward and blundering;—France and womankind love real faults better. To reinstate itself, to found a great oligarchy, the nobility of the Faubourg should have searched in good faith to find in its own pockets the coins of Napoléon, should have eviscerated itself if necessary to give birth to a constitutional Richelieu; if this genius was not to be found within itself, it should have gone to seek it even in the cold garret where it might be dying, and have assimilated it, as the English House of Lords constantly assimilates to itself the new creations of the aristocracy,—then to have required of this man implacable firmness, the pruning off all the dead branches, the trimming down to the ground of the tree of the aristocracy. But in the first place, the great system of English Toryism is too immense for little heads; and its importation would have taken too much time for the French, for whom a gradual success is no more than a *fiasco*. Moreover, far from having that redeeming policy which seeks strength wherever God himself has put it, these little-great personages hated all strength outside of their own; in short, far from renewing its youth, the Faubourg Saint-Germain grew aged. Etiquette, an institution of secondary importance, could have been maintained if kept for great occasions; but etiquette became a daily warfare, and instead of being merely a matter of art or of magnificence, it became a question of the maintenance of power. If at first the throne was in need of one of those counselors equal to the importance of the circumstances, the Aristocracy lacked above all that due knowldege of its own general interests which might have supplied all other deficiencies. It came to a halt before the marriage of Monsieur de Talleyrand, the only man with one of those metallic heads in which are forged anew the political systems capable of gloriously reviving the nations. The Faubourg mocked at ministers who were not nobles, and furnished no nobles capable of being ministers; it might have rendered veritable service to the country by raising the status of the justices of the peace, by fertilizing the soil, by constructing roads and canals, by making itself an active territorial power; but it sold its estates to gamble on the Bourse. It might have drawn from the bourgeoisie men of action and of talent, whose ambition undermined its power, by opening to them its ranks; it preferred to combat them, and without arms; for it now possessed only as a tradition, that which it had formerly held in reality. For the misfortune of this nobility, it retained precisely enough of its various fortunes to sustain its haughty pride. Content with these souvenirs, not one of these families thought seriously of selecting arms for their eldest sons among the *fasces* which the nineteenth century threw down in the public place. Their youth, excluded from public affairs, danced at the balls of Madame, instead of continuing at Paris under the influence of the fresh, young, conscientious talents of the Empire and of the Republic, the work which the chiefs of each of these families should have begun in all departments by there conquering acknowledgment of their titles by continual demands in favor of local interests, by conforming to the spirit of the age, by remodeling their caste according to the demands of the century. Concentrated in its Faubourg Saint-Germain, where still dwelt the spirit of old feudal opposition mingled with that of the old Court, the aristocracy, only slightly connected with the Tuileries, was more easily vanquished, existing as it did only on one ground, and, above all, as badly constituted as it was in the Chamber of Peers. Had it become an integral part of the country, it would have been indestructible; but cornered in its Faubourg, backed against the château, spread on the budget, one blow of the axe was sufficient to cut the thread of its expiring life, and the flat figure of a petty lawyer came forward to deal this stroke of the axe. Notwithstanding the fine speech of Monsieur Royer-Collard, the hereditary rights of the peerage and its entailed estates fell before the pasquinades of a man who boasted that he had saved many heads from the executioner, but who now killed, awkwardly enough, great institutions. There may be found in this warnings and instruction for the future. If the French oligarchy is to have no future life there would be an inexpressibly sad cruelty in thus torturing it after its death, and there should be thought only to bury it with honors; but if the scalpel of the surgeons is sharp to feel, it often gives life to the dying. The Faubourg Saint-Germain may find itself more powerful under persecution than it ever was in its triumph, —if it find for itself a head and a system.

At present, it is easy to sum up this semi-political sketch. This lack of broad views and this vast assemblage of small errors; the desire of reëstablishing large fortunes with which everyone was preoccupied; a real need of a creed to sustain political action; a thirst for pleasure which lowered the religious tone, and necessitated hypocrisies; the partial opposition of certain nobler spirits who saw clearly and who were displeased by the rivalries of the Court; the nobility of the provinces, often purer of race than the Court nobles, but who, too often slighted, became disaffected,—all these causes combined to give the Faubourg Saint-Germain the most discordant elements. It was neither compact in system nor consistent in its acts, neither truly moral nor openly licentious, neither corrupted nor corrupting; it did not wholly abandon the questions which worked to its injury and it did not adopt ideas which might have saved it. In short, however weak its personality may have been, the party was nevertheless armed with all those grand principles which are the life of nations. Therefore, how was it that it perished in its vigor? It was exacting in its selection of those whom it received; it had good taste, much elegant superciliousness; yet its fall had certainly nothing of the brilliant or chivalric about it. The emigration of '89 was brought about by strong sentiments; the domestic emigration of 1830 only by self-interest. The names of some men illustrious in literature, the triumphs of oratory, Monsieur de Talleyrand in the congresses, the conquest of Algiers, and certain names which became again historic on battlefields,—all these revealed to the aristocracy of France the means which remained to it to nationalize itself and to win back the recognition of its rights, if only it would deign to take them. In all organized beings there is manifested the workings of an inward harmony. If a man is lazy, indolence betrays itself in every one of his movements. In like manner the physiognomy of a class conforms to its general spirit, to the soul which animates its body. Under the Restoration the woman of the Faubourg Saint-Germain displayed neither the proud hardihood which the ladies of the Court formerly carried into their transgressions, nor the modest dignity of the tardy virtues with which they expiated their faults, and which diffused around them such a vivid lustre. She had nothing that was very frivolous, nothing that was very grave. Her passions, with a few exceptions, were hypocritical; she made terms, as it were, with their enjoyment. A few of these families lived the bourgeoise life of the Duchesse d'Orléans, whose conjugal bed was so absurdly shown to visitors of the Palais-Royale; two or three kept up with difficulty the habits of the Regency and inspired a sort of disgust in women more adroit than they. This new great lady had no influence whatever on the manners of the times; she could have nevertheless done much, she could, in despair of cause, have offered the imposing spectacle of the women of the English aristocracy; but she hesitated stupidly among her old traditions, was devout from compulsion, and concealed everything, even her good qualities. Not one of these French women could create a salon to which the leaders of society might come to acquire lessons in taste and elegance. Their voices, once so potent in literature—that living expression of all societies—were now absolutely without sound. When a literature has no general system it has no body, and disappears with its day. Whenever, in any age, there is found in the midst of a nation a body of people apart, thus constituted, the historian nearly always finds among them some principal personage who illustrates in himself the virtues and the defects of the society to which he belongs,—Coligny among the Huguenots, the Coadjutor in the bosom of the Fronde, the Maréchal de Richelieu under Louis XV., Danton in the Terror. This identity of physiognomy between a man and his historical train is in the nature of things. To lead parties, must we not be in harmony with their ideas? to shine in an epoch, must we not represent it? From this constant obligation laid upon the sagacious and prudent leaders of the people to consider the prejudices and follies of the masses which follow them, come the acts for which certain historians blame these leaders, when—at a safe distance from terrible popular convulsions—they judge in cold blood the passions which are most necessary to conduct great secular struggles. That which is true of the historical comedy of the ages is equally true in the narrower sphere of those partial scenes in the national drama which are called its *manners and customs*.

✽

At the beginning of the ephemeral life which the Faubourg Saint-Germain led under the Restoration, and to which—if the preceding considerations are true—it did not know how to give stability, a young woman was for a time the most complete type of the nature, at once superior and feeble, grand and petty, of her caste. She was a woman artificially educated, really ignorant; full of elevated sentiments, yet lacking one thought to bring them into co-ordination; expending the richest treasures of her soul on conventionalities; ready to defy society, but hesitating and falling into artifice as the natural consequence of her scruples; having more positiveness than character, more infatuation than enthusiasm, more head than heart; eminently a woman and eminently a coquette, above all Parisian; loving brilliancy, festivities; reflecting not at all, or reflecting too late; of an imprudence which came near being poetical; charmingly insolent, but humble in the depths of her heart; asserting strength like a reed erect, but like this reed ready to bend beneath a strong hand; talking much of religion, yet not loving it, and yet ready to accept it as an issue. How shall we explain a creature so veritably many-sided, capable of heroism, and forgetting to be heroic for the sake of uttering some malicious saying; young and agreeable, less old in heart than aged by the maxims of the world about her, and comprehending their egotistical philosophy without ever having applied it; having all the vices of the courtier and all the nobility of adolescent womanhood; distrusting all things, and yet yielding herself up at moments to the fulness of faith? Must not forever remain this unfinished portrait of this woman, in which the most changeable tints clashed while yet producing a poetic confusion, for there was in it a divine light, a gleam of youth, which blended these confused tints into a sort of harmonious whole? Her grace served her for unity. Nothing in her was feigned. These passions, these half-passions, these slight indications of grandeur, this reality of pettiness, these cold feelings and these warm impulses, were natural to her and sprang as much from her personal position as from that of the aristocracy to which she belonged. She alone fully comprehended herself, and she held herself proudly above the world, in the shelter of her great name. There was something of the *I* of Medea in her life, as in that of the aristocracy, which was dying without being willing to rouse itself, or extend its hand to any political physician, or to touch, or to be touched, so profoundly did it feel itself fainting or already dust. The Duchesse de Langeais, as she was named, had been married about four years at the consummation of the Restoration, that is to say in 1816, that epoch in which Louis XVIII., enlightened by the revolution of the Hundred-Days, comprehended his situation and his century, in spite of his advisers, who nevertheless triumphed later over this Louis XI. without an axe—as soon as he was struck down by disease. The Duchesse de Langeais was a Navarreins, a ducal family which from the time of Louis XIV. had maintained the principle of never abdicating its own title in its marriages. The daughters of this house were all to have, sooner or later, like their mother, the right to be seated in the royal presence. At the age of eighteen Antoinette de Navarreins issued from the deep seclusion in which she had been brought up to marry the eldest son of the Duc de Langeais. The two families were then living isolated from the world; but the invasion of France promised to the Royalists the return of the Bourbons as the only possible conclusion to the misfortunes of war. The Ducs de Navarreins and de Langeais, remaining faithful to the Bourbons, had nobly resisted all the seductions of the imperial glory, and in the circumstances in which they found themselves at the period of this marriage they were naturally obliged to follow the ancient policy of their families. Mademoiselle Antoinette de Navarreins, beautiful and poor, was therefore married to the Marquis de Langeais, whose father died a few months after this marriage. On the return of the Bourbons the two families resumed their rank, their functions, and their court dignities, and again entered the social world from which they had long held themselves aloof. They now stood at the summit of this new political world. In that period of cowardice and of false conversions the public conscience was gratified to recognize in these two families spotless fidelity, the harmony between private life and political character to which all parties render involuntary homage. But, by a misfortune not uncommon in times of transformation, the most upright personages, those who by the elevation of their views, the wisdom of their principles, would have brought about in France a belief in the generosity of a new and bold policy, were pushed aside from the conduct of affairs, which fell into the hands of those who were interested in carrying principles to an extreme as a pledge of their devotion. The de Langeais' and de Navarreins' families remained in the highest sphere of court life, condemned to the duties of its etiquette as well as exposed to the reproaches and the ridicule of liberalism, accused of gorging themselves with honors and wealth while in point of fact their patrimony had in no wise increased and their receipts from the civil list were consumed by the mere cost of appearance,—a necessity in all European monarchies, even in those which are republican. In 1818, Monsieur le Duc de Langeais held the command of a military division, and the duchess had a position with a princess which enabled her to live in Paris, far from her husband, without scandal. The duc had in addition to his command, a function at Court, to which he sometimes came, leaving on such occasions his command to a field marshal. The duc and the duchesse thus lived entirely separated from each other, both in fact and in heart, though unknown to the world. This marriage of convention had resulted as such family compacts usually do. Two characters, the most uncongenial in the world, were brought together, they secretly irritated each other, were both secretly wounded, and separated forever. Then each had followed his own nature and the habits of the world. The Duc de Langeais, as methodical in mind as the Chevalier de Folard, gave himself up systematically to his tastes and his pleasures, and left his wife free to follow her own, after having recognized in her an eminently proud spirit, a cold heart, a deep submission to the usages of the world, a youthful loyalty which was likely to remain unsullied under the eyes of her great relatives and in the atmosphere of a Court at once pious and prudish. He adopted then, deliberately and coolly, the part of a grand seigneur of the preceding century, abandoning to herself a young woman of twenty-two, deeply offended, and who had in her character an alarming quality, that of never pardoning an offense when all her feminine vanities, when her self-love, her virtues, perhaps, had been misunderstood, secretly wounded. When an outrage is public, a woman likes to forget it, it gives her an opportunity to exalt herself, she is a woman in her forgiveness; but they never forgive secret wrongs, because they love neither concealed cowardice, nor virtue, nor love.

Such was the position, unknown to the world,

in which Madame la Duchesse de Langeais found herself, and on which she wasted no reflections when the fêtes in honor of the marriage of the Duc de Berri took place. On this occasion the Court and the Faubourg Saint-Germain came out of their apathy and their reserve. This event was the real commencement of that unheard-of splendor so uselessly displayed by the government of the Restoration. At this period, the Duchesse de Langeais, from policy or from vanity, never appeared in the world without being surrounded or accompanied by three or four women as distinguished by their names as by their position. Queen of society, she had her ladies-in-waiting who reproduced elsewhere her manners and her wit. She had skilfully chosen them from among those who were closely allied neither with the Court nor with the Faubourg Saint-Germain, but who aspired to both positions; simple dominions which wished to elevate themselves to the edge of the throne and to mingle with the seraphic powers of that high sphere called *le Petit Château*. In such a position, the Duchesse de Langeais was stronger, ruled better and, moreover, was more secure. Her *ladies* defended her against calumny and aided her to play the contemptible rôle of a woman of fashion. She could at her ease laugh at men, at their passions, excite them, gather in the homage which nourishes all female natures, and remain mistress of herself. At Paris and in the highest circles woman is always woman; she lives by incense, flatteries and honors. The truest beauty, the most admirable face, is nothing if it is not admired; a lover, the sycophancy of adulation, are the attestations of her power. What is power if unknown? Nothing. The very prettiest woman alone in a corner of the salon is unhappy. When one of these creatures is at the centre of social magnificence she desires then to reign in all hearts, often from lack of power to be the happy sovereign in one alone. These toilets, these charms, these coquetries, were all provided for the most paltry beings that were ever found in any society, fops without mind, men whose sole merit was a handsome face, and for whom all women compromised themselves without profit; veritable idols of wood gilded, which, with a few exceptions, had neither the antecedents of the coxcombs in the days of the Fronde, nor the good solid value of the heroes of the Empire, nor the wit and manners of their grandfathers, but who assumed nevertheless to possess these advantages gratis; who were brave, as is the French youth; they had ability, doubtless, if put to the proof, but they could accomplish nothing under the reign of the worn-out old men who held them in leash. It was a cold, petty and unpoetical epoch. Perhaps it requires a good deal of time for a restoration to become a monarchy.

For eighteen months the Duchesse de Langeais had been leading this empty life, filled exclusively with balls, and visits concerning balls, with triumphs without an object, with ephemeral passions born and dead in a night. When she entered a room all eyes turned upon her, she gathered a harvest of flattering words, sometimes passionate expressions which she encouraged with a gesture, a glance, and which could never penetrate her fair exterior. Her tone, her manner, everything about her marked authority. She lived in a sort of fever of vanity, of perpetual amusement which made her giddy. In her conversation she would go to great lengths, she listened to everything, and depraved—so to speak—the surface of her heart. When alone she often blushed over the recollection of things at which she had laughed, of some scandalous story the details of which had aided her in discussing theories of love of which she knew nothing, and the subtle distinctions of modern passion which obliging hypocrites of her own sex explained to her; for women, able to say everything to each other, lose more among themselves than they do by men's corruption. There came a time when she comprehended that the woman beloved was the only one whose beauty, whose spirit, could be universally recognized. What did a husband prove? Merely that a young girl, a woman either with a rich portion or well brought up, had had a clever mother, or that she satisfied a man's ambition; but a lover is a constant announcement of her personal perfections. Madame de Langeais learned, young as she was, that a woman could allow herself to be loved ostensibly without sharing in love, without sanctioning it, without gratifying it except by the most meagre service of love, and more than one demure hypocrite revealed to her the method of playing these dangerous comedies. The duchess therefore had her court, and the number of those who adored her or courted her was a guarantee of her virtue. She was coquettish, gracious, seductive to the end of the fête, of the ball, of the soirée; then when the curtain fell she became again solitary, cold, careless, and yet, nevertheless, revived the next morning for other emotions equally superficial. There were two or three young men, completely deceived, who really loved her, and whom she derided with a perfect lack of feeling. She would say to herself "I am loved—he loves me!" This certainty sufficed her. Like the miser, content in the knowledge that his whims can be satisfied, she did not go, perhaps, so far as to desire.

One evening she was at the house of one of her intimate friends, Madame la Vicomtesse de Fontaine, one of her humble rivals, who hated her cordially and accompanied her everywhere;—a species of armed friendship in which each is suspicious, and in which the confidences are skilfully discreet, sometimes perfidious. After distributing a few patronizing recognitions, affectionate or disdainful, with the natural air of a woman who knows all the value of her smiles, her eyes chanced to fall upon a man wholly unknown to her, but whose large and grave figure surprised her. She felt in looking at him, an emotion sufficiently like that of fear.

"My dear," she asked of Madame de Maufrigneuse, "who is that newcomer?"

"A man of whom you have no doubt heard, the Marquis de Montriveau."

"Ah! it is he."

She took her eyeglass and examined him somewhat insolently, as she would have looked at a portrait which receives all glances and can return none.

"Present him to me, he must be amusing."

"No one could be more tiresome nor more gloomy, my dear. But he is all the fashion."

*

Monsieur Armand de Montriveau was at this time, though unaware of it, the object of a general curiosity, and he was worthy of it much more than any of those passing idols of which Paris has need and with which it is enamored for a few days in order to satisfy that passion of infatuation and of factious enthusiasm with which it is periodically afflicted. Armand de Montriveau was the only son of Général de Montriveau, one of those *ci-devant* who nobly served the Republic, and who fell, killed by the side of Joubert, at Novi. The orphan was placed through the care of Bonaparte in the military school at Châlons, and taken, with several other sons of generals killed in battle, under the protection of the French Republic. On leaving this school, without fortune, he entered the artillery, and was only in command of a battalion at the time of the disaster of Fontainebleau. The arm to which he belonged offered few chances of promotion. In the first place, the number of officers is more limited than in any other branch of the service; in the second the liberal, and almost republican, opinions prevalent among the artillery, the fears inspired in the Emperor's mind by a body of skilled men, accustomed to reflection, hindered the military fortunes of the most of them. Therefore, contrary to the usual rule, officers advanced to the grade of general were not always the most distinguished members of this arm, for, being mediocrities, they gave rise to fewer fears. The artillery was a corps apart in the army, and belonged to Napoléon only on the field of battle. To these general causes which may explain the checks encountered in his career by Armand de Montriveau, were joined others inherent in his person and his character. Alone in the world, thrown at the age of twenty years into that tempest of men in the midst of which Napoléon lived, and having no interest outside of himself, prepared to meet death day by day, he accustomed himself to live only by an inward esteem and by the consciousness of duty fulfilled. He was habitually silent, as are all timid men; but his timidity did not come from lack of courage, it was a sort of modesty which forbade in him all vain demonstration. His intrepidity on the battle-field was never ostentatious; he saw everything, could tranquilly give good advice to his comrades, and advance in face of the bullets, stooping at the right moment to avoid them. He was kind, but his countenance made him seem haughty and severe. Of mathematical strictness in everything, he admitted no hypocritical compromise, neither with the duties of a position nor with the consequences of a deed. He lent himself to nothing shameful, never asked anything for himself; in short, he was one of those great unknown men, philosophical enough to despise glory, and who live without attachment to life because they find no way to develop their powers or their opinions to their full extent. He was feared, held in esteem, but little loved. Men will permit us indeed to rise above them, but they will never forgive us for not descending to their level. Thus their sentiments towards great characters are never without a little of hatred and of fear. To be too honorable is for them a tacit censure, which they forgive neither to the living nor the dead. After the parting at Fontainebleau, Montriveau, though noble and titled, was placed on half pay. His antique integrity alarmed the ministry of war, where his faithfulness to his oath taken to the imperial eagle was well known. During the Hundred-Days he was appointed colonel of the Guard, and was left behind on the field of Waterloo. His wounds having detained him in Belgium, he was not with the army of the Loire; but the royal government refused to recognize the ranks bestowed during the Hundred-Days, and Armand de Montriveau left France. Led by his spirit of enterprise, by that nobility of mind which up to this time the chances of war had satisfied, and possessed by his instinctive rectitude to undertake projects of great utility, Général de Montriveau embarked in the design of exploring Upper Egypt and the unknown parts of Africa, the central countries particularly, which to-day excite so much interest among men of science. His scientific expedition was long and unfortunate. He had gathered many valuable notes which would have aided in the solution, so ardently sought for, of many geographical or industrial problems, and he had penetrated, not without having surmounted innumerable obstacles, to the heart of Africa, when he fell by treason into the power of a savage tribe. He was stripped of everything, held in slavery, and driven for two years across the deserts, threatened with death at every moment and treated worse than an animal made the sport of pitiless children. His bodily strength and his constancy of soul enabled him to endure all the horrors of his captivity; but he almost completely exhausted his energy in effecting his escape, which was nothing less than miraculous. He reached the French settlement of the Senegal half-dead, in rags, having no longer anything but confused recollections. The immense sacrifices of his journey, the study of African dialects, his discoveries and observations, were all lost. A single fact will serve to illustrate his sufferings: During several days the children of the Sheik of the tribe in which he was a slave amused themselves by taking his head for the target in a game which consisted of throwing from a sufficient distance the small bones of horses and making them stick in this target. Montriveau returned to Paris about the middle of the year 1818, ruined in prospects, without patrons and seeking none. He would have died twenty times rather than solicit a favor, no matter what it might be, not even the recognition of his own rights. Adversity and suffering had developed his energy even in small things, and the habit of maintaining his dignity as a man in presence of that moral being which we call conscience, gave importance in his mind to acts apparently the most insignificant. Nevertheless, his connection with the principal scientific men of Paris and with a few military men of attainments made known his merits and his adventures. The particulars of his captivity and his escape, those of all his travels in fact, revealed so much intelligence, courage and self-possession that he acquired, without being aware of it, that fleeting celebrity of which the salons of Paris are so prodigal, but which demands unheard-of efforts from those artists who may wish to perpetuate it. Toward the end of this year his position suddenly changed. From poor he became rich, or at least he had all the external advantages of wealth. The royal government, which sought to attach to itself the men of merit in order to give real strength to the army, began to make some concessions to those old officers whose loyalty and known character offered guarantees of fidelity. Monsieur de Montriveau was reëstablished in his rank on the army lists, received all his back pay, and was admitted to the Royal Guard. These favors were successively shown to him without any request on his part. His friends spared him all personal efforts, which he certainly would never have made for himself. Then, contrary to his habits, which suddenly changed, he began to go into society, where he was favorably received and where he met on all sides evidences of high esteem. He seemed to have reached some end in his life; but in him all took place within his own breast and he made no external demonstration. He bore in society a grave and reserved manner, he was silent and cold. He had therein much success, just because he presented a sharp contrast to the mass of conventional physiognomies which furnished the salons of Paris, —where, in fact, he was entirely strange. His speech had the conciseness of the language of solitary men and savages. His shyness was taken for pride and pleased greatly. He was something strange and grand, and women were so much the more generally taken with this original character because he escaped from their adroit flatteries, from those manœuvres by which they circumvent the most powerful men and soften the most inflexible minds. Monsieur de Montriveau did not in the least understand these little Parisian tricks, and his soul could only respond to the sonorous vibrations of lofty sentiments. He would promptly have been dropped were it not for the romance of his adventures and his life, for the praises which were sounded behind his back without his knowledge, and for that triumph of vanity which was waiting for the woman who was destined to occupy his thoughts. Thus the curiosity of the Duchesse de Langeais was as lively as it was natural. As it happened, she had become interested in this man the night before, for she had heard the narration of one of the scenes in the travels of Monsieur de Montriveau which was most calculated to impress the lively imagination of a woman. In an excursion toward the sources of the Nile, he had with one of his guides the most extraordinary struggle known in the annals of travel. There was a desert which could only be crossed on foot in order to reach a region he was anxious to explore. There was but one guide capable of leading him there. Up to that time no traveler had been able to penetrate to this region, in which the intrepid officer believed he should find the solution of several scientific problems. In spite of the representations made to him by the old men of the country and by his guide, he undertook this terrible journey. Arming himself with all his courage, sharpened moreover by the assurance of the terrible difficulties to overcome, he started early one morning. After marching for the entire day he slept that night upon the sand, a prey to an extraordinary fatigue caused by the shiftiness of the sand, which gave way under his foot at every step. However, he knew that on the morrow he must resume his route, and his guide had assured him that by the middle of the day he should reach his goal. This assurance gave him courage and renewed his strength, and in spite of his sufferings he continued his march, cursing science a little, but, ashamed to complain openly before his guide, he kept his sufferings secret. He had traveled for a third of the day when, conscious of his exhausted strength and with his feet bleeding from the journey, he asked if they would soon arrive. "In an hour," said the guide. Armand roused his strength for one hour more, and went on.

The hour passed by and he was not able to see, even on the horizon, a horizon of sand as broad as that of the open sea, the palm trees and the mountains whose tops should announce the end of his journey. He stopped, refused to go farther, threatened his guide, reproached him as his murderer, for having deceived him; tears of rage and of fatigue ran down his scorched cheeks; he was overwhelmed with the increasing suffering of the march and his throat seemed closing with the thirst of the desert. The guide, unmoved, listened to his reproaches with an ironical air while seeming to study, with the apparent indifference of an Oriental, the imperceptible irregularities of the sand, almost blackish like burnished gold.

"I was mistaken," he said coldly. "It is too long since I have followed this road for me to be able to recognize the landmarks; we are in the right way, but we shall have to march two hours more."

"The man is doubtless right," thought Monsieur de Montriveau.

Then he resumed his route, following painfully the pitiless African, to whom he seemed tied by a rope, as a condemned man is invisibly to his executioner. But the two hours passed, the Frenchman had expended the last drops of his energy and the horizon was still clear, he saw on it neither palms nor mountains. He had no strength left for cries or murmurs, he stretched himself on the sand to die; but his look might have terrified the most intrepid man, it seemed to announce that he would not die alone. His guide, like a veritable demon, replied with a calm glance, full of power, and left him where he lay,—taking care to place himself at a distance which would permit him to escape his victim's despair. Finally, Monsieur de Montriveau gathered his strength for a last imprecation. The guide drew nearer, looked at him fixedly, motioned him to silence, and said:

"Did you not insist, in spite of us, on going to the place to which I am now guiding you? You reproach me with deceiving you; if I had not done so, you would not have come as far as this. Do you wish for the truth, here it is. We have still five hours of march before us, and we cannot turn back on our steps. Sound your heart, if you have not enough courage, here is my poniard."

Surprised by this frightful comprehension of suffering and of human strength, Monsieur de Montriveau would not fall below the standard of a barbarian; and, drawing from his European pride a fresh draught of courage, he rose to follow his guide. The five hours passed by, Monsieur de Montriveau still perceived nothing, he turned a dying eye upon his guide; but at the same moment the Nubian took him on his shoulders, lifted him up a few feet and showed him at the distance of a hundred steps a lake surrounded by verdure and a noble forest lit up by the rays of the setting sun. They had arrived within a short distance of an immense granite ledge beneath which this sublime landscape lay, as it were, buried. Armand felt himself born again, and his guide, this giant of intelligence and courage, ended his labor of devotion by carrying him across the burning and polished paths scarcely traced on the granite. He saw on one side the hell of sand and on the other the terrestrial paradise of the most beautiful oasis in these deserts.

The duchess, already struck by the aspect of this romantic personage, was still more interested when she learned that she saw in him the Marquis de Montriveau of whom she had dreamed during the night. To have found herself in the burning sands of the desert with him, to have had him for the companion of her nightmare, was not this for a woman of her nature a delightful presage of amusement? No man ever better expressed his character in his person than Armand de Montriveau, or challenged more inevitably the thoughts of others. His head, which was large and square, had for its principal characteristic trait an enormous and abundant mass of black hair which surrounded his face in a way that perfectly recalled General Kléber, whom he also resembled by the vigor expressed in his forehead, by the shape of his face, by the tranquil courage of his eyes, and by the ardor expressed in his strong features. He was small of stature, broad in the chest, muscular as a lion. When he walked, his carriage, his step, his least gesture, indicated an inexpressible consciousness of power which was imposing and had something despotic in it. He seemed to know that nothing could oppose his will, perhaps because he willed only that which was right. Nevertheless, like all men really strong, he was gentle in his speech, simple in manner and naturally kind. Only it seemed that all these fine qualities might disappear under certain grave circumstances in which the man would become implacable in his convictions, fixed in his resolves, terrible in his action. A close observer would have been able to see at the closing line of his lips a slight upward curve which was habitual and which betrayed his disposition to irony.

*

The Duchesse de Langeais, knowing the passing value of the conquest of such a man, resolved, during the few moments that the Duchesse de Maufrigneuse took to bring him up for presentation, to make him one of her lovers, to give him precedence over all the others, to attach him to her suite and to display for him all her coquetry. It was a whim, the pure caprice of a duchess with which Lope de Véga or Calderon would have made *The Gardener's Dog*. She resolved that this man should belong to no other woman, but she did not imagine that she might belong to him. The Duchesse de Langeais had received from nature all the qualities necessary to play the rôle of a coquette and her education had perfected them. Women had good reason to envy her, and men to love her. Nothing was lacking in her which could inspire love, which could justify it, and which could perpetuate it. Her style of beauty, her address, her attitudes, all combined to give her the grace of natural coquetry which in a woman seems to be the consciousness of her power. She was well formed and her movements perhaps had in them a little too much ease, the only affectation with which she could be reproached. Everything about her was in harmony, from the least little gesture to the particular turn of her phrases, to the hypocritical manner in which she launched her glances. The predominating character of her countenance was a refined nobleness, which did not destroy her entirely French mobility of person. These ever changing attitudes had an infinite charm for men. It seemed as though she would be the most delicious of mistresses when she laid aside her corset and all the paraphernalia of her outward show. In fact, the germs of all the joys of love were in the freedom of her expressive glance, in the caressing tones of her voice, in the grace of her words. She let it be seen that there was in her a noble courtesan, vainly denied by the religion of the duchess. Whoever passed an evening beside her found her alternately gay and melancholy, without her ever having the air of pretended gaiety or gravity. She seemed able to be at will courteous, contemptuous, sarcastic or confiding. She seemed kind, and really was so. In her position, nothing obliged her to descend to maliciousness. At times she showed herself alternately trustful and distrustful, easily moved to tenderness, then hard and chilling enough to break a heart. But to properly paint her would it not be necessary to gather together every feminine antithesis; in a word, she was everything she wished to be or seem. Her face, which was perhaps a trifle too long, had in it a grace, something spiritual, slender, which recalled the faces of the Middle Ages. Her skin was pale with delicate rose tints. Everything in her erred, so to speak, through excessive delicacy.

Monsieur de Montriveau allowed himself very

willingly to be presented to the Duchesse de Langeais who, with the exquisite tact that avoids commonplaces, received him without overwhelming him with questions or compliments, but with a certain respectful grace which should flatter a superior man, for superiority in a man implies a little of that tact which enables women to divine so surely in all matters of sentiment. If she showed some curiosity it was only in her glance; if she flattered, it was only by her manner; and she displayed that prettiness of speech, that delicate desire to please, which she knew how to show better than anyone else. But all her conversation was, in some sort, only the body of the letter; there was to be a postscript in which the real thought would be uttered. When after half an hour of light conversation in which the accent, the smiles alone, gave any value to the word, Monsieur de Montriveau seemed to wish to retire discreetly, the duchess retained him by an expressive gesture.

"Monsieur," she said to him, "I do not know if the few moments during which I have had the pleasure of conversing with you have offered you sufficient attraction to justify me in inviting you to come and see me; I am afraid that there would be a great deal of egotism in wishing to claim you. If I have been so happy as to make the prospect agreeable to you, you will always find me in the evening until ten o'clock."

These words were said so softly that Monsieur de Montriveau could do no less than accept the invitation. When he fell back among the group of men who stood at some distance from the women several of his friends congratulated him, half in jest and half in earnest, on the unusual welcome that had been accorded him by the Duchesse de Langeais. This difficult, this illustrious conquest they declared was undoubtedly made, and the glory thereof had been reserved for the artillery of the Guard. It is easy to imagine the good and evil pleasantries which this topic, once launched, suggested in one of these Parisian salons where amusement is so eagerly sought and where the jests are of such brief duration that each one hastens to gather the flower while it blooms.

These foolishnesses flattered the general unconsciously. From the place where he stationed himself his eyes were drawn to the duchess by many confused impulses; and he could not help admitting to himself that, of all the women whose beauty had charmed his eyes, not one had ever offered him a more delightful expression of the virtues, the defects, the harmonies which the most juvenile imagination in France could desire in a mistress. What man, in whatever rank fate has placed him, has not felt in his soul an indefinable joy in finding in a woman whom he chooses, even in his dreams, for his own, the triple perfections, moral, physical and social, which permit him always to see in her all his wishes accomplished? If it is not a cause of love, this flattering union of qualities is assuredly one of the greatest incentives to feeling. Without

LA DUCHESSE AND M. DE MONTRIVEAU

*The Duchesse de Langeais, knowing the passing value of the conquest of such a man, resolved * * * to make him one of her lovers, to give him precedence over all the others, to attach him to her suite and to display for him all her coquetry. It was a whim, the pure caprice of a duchess with which Lope de Vega or Calderon would have made* The Gardener's Dog. *She resolved that this man should belong to no other woman, but she did not imagine that she might belong to him.*

Copyright, 1890, by George Barrie & Son.

vanity, said a great moralist of the last century, love is a convalescent. There is undoubtedly, for man as for woman, a treasure-house of delight in the superiority of the being beloved. Is it not a great deal, not to say everything, to know that our self-love can never be wounded through her; that she is sufficiently noble never to be wounded by a contemptuous glance, sufficiently wealthy to be surrounded by a splendor equal to that in which the ephemeral sovereigns of finance wrap themselves, sufficiently witty never to be humiliated by a fine jest, and beautiful enough to be the rival of all her sex? Such reflections as these a man makes in a twinkling of an eye. But if the woman who inspires them offers him at the same time, for the future of his sudden passion, the changing charms of grace, the ingenuousness of a virgin soul, the thousand changes of the toilets of coquettes, the perils of love, will not the heart of the coldest man be stirred? Here is the situation which Monsieur de Montriveau occupied at this period with relation to women, and his past life was in a measure responsible for the oddness of the circumstance. Thrown while young into the tempest of the French wars, living always on fields of battle, he knew woman only as a hurried traveler passing from inn to inn knows the country through which he travels. Perhaps he could have said of his life, as Voltaire at the age of eighty said of his, and had he not thirty-seven follies with which to reproach himself? He was, at his age, as new to love as the young man who has just read *Faublas* in secret. Of woman, he knew all; but of love, he knew nothing; and the virginity of his sentiment thus furnished him new desires. Some men, engrossed by labors to which they have been condemned by poverty or ambition, art or science, as Monsieur de Montriveau had been carried away by the fortunes of war and the events of his life, know this singular situation, though they seldom avow it. In Paris, every man is supposed to have loved. No woman desires him for whom no other woman has sighed. From the fear of being thought an imbecile spring the falsehoods of self-conceit so common in France, where to be taken for an imbecile is not to be of the fatherland. At this moment Monsieur de Montriveau was a prey to a passionate desire, a desire aggrandized by the burning sun of the deserts and by a swelling of the heart of which he had never before known the fiery embrace. As strong as he was passionate, this man knew how to suppress his emotions; but even while conversing about trifling subjects he withdrew into his own mind and swore to himself that he would win that woman, the only thought through which he could enter into love. His desire became an oath, sworn after the manner of the Arabs with whom he had lived, for whom an oath is a contract made between them and their whole destiny, which they stake on the success of the enterprise consecrated by the oath, and in which they count even their death as one chance the more of success. A young man would have said to himself, "I would very much like to have the Duchesse de Langeais for my mistress!" another, "The man whom the Duchesse de Langeais loves will be a very happy fellow!" But the general said to himself, "I will have for mistress Madame de Langeais." When a man, virgin in heart and for whom love becomes a religion, admits such a thought, he does not know into what a hell he sets his foot.

Monsieur de Montriveau left the salon abruptly and went home, devoured by the first access of his first fever of love. If, towards middle age, a man still retains the beliefs, the illusions, the freedom and the impetuosity of childhood, his first movement is, so to speak, to put forth his hand to seize the object of his desire; then when he has measured the distance, almost impossible to cross, which separates him from it, he is seized, like children, with a sort of astonishment or of impatience which gives new value to the object desired; he trembles or he weeps. Thus it happened that on the morrow, after the most stormy reflections which had ever shaken his soul, Armand de Montriveau found himself under the dominion of his emotions, concentrated by the pressure of a true love. This woman, so cavalierly treated the night before, had now become for him the most sacred, the most feared of powers. She was thenceforward for him life and the world. The mere recollection of the slightest emotion she had caused him paled the greatest joys, the keenest pains, of his past life. The most rapid revolutions trouble only the interests of man, but one passion can overthrow all his sentiments. Thus, for those who live rather by feelings than by interests, for those who have more of soul and blood than of mind and lymph, true love changes the whole course of existence. With one stroke, with one thought, Armand de Montriveau effaced his whole past life. After having asked himself twenty times, like a child, "shall I go? shall I not go?" he dressed and went to the Hôtel de Langeais, about eight in the evening, and was admitted to the presence of the woman, no, not the woman, but the idol, he had seen the night before under the blaze of lights, like a fresh and pure young girl, clothed in white, in gauze and in veils. He arrived impetuously to declare his love, as if it were an affair of the first cannon shot on a field of battle. Poor neophyte! he found his vaporous sylphid enveloped in a peignoir of brown cashmere, skilfully flounced, languidly lying upon a divan in a dusky boudoir. Madame de Langeais did not even rise, she showed only her head, with the hair somewhat in disorder though covered by a veil. With a hand which in the faint light produced by the trembling flame of a single wax candle placed at a distance from her, seemed to the eyes of Montriveau as white as a hand of marble, she made him a sign to be seated, and said in a voice as soft as the light:

"If it were anyone but you, Monsieur le Marquis, if it had been a friend with whom I could take a liberty or some indifferent acquaintance who would only slightly interest me, I should have sent you away. You find me suffering fearfully."

Armand said to himself:

"I must go."

"But," she added with a glance at him the fire of which the ingenuous soldier attributed to fever, "I do not know whether it is from a presentiment of your kind visit, of the promptness of which I cannot be more sensible, but for the last few minutes I have seemed to feel my head clear itself."

"I may then remain?" said Montriveau to her.

"Ah! I should be sorry indeed to have you go. I said to myself this morning that I could not have made any impression upon you; that you had doubtless taken my invitation for one of those meaningless phrases of which Parisian women are so prodigal, and I pardoned your ingratitude in advance. A man who comes from the desert is not expected to know how exclusive in its friendships our Faubourg is."

These gracious words, half murmured, fell one by one and were as if freighted with the pleased feeling that seemed to dictate them. The duchess wished to have all the benefits of her headache, and her speculation was a complete success. The poor soldier suffered really from the pretended suffering of this woman. Like Crillon, hearing the story of the passion of the Saviour, he was ready to draw his sword against the headache. Ah! how could he now dare to speak to this invalid of the love which she inspired? Armand comprehended already that he would be ridiculous to fire his love point-blank at so superior a being. He comprehended by one thought all the niceties of feeling and the exigencies of the soul. To love, is it not to know how to plead, to crave, to wait? If he felt this love, must he not prove it? He found himself silenced, chilled, by the proprieties of the noble Faubourg, by the majesty of the headache, and by the timidities of genuine love. But no power on earth could have veiled the look in his eyes in which flamed the glow, the infinitude of the desert, eyes calm like those of panthers, and over which the lids rarely fell. She liked much this fixed look which bathed her in light and in love.

"Madame la Duchesse," he replied, "I should fear to express to you badly my gratitude for your goodness. At this moment I wish for but one thing, the power to dissipate your suffering."

"Permit me to get rid of this, I am now too warm," she said, throwing off by a movement full of grace the cushion that had lain upon her feet, which she now showed in all their splendor.

"Madame, in Asia your feet would be valued at nearly ten thousand sequins."

"Travelers' flattery," she said smiling.

This bright creature took delight in drawing the stern Montriveau into a conversation full of trifling, of commonplaces and of nonsense, in which he manœuvred, to use a military phrase, like Prince

Charles when pitted against Napoléon. She amused herself maliciously in recognizing the extent of this new passion by the number of foolish things wrested from this novice whom she led, step by step, into an inextricable labyrinth in which she proposed to leave him, very much ashamed of himself. She began therefore by laughing at him, pleasing herself nevertheless by making him forget the time. The length of a first visit is often a flattery, but in this Armand was not her accomplice. The celebrated traveler had been in her boudoir an hour, talking of everything, having said nothing, conscious that he was only an instrument in the hands of this woman who was playing upon him, when she moved, sat up, threw around her neck the veil which she had on her head, leaned on her elbows, did him the honors of a complete recovery, and rang for lights. To the absolute inaction in which she had been lying succeeded movements full of grace. She turned towards Monsieur de Montriveau and said in reply to a confidence which she had just wrung from him and which seemed to give her a lively interest:

"You are laughing at me when you try to make me believe that you have never loved. That is a favorite pretence of men before us. We believe them. Pure politeness! Do we not know how much of this to believe? Where is the man who has never encountered in his life one single occasion to be in love? But you delight to deceive us, and we let you do it, silly fools that we are, because your deceptions are still a homage paid to the superiority of our sentiments, which are always pure."

This last phrase was pronounced with an accent full of haughtiness and of pride which made of this novice of a lover a ball flung down to the bottom of an abyss and of the duchess an angel floating upward towards her own particular heaven.

"The deuce," cried Armand de Montriveau within his soul, "how shall I ever tell this far-off being that I love her?"

He had already told her so twenty times, or rather the duchess had twenty times read it in his eyes and perceived in the passion of this truly great man an amusement for herself, an interest in a life hitherto devoid of interest. She was therefore prepared already to throw up, with the greatest skill, a certain number of redoubts around her which she would give him to carry, one by one, before he would be permitted to enter the citadel of her heart. Plaything of her caprices, Montriveau was to be kept stationary while all the time surmounting obstacle after obstacle, as an insect tormented by a child jumps from one finger to another, thinking it is getting away, while its malicious executioner keeps it at the same place. Nevertheless, the duchess recognized with an inexpressible pleasure that this man of character had not lied in his assertion. Armand had, in fact, never loved. He was about to take his leave, discontented with himself, still more discontented with her; but she saw with delight an ill-humor which she knew how to dissipate with a word, a look, a gesture.

"Will you come to-morrow evening?" she said to him. "I am going to a ball, I shall expect you up to ten o'clock."

*

The greater part of the next day was spent by Montriveau seated in the window of his study and smoking an indefinite number of cigars. He could only thus wait for the hour in which to dress and to go to the Hôtel de Langeais. It would have been pitiful for those who knew the noble worth of this man to see him thus so belittled, so agitated, to know that this mind whose faculties might embrace worlds was now contracted to the limits of the boudoir of an exquisitely elegant woman. But he felt himself already so fallen, in his happiness, that to save his life he would not have confided his love to his most intimate friend. In the modesty which takes possession of a man when he loves, is there not always some sense of shame, and is it not his littleness which swells the pride of a woman? In short, is there not a crowd of motives of this species, but which women never explain to themselves, which lead almost all of them to be the first to betray the secret of their love, a secret of which they weary, perhaps?

"Monsieur," said the valet de chambre, "Madame la Duchesse is not yet visible, she is dressing, and begs you to wait for her."

Armand walked about the salon, studying the taste displayed in the least details. He admired Madame de Langeais in admiring the things which were hers and which betrayed her habits, even before he was fully conscious of her individuality or of her thoughts. After waiting about an hour the duchess came from her chamber, softly, without noise. Montriveau turned, saw her walking with the lightness of a shadow and quivered. She came to him without saying as a bourgeoise might have done, "What do you think of me?" She was sure of herself, and her steadfast look said, "I have adorned myself thus to please you." Some old fairy godmother of some hidden princess, alone could have wound about the throat of this charming creature the cloud of gauze whose folds held brilliant tones which lit up still more the clearness of her satin skin. The duchess was dazzling. The delicate blue of her gown, whose ornaments were repeated in the flowers in her hair, seemed, by the richness of its color, to give substance to its frail texture, at times quite aerial; for in advancing rapidly towards Armand she caused to float behind her the two ends of the scarf which hung at her side, and the gallant soldier could not but compare her with those pretty blue insects which hover above the waters, among the flowers, with which they seem to blend.

"I have made you wait," she said in the voice which women know how to assume for the man they wish to please.

"I would wait patiently an eternity if I could find a divinity beautiful as you; but it is not a compliment to speak to you of your beauty, you can accept nothing less than adoration. Let me then only kiss your scarf."

"Ah, fie!" she said with a proud gesture, "I esteem you enough to offer you my hand."

And she held out to him her still moist hand. The hand of a woman, at the moment when she issues from her perfumed bath, retains an inexpressibly tender freshness, a velvety softness, of which the tingling impression goes from the lips to the soul. Thus, in a man already charmed, who has in his senses as much voluptuousness as he has love in his heart, this kiss, chaste in appearance, may excite redoubtable storms.

"Will you always offer it to me thus?" said the general, humbly kissing with respect this dangerous hand.

"Yes; but we will go no farther," she said smiling.

She sat down and seeemd to be curiously awkward in putting on her gloves and in slipping the kid which was at first too tight, around her slender fingers, looking at the same time at Monsieur de Montriveau, who admired alternately the duchess and the grace of her repeated gestures.

"Ah, this is well," she said, "you have been punctual, I love punctuality. His Majesty says that it is the politeness of kings; but, in my opinion, between us, I think it the most respectful of flattery. Eh! is it not so? Don't you think so?"

Then she looked at him sideways again to express to him a deceiving friendship, finding him mute with pleasure, and positively happy with these nothings. Ah! the duchess understood marvelously well her business as a woman, she knew admirably how to lift a man up in proportion as he humbled himself, and to reward him with hollow flatteries at each step that he took in descending to the sillinesses of sentimentality.

"You will not forget to come always at nine o'clock."

"No, but do you go to a ball every night?"

"How can I tell?" she replied, shrugging her shoulders with a little childish gesture, as if to avow that she was all caprice and that a lover must take her as he found her. "Besides," she added, "what does it matter to you? you shall take me there."

"For this evening," he said, "it would be difficult, I am not suitably dressed."

"It seems to me," she replied looking at him haughtily, "that if anyone would suffer for your dress it would be I. But know, Monsieur, the traveler, that the man whose arm I accept is always above fashion, no one will dare to criticise him. I see that you do not know the world; I like you the better for it."

And she was already dragging him into the pettinesses of the world, in endeavoring to initiate him into the vanities of a woman of fashion.

"If she chooses to commit a folly for me," Armand said to himself, "I should be a great fool to prevent her. She undoubtedly likes me, and certainly she cannot despise the world more than I despise it myself; so here goes for the ball!"

The duchess doubtless was thinking that when the general was seen following her to the ball in boots and a black cravat no one would hesitate to believe him passionately in love with her. The general, on the other hand, delighted to see the queen of the elegant world willing to compromise herself for him, found his wit rising with his hopes. Conscious that he pleased, he displayed his ideas and his feelings without experiencing the constraint that had troubled his heart the night before. This genuine conversation, animated, filled with those first confidences as pleasant to utter as to hear, did it really charm Madame de Langeais, or had she planned this delightful coquetry; nevertheless, when midnight sounded, she glanced mischievously at the clock.

"Ah! you are making me lose the ball!" she said with an expression of surprise and of vexation at having forgotten herself.

Then she justified to herself the exchange of her pleasures by a smile which made Armand's heart leap.

"I certainly did promise Madame de Beauséant," she added. "They are all expecting me."

"Well then, let us go."

"No, go on," she said. "I shall stay here. Your adventures in the East charm me. Tell me all your life. I love to share the sufferings of a brave man, for I do feel them, truly!"

She played with her scarf, twisting it, tearing it by impatient movements which seemed to express some inward discontentment and serious thought.

"We are worth nothing, we women," she resumed. "Ah! we are unworthy beings, selfish, frivolous. All we know is how to weary ourselves with amusement. Not one of us comprehends the rôle of her life. Formerly, in France, women were beneficent lights, they lived to comfort those who weep, to encourage the great virtues, to reward artists and animate their life by noble thoughts. If the world has become so little, the fault is ours. You make me hate this world and the ball. No, I have not sacrificed much to you."

She ended by destroying her scarf, like a child who, playing with a flower, finishes by tearing off all the petals; then rolling it up she threw it from her, thus disclosing her swan-like neck. She rang the bell.

"I shall not go out," she said to her valet de chambre.

Then she turned her long blue eyes on Armand timidly so as to make him accept by the fear which they expressed, this order as an avowal, as a first, as a great favor.

"You have had many sufferings," she said after a pause full of thought and with that tenderness which is often in the voice of a woman when it is not in her heart.

"No," answered Armand. "Until to-day I did not know what happiness was."

"You know it then?" said she, looking up at him with a hypocritical and subtle air.

"But happiness for me henceforth, will it not be to see you, to listen to you?—Up to the present time, I have only suffered, and now I comprehend that I may be unhappy—"

"Enough, enough," she cried, "now go, it is midnight, let us respect the proprieties. I did not go to the ball, but you were there. Let us not give occasion for gossip. Adieu. I do not know what I shall say, but the headache is a good person and never contradicts us."

"Is there a ball to-morrow?" he asked.

"You will get accustomed to them, I think. Well, yes, to-morrow we will go to another ball."

Armand went away the happiest man on earth; and he returned every evening to Madame de Langeais at the hour which, by a sort of tacit understanding, was reserved for him. It would be tedious, and for those numerous young people who have so many of these beautiful souvenirs superfluous, to make this recital advance step by step as did the poem of these hidden conversations, the course of which checked or widened at a woman's pleasure by a dispute over words when the sentiment went too far, by a complaint of the sentiment when words would not answer to her thought. To mark the progress of this Penelope's web, perhaps it would be better to restrict ourselves to the material gains which the sentiment was allowed to make. Thus, a few days after the first meeting of the duchess and Armand de Montriveau, the assiduous general had conquered in all propriety the right to kiss the insatiable hands of his mistress. Wherever Madame de Langeais appeared Monsieur de Montriveau was certain to be seen also, so that certain people called him in jest "the orderly of the Duchess." Already his position had brought him envy, jealousy and enemies. Madame de Langeais had attained her object. The marquis was confounded with her numerous other admirers, and he served her to humiliate those who boasted of being in her good graces by publicly giving him the precedence.

"Decidedly," said Madame de Sérizy, "Monsieur de Montriveau is the man whom the duchess most distinguishes."

Who does not know what this expression means in Paris, *to be distinguished by a woman?* The circumstances were thus perfectly well regulated. The stories told of the general rendered him so redoubtable that the clever young men tacitly abandoned all pretensions to the duchess, and only continued to revolve in her sphere that they might make the most of the importance it lent them, use her name, her reputation, to better ingratiate themselves with certain powers of the second rank, delighted to carry off one of the lovers of Madame de Langeais. The duchess had quite enough perspicacity to perceive all these desertions and these treaties, of which her pride would not permit her to be the dupe. And she knew very well, as Monsieur le Prince de Talleyrand who was much in love with her said, how to gather an aftermath of vengeance with a two-edged scoff at such morganatic espousals. Her disdainful satire contributed not a little to the fear she inspired and to her reputation for keen wit. She thus strengthened her reputation for virtue, all the while entertaining herself with the secrets of others without ever permitting her own to be penetrated. Nevertheless, after two months of this assiduity she began to feel in the depths of her heart a vague fear as she saw that Monsieur de Montriveau comprehended nothing of the refinements of the coquetry of the Faubourg Saint-Germain and took quite seriously the pretty little Parisian ways.

"My dear duchess," the old Vidame de Pamiers said to her one day, "your friend is first cousin to the eagles, you will never tame him, and he will carry you off to his eyrie some day if you do not take care."

*

The day after the evening in which the worldly-wise old man had made her this speech, which Madame de Langeais feared was only too prophetic, she began a serious effort to make herself hated, and showed herself hard, exacting, fidgety, detestable, to Armand, who disarmed her by an angelic mildness. This woman knew so little of the great kindness of noble natures that she was touched and surprised by the courteous pleasantries with which her ill-humor was at first met. She was seeking a quarrel, and found only fresh proofs of affection. Nevertheless she persisted.

"In what respect," said Armand to her, "has a man who idolizes you been so unfortunate as to displease you?"

"You don't displease me," she replied, becoming suddenly sweet and submissive; "but why do you wish to compromise me? You can only be a *friend* for me. Do you not know it? I would wish to find in you the instinct, the delicacy of true friendship, so that I need not be forced to lose either your regard or the pleasure I experience when near you."

"To be only your *friend!*" cried Monsieur de Montriveau, to whom this terrible word was like an electric shock. "On the faith of all those sweet hours which you have granted me I have rested, and I thought to have awakened in your heart; and to-day, without motive, you take gratuitous pleasure in killing the secret hopes by which I live. After having made me promise such constancy and after showing such horror of women who have only caprices, do you wish me to understand that, like all the other women of Paris, you have only passions and no love? Why, then, have you asked of me my life, and why have you accepted it?"

"I was wrong, my friend. Yes, a woman is wrong when she yields to such intoxication which she has neither the power nor the right to reward."

"I understand, you have only been a little coquettish and—"

"Coquettish? I hate coquetry. To be a coquette, Armand, is to promise one's self to many men and to give one's self to none. To give one's self to all is to be a libertine. That is how I understand our ethics. But to be sad with the melancholy, gay with the careless, politic with the ambitious, to listen with feigned admiration to the chatterers, to be military with the soldiers, to grow passionate for the good of the country with the philanthropists, to give to each his little dose of flattery, all this seems to me as necessary as to put flowers in our hair, as diamonds, gloves or clothes. Conversation is the moral part of our toilet; we put it on and take it off with the feathers in our hair. Do you call that coquetry? But I have never treated you as I have the rest of the world. With you, my friend, I am true. I have not always agreed with your ideas, and when you have convinced me after a discussion, have you not seen me perfectly happy? In fact I love you, but only as a pure and religious woman should love. I have been thinking over it. I am married, Armand. If the terms on which I live with Monsieur de Langeais leave me free to dispose of my heart as I please, the laws, the conventions of society have taken from me the right to dispose of my person. In whatever rank a woman is placed, a dishonored woman is driven from society, and I have never yet seen the man who could understand the full meaning of our sacrifices. Even more, the rupture which everyone foresees between Madame de Beauséant and Monsieur d'Ajuda who, they say, is going to marry Mademoiselle de Rochefide, proves to me that these same sacrifices are almost always the reasons of men abandoning us. If you love me sincerely you will cease to see me, at least for some time! For you I lay aside all vanity; is not that something? What does the world not say of a woman to whom no man is attached? That she has no heart, no mind, no soul, and above all no charm. Oh! the coquettes will not spare me, they will take away from me all the qualities which they have been offended at finding in me. So long as I preserve my reputation, what does it matter to me to see the contest of my rivals for my advantages?— They certainly will not inherit it. Come, my friend, give something to one who sacrifices so much for you! Call on me less often, I will not love you the less for it."

"Ah!" replied Armand with the profound irony

of a wounded heart, "love, according to the scribblers, is fed only on illusions! Nothing is more true, I see it, I am to imagine myself loved. But truly, there are thoughts like wounds from which there is no recovery: You were one of my last beliefs, and I now see that all things here below are false."

She smiled.

"Yes," continued Montriveau in an altered voice, "your Catholic faith to which you have tried to convert me is a lie that men make to themselves, hope is a lie based upon the future, pride is a lie between us; pity, wisdom, fear are all lying calculations. My happiness is then also to be a lie, I am to cheat myself and consent to give forever gold for silver. If you can so easily dispense with my presence, if you will acknowledge me neither for your friend nor your lover, you do not love me! And I, poor fool, I say this to myself, I know it, and I love you!"

"But, *Mon Dieu!* my poor Armand, how you go to extremes."

"To extremes?"

"Yes, you think that everything is at an end because I speak to you of prudence."

In her heart she was enchanted with the anger that overflowed in her lover's eyes. At this moment she was tormenting him; but at the same time she judged him, and noticed every alteration in his countenance. Had the general been so unfortunate as to show himself generous without discussion, as sometimes happens to these candid souls, he would have been banished forever, impeached and convicted of not knowing how to love. The greater number of women like to feel their moral convictions violated. Is it not one of their flatteries to yield only to superior force? But Armand was not wise enough to perceive the net skilfully spread for him by the duchess. Strong men who love have so much of the child in their souls!

"If you only wish to keep up appearances," he said artlessly, "I am ready to—"

"Keep up appearances!" she cried, interrupting him; "what sort of ideas do you have of me? Have I given you the smallest reason to think I could ever be yours?"

"Ah, then, what are we talking about?" demanded Montriveau.

"But, Monsieur, you frighten me—No, pardon, thank you," she continued in a freezing tone, "thank you Armand,—you call my attention in time to an imprudence quite involuntary, believe it, my friend. You know how to suffer, you say! I also, I will learn how to suffer. We will cease to see each other; and then, when we have both recovered some calmness, well, then we will try to arrange for ourselves some sort of happiness approved by the world. I am young, Armand, a man without delicacy might do many things to compromise a woman of twenty-four. But, you! you will always be my friend—promise me."

"The woman of twenty-four," he replied, "is old enough to calculate."

He sat down on the divan of the boudoir and held his head between his hands.

"Do you love me, Madame?" he demanded lifting his head and showing a face full of resolution. "Answer fearlessly, yes or no!"

The duchess was more frightened by this interrogation than she would have been by a threat of death,—a common trick which easily frightens women of the nineteenth century who no longer see men wearing their swords by their sides; but are there not effects of the eye-lashes, the eyebrows, contractions in the look, tremblings of the lips, which communicate the fear which they express so keenly, so magnetically?

"Ah!" she said, "if I were free, if—"

"Eh! is it only your husband that is in the way?" cried the general joyfully, walking with great strides up and down the boudoir. "My dear Antoinette, I possess a more absolute power than that of the autocrat of all the Russias. I am on good terms with fate: I can, socially speaking, advance it or put it back at my will like the hands of a watch. To guide fate in our political machine, is it not simply to know the mechanism? In a little while you will be free, remember then your promise."

"Armand," she cried, "what do you mean? Good God! Do you think that I could be the reward of a crime? do you wish my death? Have you no religion at all? For myself, I fear God. Although Monsieur de Langeais has given me the right to hate him, I wish him no ill."

Monsieur de Montriveau, who was beating a tattoo mechanically with his fingers on the marble of the chimney-piece, contented himself by looking at the duchess with a calm air.

"My friend," she said, continuing, "respect him. He does not love me, he has not been good to me, but I have duties to fulfil towards him. To spare him the misfortunes with which you threaten him, what would I not do?—Listen," she resumed after a pause, "I will not talk to you any more of separation, you shall come here as in the past, I will always offer you my forehead to kiss; if I refused it sometimes it was pure coquetry, in truth. But let us understand each other," she said, seeing him approach. "You will permit me to increase the number of my followers, to receive them in the morning even more than I have been doing,—I will increase my frivolities, I will treat you very badly in appearance, and feign a rupture; you will come a little less often; and then, afterwards—"

As she said these words she permitted him to pass his arm around her and seemed to feel, thus pressed in his embrace, the excessive pleasure which most women find in this pressure, in which all the enjoyments of love seem to be promised; then she doubtless wished to inspire some confidence, for she stood on tiptoe to bring her forehead under the burning lips of Armand.

"Afterwards," resumed Montriveau, "you will talk to me no more of your husband; you ought not even to think of him."

Madame de Langeais kept silence.

"At least," she said after an expressive pause, "you will do all that I ask of you, without grumbling, without being wicked, will you not, my friend? You only wished to frighten me? Come, confess it!—you are too good to ever entertain criminal thoughts. But have you then secrets that I know nothing of? What do you mean by controlling fate?"

"The moment, when you confirm the gift that you have already made me of your heart, I am too happy to know well how I should answer you. I have confidence in you, Antoinette, I shall have no doubts, no false jealousies. But if chance should set you at liberty, we are united—"

"Chance, Armand," she said, making one of those pretty gestures of the head which seem to mean so many things and which this species of women dispense so lightly, as a cantatrice plays with her voice. "Pure chance," she resumed. "Understand it well; if through you any misfortune happens to Monsieur de Langeais, I will never be yours."

They parted mutually satisfied. The duchess had made a compact which would permit her to prove to all the world by her words and her actions that Monsieur de Montriveau was not her lover. As for him, the wily creature purposed to tire him out by granting no other favors than those snatched in those little quarrels which she could arrest as she pleased. She knew so prettily how to revoke on the morrow a concession granted the night before, she was so seriously determined to remain physically virtuous, that she saw no risk to herself in these preliminaries, dangerous only to women really in love. In fact, a duchess separated from her husband offered but little to love, in sacrificing to it a marriage that had long been annulled. On his side, Montriveau, quite happy in having obtained the vaguest of promises, and of having put aside forever the objections that a wife could find in conjugal faith for refusing love, congratulated himself on having conquered a little more ground. Thus for some time he abused those rights of enjoyment which had been so reluctantly granted him. More childlike than he had ever yet been, this man gave himself up to all those childish delights which make a first love the flower of our life. He became a child again in pouring out his soul and all the cheated energies which his passion communicated, upon the hands of this woman, upon her blonde hair whose wavy curls he kissed, upon that dazzling forehead which seemed to him so pure. Inundated with love, vanquished by the magnetic outflowings of so warm a sentiment, the duchess hesitated to begin the quarrel which should separate them forever. She was more of a woman than she thought herself, this fragile creature, striving to reconcile the claims of religion with the lively emotions of vanity, with those semblances of pleasure upon which the Parisians dote. Every Sunday she heard Mass, not missing one of the Offices of the Church; every evening she plunged into the intoxicating voluptuousness which flows from desires ceaselessly repressed. Armand and Madame de Langeais resembled those fakirs of India who are rewarded for their chastity by the temptations it offers them. Perhaps also the duchess had come to persuade herself that all love might be resolved into these fraternal caresses, which would doubtless have appeared innocent in the eyes of the world but to which the fearlessness of her thoughts lent an excessive depravation. How else explain the incomprehensible mystery of her perpetual fluctuations? Every morning she resolved to close her doors to the Marquis de Montriveau; every evening at the appointed hour she allowed herself to be charmed by him. After a feeble defence she would become less forbidding; her conversation became sweet and gracious; two lovers only could be thus. The duchess displayed her most sparkling wit, her most charming coquetries; then, when she had irritated the soul and the senses of her lover, if he seized her, she would have been quite willing to have allowed herself to be broken and tormented by him, but she had her *ne plus ultra* of passion; and when he had reached this limit she always became offended if, mastered by his passion, he threatened to pass the barriers. But no woman will dare to deny herself to love without a reason, nothing is more natural than to yield; so Madame de Langeais soon surrounded herself by a second line of fortifications, more difficult to carry than the first. She invoked the terrors of religion. Never did the most eloquent father of the church plead better the commands of God; never was the vengeance of the Most High better proclaimed than by the voice of the duchess. She employed neither the phraseology of sermons nor the amplifications of rhetoric. No, she had her own *pathos*. To Armand's most ardent supplications she replied by a tearful glance, by a gesture that revealed a frightful fulness of sentiment; she silenced him by imploring mercy; a word more, she would not hear it, she would succumb, and death seemed to her preferable to a criminal happiness.

"Is it then nothing to disobey God!" she would say to him, recovering her voice made feeble by the inward conflicts over which this pretty comedienne seemed to secure with difficulty a temporary mastery. "Men, the whole world, I would gladly sacrifice for you; but you are very selfish to ask of me my whole future in return for a moment of pleasure. Come, see, now are you not happy?" she added offering him her hand and revealing herself to him in a négligé which certainly offered to her lover some consolations of which he always availed himself.

If to retain a man whose ardent passion gave her some unaccustomed emotions or if through weakness, she permitted him to snatch a rapid kiss, immediately she feigned terror, she blushed and banished Armand from the sofa at the moment when the sofa became dangerous for her.

"Your pleasures are sins that I must expiate, Armand; they cost me penitences, remorse," she cried.

When Montriveau found himself two chairs away from these aristocratic petticoats, he took to blasphemy, he cursed God. Then the duchess grew angry.

"But, my friend," she said severely, "I cannot understand why you refuse to believe in God, for it certainly is impossible to believe in men. Be silent, do not speak in that manner; your soul is too noble to espouse the follies of liberalism which pretend to do away with God."

Discussions, theological and political, served her as douches to calm Montriveau, who knew no longer how to be reconciled to love when she excited his anger by casting him a thousand leagues away from this boudoir into theories of absolutism which she defended admirably. Few women dare to be democratic, they are then too much in contradiction to their own despotism in matters of sentiment. But sometimes also the general shook his mane, ignored politics, growled like a lion, lashed his flanks, threw himself on his prey, became again terrible from love of his mistress, incapable of curbing longer his evident thought and love. If this woman then felt within her the movings of some fancy strong enough to compromise her, she was discreet enough to quit her boudoir,—she left the atmosphere so charged with desire which she there breathed, went into her salon, seated herself at the piano and began to sing the sweetest airs of modern music, and thus deceived the love of the senses which sometimes did not spare her, but which she had strength to overcome. At such moments, she was sublime in Armand's eyes; she did not feign, she was true, and the poor lover thought himself beloved. This egotistic resistance caused him to take her for a saintly and virtuous creature, and he resigned himself, and he talked of platonic love,— he, General of Artillery! When she had played religion long enough in her own interest Madame de Langeais played it over again in his; she endeavored to bring him back to Christian sentiments, she remodeled the *Genius of Christianity* for military purposes. Montriveau grew impatient, found his yoke heavy. Oh! then in a spirit of contradiction, she flung at him the terrors of God, to see if God would relieve her of a man who held to his purpose with a constancy which began to frighten her. Moreover, she wished to prolong every quarrel which might promise to lengthen out indefinitely the moral struggle, after which would come the material struggle, much more dangerous.

*

If the opposition made in the name of the marriage laws represented the *civil epoch* of this sentimental war, the present struggle constituted the *religious epoch,* and it had, like its predecessor, a crisis after which its fury must abate. One evening Armand arriving accidentally at a very early hour found Monsieur l'Abbé Gondrand, the director of the conscience of Madame de Langeais, established in an arm-chair in the chimney-corner with the air of a man who was comfortably digesting his dinner and the pretty sins of his penitent. The sight of this man, with his fresh and placid countenance, whose forehead was calm, his mouth ascetic, his glance somewhat maliciously inquisitorial, who had in his bearing a true ecclesiastical dignity and already in his vestments the Episcopal purple, caused the face of Montriveau to darken singularly; he bowed to no one and kept silence. Outside of his love the general was not wanting in judgment, he guessed therefore, in exchanging some glances with the future bishop, that this man promoted the difficulties with which the duchess fenced about her love for him. That an ambitious abbé should play fast and loose and restrain the love of a man tempered as he had been, this thought brought the blood to Montriveau's face, clenched his hands, made him rise, walk about the room, stamp about; but when he returned to his seat resolved to give open vent to his feelings, a single look from the duchess sufficed to calm him. Madame de Langeais, in no wise disturbed by the black silence of her lover, which would have embarrassed any other woman, continued to converse very intelligently with Monsieur Gondrand on the necessity of reëstablishing religion in all its ancient splendor. She demonstrated much more cleverly than the abbé could have done, the reasons why the Church should be a power at once temporal and spiritual and regretted that the Chamber of Peers had not yet its *Bench of Bishops,* as the English House of Lords had. However, the abbé, knowing that Lent would soon give him his revenge, yielded his place to the general and went away. The duchess scarcely rose to acknowledge the humble bow of her director, so occupied was she in watching Montriveau's behavior.

"What is the matter, my friend?"

"Your abbé turns my stomach."

"Why did you not take a book?" she said without caring whether the abbé who was just closing the door, heard her or not.

Montriveau remained silent a moment, for the duchess accompanied her speech with a gesture which added to its excessive impertinence.

"My dear Antoinette, I thank you for giving precedence to love over the Church; but I beg you will permit me to ask you one question."

"Ah! you ask me questions. Very well," she

replied. "Are you not my friend? I can certainly show you the depths of my heart. You will find but one image there."

"Have you spoken to that man of our love?"

"He is my confessor."

"Does he know that I love you?"

"Monsieur de Montriveau, you surely do not presume to wish to penetrate the secrets of my confession?"

"Then that man knows all our quarrels and my love for you?—"

"A man, Monsieur!—say God!"

"God! God! I should be alone in your heart. But leave God alone, there wherever He is, for the love of Him and of me. Madame, you shall not go any more to confession, or—"

"Or?" she said smiling.

"Or I will never come here again."

"Go, Armand. Adieu, adieu forever."

She rose and went into her boudoir, without casting a single glance at Montriveau, who remained standing, his hand resting on the back of a chair. How long he stood there he never knew himself. The soul has the mysterious power of extending as of contracting space.

He opened the door of the boudoir, all was dark within. A feeble voice gathered strength to say sharply:

"I did not ring. Besides, why do you enter without orders? Suzette, leave me."

"You are suffering?" cried Montriveau.

"Remove yourself, Monsieur," she cried, ringing, "and go away from here, at least for a moment."

"Madame la Duchesse rang for lights," he said to the valet de chambre, who came into the boudoir and lighted the candles.

When the two lovers were alone Madame de Langeais remained reclining on her divan, silent, motionless, precisely as if Montriveau were not there.

"Dear," he said with an accent of pain and tender kindness, "I was wrong. I certainly would not have you without religion—"

"It is fortunate," she replied in a hard voice, without looking at him, "that you recognize the necessity of conscience. I thank you, for God."

At this the general, withered by the inclemency of this woman, who knew so well how to become at will a perfect stranger or a sister for him, made a step toward the door in despair, and was about to abandon her forever without speaking a single word. He suffered, and the duchess in her heart was laughing at sufferings caused by a moral torture much more cruel than was in old times the judicial torture. But this man was not to be allowed to go. In every kind of crisis a woman is, if we may say so, pregnant with a certain quantity of words; and when she has not uttered them she experiences the sensation suggested by the sight of an unfinished thing. Madame de Langeais, who had not spoken all her mind, resumed:

"We have not the same convictions, general, I

am pained to know it. It would be terrible for a woman not to believe in a religion which allows her to love beyond the grave. I put aside Christian sentiments, you cannot understand them. Let me speak to you only of the proprieties. Would you wish to deny to a woman of the Court the *Holy Communion* when it is customary to receive it at Easter? but it is necessary nevertheless to know what stand to take. The Liberals will not kill the religious sentiment, for all their desire to do so. Religion will always be a political necessity. Would you undertake to govern a nation of pure Rationalists? Napoléon did not dare, he persecuted the Ideologists. To keep the people from reasoning, you must give them sentiments. Let us accept therefore the Catholic religion with all its consequences. If we wish that France should go to Mass, should we not commence by going there ourselves? Religion, Armand, is as you see the bond of the conservative principles which enable the rich to live in safety. Religion is intimately connected with the rights of property. It is certainly a finer thing to lead the people by moral ideas than by scaffolds, as in the days of the Terror, the only means that your detestable Revolution could invent for enforcing submission. The priest and the king, why, they are you, they are me, they are the princess, my neighbor; they are, in a word, all the interests of honest people personified. Come, my friend, be then really on your own side, you who might be its Sylla, if you had the least ambition.

As for me I am quite ignorant of politics, I only reason from feeling; but I know enough, nevertheless, to be sure that society will be upset if its base is to be called in question at every moment—"

"If your court, your government, has these opinions, I am sorry for you," said Montriveau. "The Restoration, Madame, should say like Catherine de Médicis when she thought the battle of Dreux was lost,—'Well, then, we will go to the Protestant church.' Now, 1815 is your battle of Dreux. Like the throne of those days, you have gained it in fact but lost it in law. Political protestantism is victorious in all minds. If you do not wish to make an Edict of Nantes; or if, making it, you revoke it; if you are some day tried and convicted of desiring to do away with the Charter, which is only a pledge given to maintain the interests of the Revolution,—the Revolution will rise again terrible, and will give you but one blow. It is not it that will leave France; it is its very soil. Men allow themselves to be killed, but not interests.— Eh! my God! what to us are France, the throne, legitimacy, the world itself? They are but idle tales compared with my happiness. Reign, or be overthrown, it is but little I care. Where am I then?"

"My friend, you are in the boudoir of Madame la Duchesse de Langeais."

"No, no, no more duchess, no more de Langeais, I am beside my dear Antoinette!"

"Will you do me the pleasure to stay where you

are," said she, laughing and repelling him, but without violence.

"You have never then loved me?" he said in a rage which flashed from his eyes like lightning.

"No, my friend."

This 'no' had the sound of a 'yes.'

"I am a great fool," he said, kissing the hand of this terrible queen once more become woman.— "Antoinette," he resumed, resting his head upon her feet, "you are too chastely tender to tell our happiness to anyone in the world."

"Ah! you are indeed a great fool," she said, rising with a quick and graceful movement. And without adding a word she fled into the salon.

"What is the matter with her?" asked the general, who could not guess the power of the disturbance that his burning head had electrically communicated from the feet to the head of his mistress.

As he arrived furious in the salon he heard celestial strains. The duchess was at her piano. Men of science or of poetic natures, who can at the same time comprehend and enjoy without reflection injuring their pleasure, feel that the notes and the phrases of music are the intimate instruments of the musician, just as the wood or the brass are those of the performer. For them there exists a music apart in the depths of the double expression of this sensual language of souls. *Andiamo mio ben* can bring tears of joy or piteous laughter, according to the singer. Often, here and there in the world, a young girl dying under the weight of a hidden grief, a man whose soul vibrates under the strokes of a passion, take a musical theme and become reconciled with Heaven, or speak with themselves in some sublime melody, like a lost poem. So, now the general at this moment listened to one of these poems, as unknown as could be the solitary complaint of a bird dying without companions in a virgin forest.

"*Mon Dieu!* what are you playing?" he asked in a voice of emotion.

"The prelude to a ballad called, I think, *Fleuve du Tage.*"

"I did not know that there could be such music in a piano," he said.

"Ah! my friend," she said, giving him for the first time the glance of a loving woman, "neither do you know that I love you, that you make me suffer horribly, and that I must indeed find a way to complain without being too well understood; otherwise I should be yours.—But you see nothing."

"And you will not make me happy!"

"Armand, I should die of sorrow the next day."

The general left her brusquely, but when he reached the street he wiped away two tears which he had had the strength to retain till then.

*

Religion lasted three months. At the end of that time, the duchess, weary of her repetitions, delivered, so to speak, her God bound hand and foot to her lover. Perhaps she was afraid that by dint of preaching eternity she might perpetuate the general's love in this world and in the next. For the honor of this woman we must believe that she was virgin even in heart; otherwise her conduct would be too cruel. As yet far from the age at which men and women both find themselves too near the limits of the future to lose time and to quibble with their enjoyments she was doubtless not at her first love, but among her first pleasures. Without experience whereby to compare the good with the evil, without the knowledge of suffering that might have taught her the value of the treasures poured at her feet, she was amusing herself with them. Ignorant of the delightful splendors of light, she was content to remain in the shadows. Armand, who began to comprehend this singular condition, trusted in the primary instincts of nature. He reflected every night, as he left Madame de Langeais, that no woman could accept for seven months the devotion of a man and the most tender, the most delicate, proofs of his love, or yield herself to the superficial exigencies of a passion to deceive it finally, and he patiently awaited the summer season, confident that he would gather the fruit in its prime. He perfectly understood the scruples of a married woman and religious scruples. He even rejoiced in these struggles. He thought the duchess chaste where she was only frightfully coquettish; and he would not have had her otherwise. He liked to see her raise obstacles; would he not gradually triumph over them all? And each triumph, would it not augment the slight total of amorous intimacies long withheld, then conceded by her with all the semblance of love? But he had so well tasted and appreciated all those slight and progressive conquests which satisfy timid lovers that they had become habitual to him. In the matter of obstacles he had only his own fears to overcome; for he no longer saw any hindrance to his happiness other than the caprices of the one who allowed him to call her *Antoinette.* He resolved therefore to demand more, to demand everything. Timid as a lover still young who does not dare to believe in the lowering of his idol, he hesitated long and passed through those terrible reactions of the heart, those clearly formed desires which a word annihilates, those fixed resolutions which expire at the threshold of the door. He despised himself for not having strength to say a word, and yet he did not say it. Nevertheless, at last one evening he proceeded in a sombre melancholy to put forth the rude claims to his illegally legitimate rights. The duchess did not wait the request of her slave to know his desire. Is a man's desire ever secret? Have not all women that intuitive knowledge of certain expressions of the physiognomy?

"What, would you cease to be my friend?" she asked, interrupting him at the first word and casting on him a glance made lovelier by a divine flush which flowed like a new blood under her diaphanous skin. "As a reward for my generosity, you would dishonor me. Reflect a little. I have myself reflected much; I think always of *us*. There is an integrity for women in which we should no more make default than you should fail in honor. For myself, I could not deceive. If I became yours, I could no longer be in any respect the wife of Monsieur de Langeais. You exact therefore the sacrifice of my position, of my rank, of my life, for a doubtful love which has not had seven months of patience. What! already you would wish to deprive me of the free disposition of myself? No, no, do not speak to me thus. No, say nothing to me. I will not, I can not listen to you."

Here Madame de Langeais with both hands put back her clusters of curls that heated her brow and became very animated.

"You come to a feeble creature with well defined calculations, saying to yourself: 'She will talk to me of her husband for a certain length of time, then of God, then of the inevitable consequences of love; but I will use, I will abuse the influence which I shall have acquired; I will render myself necessary; I shall have on my side the ties of habit, the arrangements recognized by the public; finally, when the world shall have finished by accepting our liaison, I shall be the master of this woman.' Be frank, these are your thoughts—Ah! you calculate, and you call that love! Fie! you are in love, ah! I really believe it! You desire me, and you wish to have me for your mistress, that is all. Well, then, no, *La Duchesse de Langeais* will not descend so low as that. Let the artless bourgeoises be the dupes of your falsehood; for myself, I never shall. Nothing assures me of your love. You speak of my beauty, I may become ugly in six months, like the dear princess, my neighbor. You are charmed with my wit, with my grace; *Mon Dieu!* you will get accustomed to them just as you get accustomed to pleasure. Have you not already made a habit for the last few months of the favors which I have had the weakness to accord you? When I am lost, some day, you will give me no other reason for your change than the decisive word: 'I no longer love you.' Rank, fortune, honor, all of the Duchesse de Langeais will be swallowed up in a hope deceived. I shall have children who will bear witness to my shame, and—. But," she resumed with an involuntary gesture of impatience, "I am too kind to explain to you that which you know better than I. Come now, let us remain as we are. I am too happy as I am to be able yet to break the bonds which you think so strong. Is there then anything so very heroic in coming to the Hôtel de Langeais to pass some time every evening with a woman whose chatter pleased you, with whom you amused yourself as with a plaything? But there are several young fops who come to see me daily, from three to five o'clock, as regularly as you come in the evening. They are then very generous! I laugh at them, they receive very tranquilly my caprices, my impertinences, and make me laugh; whilst you, you to whom I accord the most precious treasures of my soul, you wish to ruin me and cause me a thousand griefs. Keep silence, enough, enough," she said seeing him about to speak, "you have neither heart, nor soul, nor delicacy. I know what you wish to say to me. Well then, yes. I had rather appear in your eyes as a woman cold, without feeling, without devotion, without a heart even, than to appear in the eyes of the world as a common woman, than to be condemned to eternal suffering after having been condemned to your pretended pleasures, which would certainly end by wearying you. Your egotistical love is not worth so many sacrifices—"

These words represent very imperfectly those which the duchess trilled forth with the lively prolixity of a hand-organ. Certainly she might have talked on a long while, the poor Armand offered for sole reply to this torrent of soft phrases a silence teeming with painful thoughts. He perceived for the first time the coquetry of this woman, and instinctively divined that a devoted love, love shared with another, did not calculate, did not reason thus in the heart of a true woman. Then he experienced a sort of shame as he remembered that he had involuntarily made the calculations with the odious thoughts of which he had been reproached. Then, examining his conscience with a quite angelic good faith, he found nothing but selfishness in his words, in his ideas, in the answers conceived and not expressed. He blamed himself, and in his despair he thought of throwing himself out of the window. The *I* paralyzed him. What to say, in fact, to a woman who did not believe in love? 'Let me prove to you how much I love you.' Always *I*. Montriveau did not know, as in similar circumstance the ordinary heroes of the boudoir know, how to imitate the rough logician who marched before the Pyrrhonians while denying his own movement. This audacious man failed precisely in that audacity which is common to those lovers who know the formula of feminine algebra. If so many women, and even the most virtuous, fall a prey to those men skilful in love to whom the vulgar give a bad name, perhaps it is because they are grand *demonstrators*, and that love, in spite of its delightful poetry of sentiment, demands more geometry than we think for. Now, the duchess and Montriveau were alike in this respect, that they were equally inexpert in love. She knew very little of its theory, was ignorant of its practice, felt nothing and reflected on all. Montriveau knew very little of its practice, was ignorant of its theory, and felt too much to reflect. Both of them were suffering under the misfortune of this curious situation. In this supreme moment, its myriads of thoughts might be reduced to this one only: "Surrender yourself." A phrase, horribly egotistical to a woman for whom these words bore no memories and revealed no image. Nevertheless, it was necessary to reply. Although his blood was lashed by these little phrases, shot like arrows, one by one, very sharp, very cold, very steely, Montriveau was compelled to dissemble his anger that he might not lose all by some extravagance.

"Madame la Duchesse, I am in despair that God has not invented for woman any other manner of confirming the gift of her heart than by adding to it that of her person. The high price which you attach to yourself shows me that I should not attach a lesser one. If you give me your soul and all your feelings, as you say you do, what matters the rest? However, if my happiness is to you so painful a sacrifice, let us say no more about it. Only, you will pardon a man of heart for feeling humiliated in seeing himself taken for a spaniel."

The tone of this last phrase might well have frightened any other woman; but when one of these petticoat-wearers is lifted above everything else in permitting herself to be turned into a divinity, there is no power here below that is as proud as she.

"Monsieur le Marquis, I am in despair that God has not invented for man any more noble manner of confirming the gift of his heart than by the manifestation of desires prodigiously vulgar. If, in giving our persons we become slaves, a man commits himself to nothing in accepting us. Who can assure me that I shall be always loved? The love that I should be forced to show at all times to attach you closer to me might be the very reason of your desertion. I do not choose to be a second edition of Madame de Beauséant. Does any one ever know what it is that keeps you faithful to us? Our constant coldness is the secret of the constant passion of some of you; for others, a perpetual devotion is required, an adoration every minute; for these, kindness; for those, despotism. No woman has ever yet fully deciphered your heart."

There was a pause, after which she changed her tone.

"In short, my friend, you cannot prevent a woman from trembling at this question, 'shall I be always loved?' Hard as they may be, my words are dictated to me by the fear of losing you. *Mon Dieu!* it is not I, dear, who speak to you, but reason; and how is it that reason is to be found in such a light creature as I am? Indeed, I cannot tell."

To hear this answer, begun in a tone of most trenchant irony and ended with the sweetest accents which a woman can use to picture love in all its candor, was not this to pass in a moment from martyrdom to the skies? Montriveau turned pale, and for the first time in his life fell on his knees at the foot of a woman. He kissed the hem of the robe of the duchess, her feet, her knees; but for the honor of the Faubourg Saint-Germain let us not reveal the mysteries of her boudoirs in which everything is required of love excepting that which could prove love.

"Dear Antoinette," cried Montriveau in the delirium in which he was plunged by the entire surrender of the duchess who thought herself generous in permitting herself to be adored; "yes, you are right, I do not wish that you should retain any doubts. At this moment I tremble myself lest I should lose the angel of my life, and I would wish to invent for us indissoluble bonds."

"Ah!" she said in a low voice, "you see, I was right."

"Let me finish," resumed Armand, "I will with one word dispel all your doubts. Listen, if I forsake you I will merit a thousand deaths. Be entirely mine, and I will give you the right to kill me if I betray you. I will write, myself, a letter in which I will declare certain reasons that have compelled me to destroy myself; in short, I will make in it my last will. You shall hold this testament which will justify my death, and you can thus avenge yourself without having anything to fear from either God or man."

"Have I any need of such a letter? If I had lost your love, what would life be to me? If I wished to kill you, would I not follow you? No, I thank you for the idea, but I do not want the letter. Would I not think that you were faithful to me through fear, or, the danger of an infidelity, would not that be an attraction for one who thus exposed his life? Armand, that which I ask of you is the one thing difficult to do."

"And what do you wish, then?"

"Your obedience and my freedom."

"My God," he cried, "I am like a child."

"A wilful child and one well spoiled," she said, caressing the thick hair of his head which she still retained on her knees. "Oh! yes, much more loved than he thinks, and yet very disobedient. Why not stay as we are? why not sacrifice to me the desires which offend me? why not accept what I give if it is all that I can honestly grant? Are you not then happy?"

"Oh! yes," he answered, "I am happy when I have no doubts. Antoinette, to doubt in love, is it not to die?"

And he showed at a stroke what he was, and what all men are when burning with desires, eloquent, insinuating. After having tasted those pleasures sanctioned no doubt by some secret and jesuitical ukase, the duchess experienced all those cerebral emotions the habit of which had rendered the love of Armand as necessary for her as society, the ball, the opera. To see herself adored by a man whose superiority, whose character, inspired fear; to make him a child; to play with him as Poppœa played with Nero,—very many women, like the wives of Henry VIII., have paid for this perilous delight with their life's blood. Well, curious presentiment! in yielding to him the pretty blond waves of her hair through which he loved to thrust his fingers, in feeling the pressure of the loving hand of this truly great man, in playing herself with the black locks of his hair, in this boudoir where she reigned, the duchess said to herself:

"This man is capable of killing me if he once perceives that I am trifling with him."

✻

Monsieur de Montriveau remained till two in the morning beside his mistress, who, from that moment, seemed to him no longer either a duchess or a Navarreins;—Antoinette had pushed her deception so far as to seem a woman. During this delightful evening, the sweetest prelude that ever a Parisian woman gave to that which the world calls *a fault* the general was permitted to see in her, despite the affectations of a coquettish modesty, all the beauty of a young girl. He might think with reason that so many capricious quarrels were only veils with which a celestial soul clothed itself, to be lifted one by one like those with which she enveloped her adorable body. The duchess was to him the most artless, the most ingenuous of mistresses, and he made of her the one woman of his choice; he went away from her, at last, happy in having brought her finally to grant him so many pledges of love that it seemed to him impossible not to be henceforth for her a husband in secret, the choice of whom had been approved by God. With this thought, with the candor of those who feel all the obligations of love in tasting its pleasures, Armand returned slowly home. He followed the quays so that he might see the greatest possible space of heaven. He wished to enlarge the firmament and all nature as he felt his heart expand.

His lungs seemed to him to inspire more air than they had taken in the night before. As he walked he questioned himself, and he promised himself to love this woman so religiously that she should find each day an absolution for her social faults in a continued happiness. Gentle agitations of an overflowing life! Men who have sufficient strength to dye their souls with only one sentiment experience an infinite joy in contemplating by snatches a whole life-time incessantly passionate, as some recluses can contemplate the divine light in their ecstasies. Without this belief in its perpetuity, love would be nothing; constancy enlarges it. It was thus that Montriveau comprehended his passion as he walked along in the grasp of his happiness.

"We are joined one to the other forever!"

This thought was for this man a talisman which realized the desires of his life-time. He did not ask himself if the duchess would change, if this love would endure; no, he had faith, that virtue without which there is no Christian future, but which, perhaps, is still more necessary to society. For the first time, he regarded life through his feeling, he who had hitherto lived only by the excessive action of human strength, the devotion, half corporeal, of the soldier.

The next day Monsieur de Montriveau set out at an early hour towards the Faubourg Saint-Germain. He had an appointment in a house near the Hôtel de Langeais, to which, as soon as he had transacted his business, he turned his steps, as if to his own home. The general was walking with a man for whom he seemed to have a species of aversion when he encountered him in society. This man was the Marquis de Ronquerolles, whose reputation became so high in the boudoirs of Paris; a man of wit, of talent, above all of courage, and who gave the tone to all the young men of Paris; a gallant man, whose success and whose experience were equally envied, and to whom was lacking neither fortune nor birth, which add in Paris so much lustre to the qualities of a man of the world.

"Where are you going?" said Monsieur de Ronquerolles to Montriveau.

"To Madame de Langeais."

"Ah! true, I forgot that you had allowed yourself to be taken in her toils. You will lose with her a love which you had much better employ elsewhere. I could give you ten women who are worth a thousand of that titled courtesan, who does with her head what other women, more frank, do—"

"What are you saying, my dear fellow?" said Armand, interrupting him, "the duchess is an angel of purity."

Ronquerolles laughed.

"If you have got as far as that, my dear fellow," he said, "I must enlighten you. One word only! between us, it cannot matter. Is the duchess yours? In that case, I have nothing to say. Come now, confide in me. It is a question of not losing your time in attaching your fine soul to an ungrateful nature that will betray every hope you form."

When Armand had naïvely sketched the situation, in which he mentioned minutely the rights which he had obtained with so much difficulty, Ronquerolles burst into a fit of laughter so cruel that in another man it would have cost his life. But in seeing the peculiar manner in which these two men looked and spoke to each other, standing alone in the angle of a wall as far from the world of men as they would have been in the middle of a desert, it was easy to imagine that they were united by some friendship without bounds and that no human interest could embroil them.

"My dear Armand, why did you not tell me that you were involved with the duchess? I could have given you some advice that would have enabled you to bring this intrigue to a good end. You ought to know, first, that the women of our Faubourg, like all others, delight in being immersed in love; but they wish to possess without themselves being possessed. They have arranged matters with nature. The jurisprudence of the parish allows them almost everything, short of the positive sin. The favors with which your lovely duchess regales you are venial sins which she washes off with the waters of penitence. But, if you had the impertinence to demand seriously the great mortal sin to which, naturally, you attach the highest importance, you would see with what profound disdain the door of the boudoir and that of the hôtel would be incontinently shut in your face. The tender Antoinette would have forgotten everything, you would be less than nothing for her. Your kisses, my dear friend, are wiped off with the indifference that a woman brings to the details of her toilet. The duchess would sponge love away from her cheeks just as she does her rouge. We are well acquainted with that sort of woman, the pure Parisian. Have you never noticed in the streets a little grisette trotting quickly along? her head is a picture,—pretty bonnet, fresh cheeks, coquettish hair, arch smile, all the rest of her very little cared for. Is not that a good portrait? There is your Parisian woman, she knows that her head alone will be seen,—therefore for her head are all her cares, all her adornments, all her vanities. Well, your duchess is all head, she only feels by her head, she has a heart in her head, a voice in her head, she is dainty in her head. We call this poor thing an intellectual Laïs. You are played with like a child. If you doubt it, you can have the proof this evening, this morning, this instant. Go to her, try to demand, to wish imperiously that which is refused you; even though you set about it like the late Maréchal de Richelieu, not to be denied."

Armand was dumfounded.

"Do you want her enough to make a fool of yourself?"

"I want her at any price!" cried Montriveau, desperately.

"Well then, listen. Be as implacable as she will be; try to humiliate her, to pique her vanity, to interest, not her heart, not her soul, but the nerves and the lymph of this woman who is at once nervous and lymphatic. If you can rouse a desire in her, you are saved. But quit all your beautiful childish ideas. If, having caught her in your eagles' claws, you hesitate, if you yield, if one of your eyelashes quivers, if she thinks she can still control you, she will slip from your talons like a fish and escape, never to be caught again. Be as inflexible as the law. Have no more mercy than the executioner. Strike. When you have struck, strike again. Strike always, as if with a knout. Duchesses are hard, my dear Armand, and these feminine natures soften only under blows; suffering gives them a heart, and it is a work of charity to strike them. Strike therefore without ceasing. Ah! when pain has well wrung their nerves, enervated those fibres that you think so soft and tender; made that dry heart to beat, which, under this play, will resume its elasticity; when the brain has yielded, passion will enter perhaps in the metallic springs of this machine of tears, of manners, of swoonings, of melting phrases; and you will see the most magnificent of conflagrations if only the chimney takes fire. This kind of female steel will have the red heat of metal in the forge! a heat more durable than any other, and this incandescence will perhaps become love. Nevertheless, I doubt it. And then, is the duchess worth so much trouble? Between ourselves, she would have done better to have been primarily formed by a man like myself, I would have made of her a charming woman, she has race; but as for you two, you will stay always at the A, B, C of love. But you are in love, and you do not share at this moment my ideas on the subject.—All happiness to you, my children," added Ronquerolles laughing and after a pause. "For my part, I declare in favor of easy women; at least they are tender, they love naturally, and not with all these social condiments. My poor boy, a woman who quibbles, who only wishes to inspire love? well, it is well to have one as a matter of luxury, as you have a riding horse; to see only in her the little game of the confessional against the sofa, or of white against black, of the queen against the bishop, of scruples against pleasure, a very diverting game of chess. A man ever so little of a roué, who knows the game, would give mate in three moves, at will. If I undertook a woman of that kind, I would make it my object to—"

He whispered a word in Armand's ear and left him abruptly that he might not hear his answer.

As for Montriveau, he made one bound across the courtyard of the Hôtel de Langeais, went up to the duchess's apartments and, without having himself announced, entered and went into her bedroom.

"But this is not the thing," she said, gathering her dressing-robe about her hastily; "Armand, you are an abominable man. Go away, leave me, I beg of you. Go, go. Wait for me in the salon. Go."

"Dear angel," he said to her, "has a husband no privileges?"

"But it is detestable taste, Monsieur, either in a bridegroom or in a husband, to surprise his wife in this way."

He came up to her, took hold of her and clasped her in his arms:

"Forgive me, my dear Antoinette, but a thousand evil suspicions fill my heart."

"Suspicions, fie—ah! fie, fie, then!"

"Suspicions which seem almost justified. If you loved me, would you now quarrel with me? Would you not be happy to see me? Would you not have felt some, I know not what, movement of the heart? Why I, who am not a woman, I feel an inward trembling at the very sound of your voice. The desire to fall upon your neck has often assailed me in the midst of a ball."

"Oh! if you have as many suspicions as the times I have not fallen on your neck before all the world, I fear that I shall be under suspicion all my life; but in comparison with you Othello was a baby!"

"Ah," he said in despair, "I am not loved—"

"At least, at this moment, admit that you are not lovable."

"I have, then, still to seek to please you?"

"Ah! I believe it. Come," she said with a little imperative air, "go, leave me. I am not like you; I do seek to please you—"

Never did any woman know better than Madame de Langeais how to put so much grace into her insolence; and is this not to double its effect? is this not to make the coldest man furious? At this moment her eyes, the tone of her voice, her attitude, all expressed a species of perfect liberty which is never found in a loving woman when she is in the presence of the one the sight of whom alone should make her palpitate. Armand, his mind somewhat disabused by the counsels of the Marquis de Ronquerolles and still farther enlightened by that rapid perception with which passion momentarily endows the least sagacious of men, but which is found so complete in strong minds, defined at once the terrible truth which the self-possession of the duchess betrayed, and his heart swelled with a storm like a lake ready to burst its bounds.

"If you spoke the truth yesterday, be mine, my dear Antoinette," he cried, "I will—"

"In the first place," she said, repelling him calmly and with strength when she saw him advance, "do not compromise me. My waiting-woman might hear you. Respect me, I beg of you. Your familiarity is very well in the evening in my boudoir; but here,—no. And pray what signifies your 'I will'? I will! No one has ever said that word to me. It seems to me very ridiculous, perfectly ridiculous."

"You will not yield to me on this point?" said he.

"Ah! you call it a point, the free disposition of ourselves; a point of great importance, in fact; and you will permit me to be on this point entirely my own mistress."

"And if, trusting to your promises, I exact it?"

"Then you will prove to me that I have been very wrong in making you the slightest promise, I shall not be foolish enough to keep it, and I shall entreat you to let me alone."

The general turned pale, was about to spring forward; Madame de Langeais rang, her maid entered, and smiling at him with a mocking grace, the duchess said to Armand:

"Have the kindness to come back when I am ready to be seen."

Montriveau felt at this moment all the hardness of this woman; cold and cutting as steel, she was crushing in her scorn. In one moment she had broken the bonds that were strong only for her lover. The duchess had read on Armand's brow the secret exigencies of this visit and had judged that the moment had come to make this imperial soldier know that duchesses might well lend themselves to love, but not give themselves, and that their conquest was more difficult to make than had been that of Europe.

"Madame," said Armand, "I have not the time to wait. I am, as you said yourself, a spoiled child. When I seriously wish for that of which we were speaking just now, I will have it."

"You will have it?" she said with a haughty manner in which was mingled some surprise.

"I will have it."

"Ah! how good of you to will it. As a matter of curiosity, I should like to know how you intend to get it—"

"I am enchanted," replied Montriveau, laughing in such a manner that it frightened the duchess, "to be able to give an interest to your life. Will you permit me to come to take you to the ball to-night?"

"A thousand thanks, Monsieur de Marsay has preceded you, I have made an engagement."

Montriveau bowed gravely and withdrew.

"Ronquerolles was right," he thought, "we are going to play henceforth a game of chess."

From that moment he hid his emotions under an appearance of perfect calmness. No man is strong enough to be able to support these changes which transport the soul rapidly from the highest happiness to supreme despair. Had he not caught a glimpse of a life of happiness only to feel more deeply the void of his previous existence? It was a terrible storm; but he knew how to suffer, and he received the rush of his tumultuous thoughts as a granite rock receives the waves of an angry ocean.

"I could say nothing to her; in her presence I have no longer any wits. She does not know how vile and despicable she is. No one has ever dared to put this creature face to face with herself. She has doubtless trifled with many men, I will avenge them all."

For the first time, perhaps, in the heart of a man love and revenge were so equally mingled that it was impossible for Montriveau himself to know whether it was love or vengeance which had the ascendancy. He went that same evening to the ball where he knew she would be, and he almost despaired of being able to touch this woman to whom he was tempted to ascribe something demoniacal: She showed herself very gracious to him, and smiled on him pleasantly, she doubtless did not wish the world to believe that she had compromised herself with Monsieur de Montriveau. A mutual coolness would have betrayed love. But that the duchess should change nothing in her manner while the marquis appeared sombre and vexed, would not that make it apparent that Armand had obtained nothing from her? The world is quick to recognize the unhappiness of a rejected man, and never confounds this with the discontent which some women order their lovers to affect in the hope of concealing a mutual love. And every one smiled at Montriveau, who, not having consulted his new elephant-driver, remained dreamy, suffering; while Monsieur de Ronquerolles would perhaps have advised him to compromise the duchess by replying to her false courtesies with passionate demonstrations. Armand de Montriveau left the ball, holding all human nature in horror, and yet hardly able to believe in such utter perversity.

"Since there are no public executioners for such crimes," he said, looking at the lighted windows of the salons in which were dancing, talking and smiling the loveliest women in Paris, "I will take you by the nape of your neck, Madame la Duchesse, and I will make you feel a sharper blade than the knife of the Place de la Grève. Steel against steel, we shall see which heart can bear most."

*

For about a week, Madame de Langeais hoped to see the Marquis de Montriveau again; but Armand contented himself by sending his card every morning to the Hôtel de Langeais. Each time that this card was brought to the duchess she was unable to repress a shudder, she was filled with sinister thoughts, but indistinctly, like a presentiment of misfortune. When she read that name at times she seemed to feel in her hair the powerful hand of this implacable man, at times this name threatened vengeances which her active fancy imagined as atrocious. She had studied him too closely not to fear him. Would she be assassinated? This man with the neck of a bull, would he tear her open in tossing her over his head? would he trample her under foot? When, where, how would he seize her? would he make her suffer much, and what species of suffering was he now preparing for her? She repented. There were moments when, if he had come, she would have flung herself into his arms in complete surrender. Every night as she fell asleep she saw his image under some new aspect. Sometimes his bitter smile, sometimes his brows knitted like Jupiter's, his lion-look, or some proud motion of his shoulders, made him terrible to her. The next morning the card would seem to her covered with blood. She lived agitated by that name more than she had ever been by the fiery, obstinate, exacting lover. Then, as the silence was prolonged, her apprehensions deepened; she was forced to prepare herself, without outside help, for a horrible struggle, of which she was not permitted to speak. This soul, proud and hard, was more sensible to the sting of hate than it had recently been to the caresses of love. Ah! if the general could have seen his mistress as she knit her brows in bitter thoughts in the recesses of that boudoir in which he had tasted so many joys, perhaps he would have been filled with great hopes. Is not pride, after all, one of those human emotions which can give birth to none but noble actions? Although Madame de Langeais kept the secret of her thoughts, we may suppose that Monsieur de Montriveau was no longer indifferent to her. Is it not an immense conquest for a man to absorb a woman's mind? Once there, he must necessarily make progress one way or the other. Put the feminine creature under the heels of a furious horse, before some terrible animal, and she will certainly fall on her knees, she will expect death; but if the beast be merciful and does not kill her at once, she will love the horse, the lion, the bull, she will speak to it with composure. The duchess felt herself under the feet of a lion; she trembled, she did not hate. These two persons thus so strangely pitted against each other met in society three times during that week. Each time, in reply to her coquettish interrogations, the duchess received from Armand respectful salutations and smiles tinged with so cruel an irony that they confirmed all the apprehensions inspired in the morning by the visiting-card. Life is only what our feelings make of it for us, feelings had now hollowed an abyss between these two persons.

At the commencement of the following week the Comtesse de Sérizy, sister of the Marquis de Ronquerolles, gave a grand ball, at which Madame de Langeais was present. The first person the duchess saw on entering was Armand. He was waiting for her this time, at least she thought so. They exchanged looks. A cold sweat suddenly issued from every pore of her skin. She had believed Montriveau capable of some unheard-of vengeance, proportioned to their condition; this vengeance was found, it was waiting, it was hot, it seethed. The eyes of this betrayed lover darted lightnings at her, and his visage radiated a satisfied hatred. With the utmost desire to display her coldness and her superciliousness the duchess remained silent and oppressed. She moved to the side of the Comtesse de Sérizy, who could not forbear saying to her:

"What is the matter, my dear Antoinette? You look terrifying."

"A contra-dance will restore me," she answered, taking the hand of a young man who came forward.

Madame de Langeais began to waltz with a sort of nervous frenzy that increased the lowering look on Montriveau's face. He remained standing, somewhat in advance of those who were amusing themselves by watching the waltzers. Each time that his mistress passed before him his eyes seized upon this revolving head like those of a tiger sure of its prey. The waltz over, the duchess came and seated herself near the countess, and the marquis did not cease to watch her as he conversed with a stranger.

"Monsieur," he said, "one of the things which most struck me in this journey—"

The duchess was all ears.

"—Was the phrase used by the guard at Westminster in showing the axe with which a masked man, as it is said, had struck off the head of Charles I., in memory of the king who had said it himself to an inquirer."

"What did he say," asked Madame de Sérizy.

"*Do not touch the axe!*" answered Montriveau in a tone in which there seemed to be menace.

"Really, Monsieur le Marquis," said the Duchesse de Langeais, "you look at my neck with such a melodramatic air in repeating this old story, familiar to everyone who has been to London, that I can almost imagine I can see the axe in your hand."

These last words were said laughingly, though a cold sweat had taken possession of her.

"But this story is, on the contrary, very new," he replied.

"In what way, pray tell me? if you please, in what?"

"In this, Madame, you have touched the axe," said Montriveau to her in a low tone.

"What a delightful prophecy!" she cried with a forced smile. "And when will my head fall?"

"I do not wish your pretty head to fall, Madame. I only fear some great misfortune for you. If you were shorn, would you not regret your charming blond hair which you make so much of?—"

"But there are those for whom women are glad to make such sacrifices, and often even for men who do not know how to overlook their momentary ill humor."

"Agreed. Well, if, all at once, by some chemical process, a jester were to take away your beauty, make you seem a hundred years old when you are for us but eighteen?"

"Ah! Monsieur," she said, interrupting him, "the small-pox is our Battle of Waterloo. The day after, we know those who truly love us."

"Would you not regret that delightful countenance which?—"

"Oh! very much; but less for myself than for him who might care for it. Still, if I were sincerely loved always, faithfully, what would my beauty matter?—What do you think, Clara?"

"It is a dangerous subject," replied Madame de Sérizy.

"Might one ask of His Majesty, the King of the Sorcerers," continued Madame de Langeais, "when I committed the sin of touching the axe,—I who have never been to London—"

"*No so*," he answered with a mocking laugh.

"And when will the execution commence?"

Upon which Montriveau coolly drew out his watch and looked at the hour with an air of conviction that was really frightful.

"The day will not end until a horrible misfortune has overtaken you—"

"I am not a child to be easily frightened, or, rather, I am a child that knows no danger," said the duchess, "and I am going to dance without fear on the verge of the abyss."

"I am delighted, Madame, to know that you have so much strength of mind," he replied as he saw her go to take her place in the quadrille.

Notwithstanding her apparent disdain for Armand's sinister predictions, the duchess was a prey to mortal terror. The moral and almost physical oppression under which her lover held her scarcely ceased when he left the ball. Nevertheless, after the momentary relief of breathing at her ease, she was surprised to find herself regretting this absence of fear, so eager is the female nature for extremes of emotion. This regret was not love, but it belonged undoubtedly to the feelings that lead up to it. Then, as if she were again under the effects of the influence which Monsieur de Montriveau had upon her, she recalled the air of conviction with which he had looked at his watch, and, unable to control her terror, she left the ball. It was then about midnight. Those of her servants who were waiting for her put on her pelisse and went before her to call her carriage; once seated in it, she fell very naturally into a reverie induced by

Monsieur de Montriveau's prediction. When she arrived in her court-yard she entered into a vestibule that closely resembled that of her own hôtel; but suddenly she perceived that the stairway was not hers; then, at the moment when she turned to call her servants, several men seized her suddenly, bound a handkerchief over her mouth, tied her hand and foot, and carried her away. She cried out loudly.

"Madame, we have orders to kill you if you make a noise," said a voice in her ear.

The terror of the duchess was so great that afterwards she could not in the least remember when or how she was transported. When she recovered her senses, she found herself lying, bound hand and foot with silken cords, on the sofa in a bachelor's chamber. She could not retain a cry as she encountered the eyes of Armand de Montriveau, who, seated quietly in an arm-chair and wrapped in his dressing-gown, was smoking a cigar.

"Make no noise, Madame la Duchesse," he said coolly, taking his cigar from his lips, "I have a headache. Besides, I am about to unbind you. But listen carefully to what I am now to have the honor to say to you."

He gently loosened the cords that bound the feet of the duchess.

"What good will your cries do you? no one can hear them. You are too well bred to make useless grimaces. If you are not quiet, if you insist upon struggling with me, I will bind you again hand and foot. I believe, however, all things considered, that you will respect yourself enough to remain upon that sofa as if you were lying upon your own, —cold and indifferent still, if you will.—You have caused me to shed on that couch very many tears which I have hidden from the eyes of others."

As Montriveau spoke the duchess cast about her that furtive female glance which sees all even when it appears most abstracted. She greatly liked the appearance of this room, which bore a strong resemblance to the cell of a monk. The character and the habits of the master pervaded it. No ornament relieved the gray tone of the empty walls. On the floor was a green carpet. A black sofa, a table covered with papers, two large arm-chairs, a chest of drawers on which stood an alarm-clock, a very low bed over which was thrown a red cloth with a Grecian border in black, all proclaimed the habits of a life reduced to its simplest needs. A three-branched candlestick on the chimney-piece recalled by its Egyptian shape the immensity of the deserts in which this man had so long wandered. Beside the bed, whose feet, like the enormous paws of a Sphinx, appeared under the folds of the drapery, and the angle of one of the lateral walls of the chamber, was a door hidden by a green curtain with red and black fringes held by large rings to a pole. The door through which unknown hands had brought the duchess had a similar portière, held back by a loop. At the last glance which the duchess cast upon the two curtains to compare them she perceived that the door nearest to the bed was open, and that a ruddy light from the adjoining room shone in a narrow line at the foot of the curtain. Her curiosity was naturally roused by this mysterious light which hardly enabled her to distinguish in the obscurity some strange forms; but for the moment she did not think that her danger could come from that direction, and she wished to satisfy a more pressing interest.

"Monsieur, is it an indiscretion to ask of you what you propose to do with me?" she said offensively and with a tone of cutting mockery.

The duchess believed she heard the voice of exceeding love in Montriveau's words. Besides, to carry off a woman, does not that necessarily mean to adore her?

"Nothing at all, Madame," he answered, blowing away easily the last smoke of his tobacco. "You are here for a short time only. I wish first to explain to you what you are, and what I am. When you are attitudinizing on your divan in your boudoir, I find no words to express my ideas. Moreover, in your house, at the least word which displeases you, you pull your bell-rope, you cry out and put your lover out of the door, as if he were the worst of outcasts. Here, my mind is free. Here, no one can throw me out of doors. Here, you will be my victim for a few moments, and you will have the extreme goodness to listen to me. Fear nothing. I have not carried you off to utter insults to you, or to obtain from you by violence that which I have not been able to deserve, that which you have not been willing to freely grant me. That would be baseness. You may perhaps conceive of rape; I can not conceive of it."

He threw, with a sharp movement, his cigar into the fire.

"Madame, the smoke doubtless annoys you?"

He immediately rose, took from the fire-place a warming-pan, burnt some perfumes in it and purified the air. The astonishment of the duchess could not be compared with her humiliation. She was in the power of this man, and this man did not intend to abuse his power. Those eyes, once flaming with love, she now saw calm and fixed as the stars. She trembled. Then, the terror with which Armand inspired her was augmented by one of those petrifying sensations, analogous to those helpless and motionless agitations peculiar to nightmares. She lay gripped by fear, fancying she saw the lurid light behind the curtain grow more vivid, as if blown by bellows. Suddenly, the glow, becoming stronger, illuminated three masked men. This terrible appearance disappeared so suddenly that she took it for an optical illusion.

"Madame," resumed Armand, looking at her with contemptuous coldness, "a moment, one only, will suffice me to strike you through every moment of your life, the only eternity of which I myself can dispose. I am not God. Listen to me attentively," he said, making a pause to give solemnity to his words. "Love will always come at your will; you have over men a power that is unlimited; but recollect that one day you called love to you,—it came to you, pure and honest, as much so as it can be on this earth; as respectful as it was violent; tender as the love of a devoted woman, or of that of a mother for her child; and, finally, so grand that it was a madness. You trifled with that love, you committed a crime. Every woman has a right to refuse a love she feels she cannot share. The man who loves without making himself beloved should not be pitied, and has no cause for complaint. But, Madame la Duchesse, to draw to herself, in feigning feeling, an unfortunate deprived of all natural affection, to make him comprehend happiness in all its plenitude only to tear it from him; to rob all his future of joy; to kill him, not only for to-day but for the eternity of his life, by poisoning all his hours and all his thoughts, that is what I call a frightful crime!"

"Monsieur—"

"I cannot yet permit you to answer me. Listen to me still. Moreover, I have certain rights over you; though I only wish those of the judge over the criminal, in order to awaken your conscience. If you had no longer any conscience I should not blame you; but you are still so young! you must still feel life in your heart, I like to think so. If I believe you sufficiently depraved to commit a crime unpunishable by law I do not take you to be so degraded as not to comprehend the meaning of my words. I resume."

At this moment the duchess heard the dull sound of a bellows with which the unknown, of whom she had had a glimpse, were doubtless stirring the fire, the light of which was thrown on the curtain; but the flaming glance of Montriveau compelled her to remain quiet and palpitating, with her eyes fixed before him. However great might be her curiosity, the fire of his words interested her still more than the crackling voice of that mysterious flame.

※

"Madame," he continued after a pause, "when in Paris the executioner puts his hand upon a poor assassin and stretches him upon the plank where the law wills that an assassin shall lie to lose his head,—you know, the newspapers inform of it both the rich and the poor, the first, that they may sleep in peace, and the second, that they may take warning. Well, then, you who are religious and even somewhat devout, you go to offer masses for the soul of that man,—and yet you are of his family, you are the elder branch of it. You can remain seated in peace, you can exist happy and without care. Driven by poverty or by rage, your brother of the bagnio has only killed a man; and you! you have killed the happiness of a man, his best life, his dearest beliefs. The other has but simply waited for his victim; he killed him despite himself, notwithstanding his fear of the guillotine; but you!—you have heaped up all the crimes of your weakness upon an innocent strength; you have tamed your sufferer in order the better to devour his heart; you have baited him with caresses; you have not omitted one of those which could make him think of, dream of, desire the delights of love. You have demanded a thousand sacrifices of him to refuse him everything. You have made him see the light strongly before putting out his eyes. A noble courage! Such infamies are luxuries which are not understood by those bourgeoises at whom you sneer. They know how to give themselves and to forgive; they know how to love and to suffer. They make us all little by the grandeur of their devotion. As we go higher in society we find just as much mud as there is at the bottom; only it is hardened and gilded. Yes, to find perfection in the ignoble we must look for a fine education, a great name, a pretty woman, a duchess. To fall to the bottom of all it is necessary to be at the top of all. I express myself badly to you, I still suffer too much from the wounds which you have caused me; but do not fear that I shall complain! No. My words are the expression of no personal hope, and contain no bitterness. Rest assured, Madame, I pardon you, and this pardon is so complete that you cannot complain of coming to seek it against your will.—Only, you may make suffer other hearts as confiding as mine, and I should spare them their sufferings. You have therefore inspired me with a thought of justice. Expiate your fault here below. God will pardon you perhaps, I hope so, but He is implacable, and He will strike you."

At these words the eyes of this humbled, tortured woman filled with tears.

"Why do you weep? Be faithful to your own nature. You have watched without feeling the tortures of the heart you have broken. Enough, Madame, console yourself. I can no longer suffer. Others may tell you that you have given them life;

for myself I say to you with delight that you have given me annihilation. Perhaps you have guessed that I do not belong to myself, that I should live for my friends, and that I could then support with them the coldness of death and the griefs of life. Would you have so much kindness? would you be like the tigers of the desert who make the wound and then lick it?"

The duchess melted into tears.

"Spare yourself those tears, Madame. If I believed in them, it would be to be suspicious of them. Are they, or are they not, one of your artifices? After all those which you have employed, how could I believe that there can be anything truthful in you? Nothing in you has henceforth the power to move me. I have said all."

Madame de Langeais rose with a movement that was at once full of nobility and of humility.

"You have the right to treat me harshly," she said, holding out to him a hand which he did not take, "your words are not yet harsh enough, and I deserve this punishment."

"To punish you, Madame, I! but to punish, is not that to love? Expect nothing from me that resembles feeling. I might, indeed, on my own behalf be accuser and judge, decree and executioner; but no. I shall accomplish presently a duty, but nowise a desire for vengeance. The cruelest vengeance is, to my thinking, the disdain of a possible vengeance. Who knows? perhaps I shall be the minister of your pleasures. Henceforward, in wearing so elegantly the sad livery in which society clothes its criminals, perhaps you may be compelled to have their integrity. And then, you will love!"

The duchess listened with a submission that was neither feigned nor artfully calculated; she spoke only after an interval of silence.

"Armand," she said, "it seemed to me that in resisting love I obeyed the chaste instincts of a woman, and it was not from you that I expected such reproaches. You take all my weaknesses and impute them to me as crimes. How is it that you could not see that I might be drawn beyond my duties by all the curiosities of love, and that, on the morrow, I would be grieved, distressed at having gone so far? Alas! it was sinning through ignorance. There was, I swear to you, as much of good faith in my faults as in my remorse. My cruelties betrayed much more love than my yieldings bore witness to. And, moreover, of what is it you complain? The gift of my heart did not suffice you, you demanded brutally that of my person—"

"Brutally!" exclaimed Monsieur de Montriveau.

Then he said within himself:

"If I let myself be dragged into a war of words, I am lost."

"Yes, you came to me as though I were one of those bad women, without respect, with none of the courtesies of love. Had I not the right to pause, to reflect? Well, I have reflected. The unseemliness of your conduct is excusable,—love is its motive; let me think so and justify you to my own heart.

Ah! well, Armand, at the very moment when, this evening, you were predicting to me misfortune, I—I was believing in our happiness. Yes, I had confidence in that noble and proud character of which you had given me so many proofs.—And I was all thine," she added, bending towards his ear. "Yes, I had I know not what desire to give happiness to a man so sorely tried by adversity. Master for master, I wished for a noble man. The higher I felt myself, the less did I wish to descend. Trusting in thee I thought I saw a lifetime of love at the moment when thou didst show me death.—Strength is never without mercy. My friend, thou art too strong to be cruel to a poor woman who loves thee. If I had faults, can I not obtain forgiveness? can I not repair them? Repentance is the grace of love, I would be gracious to thee. Could I alone of all women be without their uncertainties, their fears, their timidity which it is so natural to feel when one binds one's self for life, and when you break so easily bonds of this sort? Those bourgeoises, to whom you compare me, give themselves, but they struggle. Well, I have struggled, but I am here—. Oh! God! he will not hear me!" she cried, interrupting herself.

She wrung her hands crying:

"But I love thee! but I am thine!"

She fell at Armand's feet.

"Thine! Thine! My only, my sole master!"

"Madame," said Armand, offering to raise her, "Antoinette can no longer save the Duchesse de

Langeais. I trust neither the one nor the other. You give yourself to-day, you will refuse yourself perhaps to-morrow. No power, neither in heaven nor on the earth, can assure me of the gentle fidelity of your love. The pledges of it were for the past; our past has gone forever."

At this moment a light blazed up so vividly that the duchess involuntarily turned her head towards the portière, and saw again distinctly the three masked men.

"Armand," she said, "I would not think ill of you. Why are those men here? What are you preparing to do to me?"

"Those men are as discreet as I shall be myself on all that passes here," he said. "See in them only my arms and my heart. One of them is a surgeon—"

"A surgeon," she said. "Armand, my friend, uncertainty is the cruelest of sufferings. Speak, then, tell me if you wish my life? I will give it to you, you need not take it—"

"You have not then understood me?" said Montriveau. "Did I not speak to you of justice? To quiet your fears," he added, coldly, taking up a piece of steel which lay on the table, "I will explain to you what I have decided to do to you."

He showed her a cross of two bars fastened to the end of a steel handle.

"Two of my friends are heating at this moment a cross like this one. We shall apply it to your forehead, there, between the two eyes, so that you cannot hide it with diamonds and thus escape the inquiries of the world. You will then bear upon your brow the infamous mark branded on the shoulder of your brothers the convicts. The pain will be slight, but I feared some nervous crisis, or resistance—."

"Resistance?" she said, striking her hands joyfully together. "No, no, I would that all the world were here to see it. Ah! my Armand, mark, mark quickly thy creature as a poor little thing of thine! Thou didst demand pledges of my love, they are all here in one. Ah! I see only mercy and pardon, only an everlasting happiness in thy vengeance—. When thou hast thus marked a woman for thine own, when thou wilt have a servile soul which will bear thy red cipher, ah! then thou canst never abandon it, thou wilt be forever mine. In isolating me from the world thou wilt be charged with my happiness, under penalty of being a coward, and I know thee noble, great! But the woman who loves will always mark herself—. Come, messieurs, enter and mark, mark the Duchesse de Langeais. She belongs to Monsieur de Montriveau forever. Enter quickly, and all of you, my forehead burns hotter than your iron."

Armand turned quickly that he might not see the duchess palpitating, kneeling before him. He uttered a word which caused his three friends to disappear. Women accustomed to the life of salons understand the possibilities of mirrors. Thus the duchess, eager to read clearly Armand's heart, was all eyes. Armand who did not think of his mirror thus let her see two tears quickly wiped away. All the future of the duchess was in those two tears. When he turned to lift her, he found her standing, she thought herself loved. Consequently the shock was terrible when she heard Montriveau say, with all that firmness which she herself had so often used when she was trifling with him:

"I grant you grace, Madame. You may believe me, this scene will be as if it had never taken place. But here, let us say farewell. I like to believe that you were sincere in your boudoir in your seductions, sincere here in the outpouring of your heart. Farewell. I no longer have any faith. You would torment me still, you would be always the duchess, and—. But farewell, we shall never understand each other—. What do you desire, at present?" he said, changing his tone to that of a master of ceremonies. "Will you return home or go back to Madame de Sérizy's ball? I have employed all my power to protect your reputation. Neither your servants nor the world can ever know of what has passed between us in the last quarter of an hour. Your servants think you still at the ball; your carriage has not yet left Madame de Sérizy's court-yard; your coupé is in your own. Where would you like to go?"

"What would you advise, Armand?"

"There is no Armand here, Madame la Duchesse. We are strangers to each other."

"Take me to the ball, then," she said, curious

still to put his power to the proof. "Throw back into the hell of the world a creature who has suffered there, and who will continue to suffer there, if for her there is no longer any happiness. Oh! my friend, I do love you as much as your bourgeoises can love! I love you enough to throw myself on your neck at the ball, before all the world, if you asked it. That horrible world has not corrupted me. See, I am young and I am going to renew my youth still more. Yes, I am a child, thy child, thou hast created me. Oh, do not banish me from my Eden!"

Armand made a gesture.

"Ah! if I must go, let me then take something with me from here, a trifle,—this, to put upon my heart at night," she said, picking up one of his gloves and folding it in her handkerchief—. "No," she continued, "I am not of that world of depraved women; thou dost not know it, and so thou canst not appreciate me; know it well! some of them give themselves for money; others yield to presents; all that is vile! Ah! I would wish to be a simple bourgeoise, a work-woman, if thou wouldst love better a woman who is below thee than one whose devotion is allied with human grandeur. Ah! my Armand, there are among us women who are noble, grand, chaste and pure, and then they are delicious. I would wish to possess all noble qualities to sacrifice them all to thee; misfortune made me duchess; I would I had been born near the throne that I might sacrifice everything for thee. I would be grisette for thee and queen for all others."

He listened, moistening a cigar.

"When you are ready to go," he said, "you will let me know—"

"But I desire to remain."

"That is another thing," said he.

"Look, this one is ill-made," she cried, taking a cigar and putting it eagerly to her mouth, where the lips of Armand had touched it.

"Thou wouldst smoke?" he said to her

"Oh! what would I not do to please thee?"

"Well then, go, Madame—"

"I obey," she answered, weeping.

"It will be necessary to cover your face that you may not see the way by which you have to pass."

"I am ready, Armand," she said, blindfolding herself.

"Can you see?"

"No."

He knelt softly at her feet.

"Ah! I hear thee," she said with a charming gesture, thinking that his feigned harshness was about to cease.

He offered to kiss her lips, she bent towards him.

"You can see, Madame."

"But I am a little curious."

"You deceive me then, still?"

"Ah!" she said, with the anger of an honor misunderstood, "take off this handkerchief and lead me, Monsieur, I shall not open my eyes."

Armand, convinced of her integrity by this cry, conducted the duchess, who, faithful to her word, made herself nobly blind; but as he held her hand with paternal care to show her where now to ascend and now to descend, he studied the quivering pulsations which agitated the heart of this woman, so surely conquered by a true love. Madame de Langeais, happy in being able to speak to him thus, pleased herself by telling him all, but he remained inflexible; and when her hand questioned his, his gave no answering pressure. Finally, after having thus proceeded some time together, Armand told her to step forward, she did so and perceived that he held back her dress that it might not brush against the walls of some opening, doubtless narrow. Madame de Langeais was touched by this care, it betrayed a little lingering love; but it was in some sort Montriveau's farewell, for he left her without a word. When she felt herself in a warm atmosphere, she opened her eyes. She found herself alone, before the chimney-piece of the boudoir of the Comtesse de Sérizy. Her first care was to arrange the disorder of her toilet; she promptly readjusted her dress and reëstablished the arrangement of her coiffure.

"Well, my dear Antoinette, we have been looking for you everywhere," said the countess, opening the door of the boudoir.

"I came here for a little fresh air," she said, "it is so intolerably warm in the salon."

"It was thought you had left; but my brother Ronquerolles told me that he had seen your servants still waiting for you."

"I am very tired, my dear, let me rest here a moment."

And the duchess seated herself on the divan.

"What is the matter? You are trembling all over!"

The Marquis de Ronquerolles entered.

"I fear, Madame la Duchesse, that some accident may happen to you. I have just seen your coachman as drunk as the 'Twenty-two Cantons.'"

The duchess did not answer, she was looking at the chimney, the mirrors, striving to detect the opening through which she had passed; then she experienced an extraordinary sensation in finding herself again in the midst of the gaieties of a ball after the terrible scene which had just changed forever the course of her life. She began to tremble violently.

"My nerves are shaken by that prediction which Monsieur de Montriveau made me here. Although it was a jest, I am going home to see if his London axe will pursue me in my dreams—. Adieu then, dear.—Adieu, Monsieur le Marquis."

She traversed the ball-room, where she was detained by flatterers whom she looked at with pity. She felt how small her world was when she, its queen, was thus humbled and abased. And oh! what were all these men compared with him whom she truly loved and whose character had resumed the gigantic proportions momentarily lessened by her, but which she now perhaps unduly exaggerated. She could not forbear looking at that one of her servants who had accompanied her, and found him very sleepy.

"You have not gone away from here this evening?" she asked him.

"No, Madame."

As she got into her carriage she saw, in fact, that her coachman was in a state of intoxication at which she would have been frightened under any other circumstances; but the great shocks of life destroy all vulgar fears. However, she reached home without accident; but she felt herself changed, and in the grasp of entirely new emotions. For her there was henceforth but one man in the world, that is to say, for him only did she desire henceforth to have some value. If physiologists can promptly define love by its connection with the laws of nature, moralists find much more difficulty in explaining it when they wish to consider it in all the developments given to it by society. Nevertheless there exists, in spite of the heresies of the thousand sects that divide the church of love, a straight and clear-cut line passing sharply through their doctrines, a line which discussions can never bend and the inflexible application of which explains the crisis into which, like almost all other women, the Duchesse de Langeais was now plunged. She did not love as yet, she had a passion.

*
Love and passion are two different states of the soul which poets and men of the world, philosophers and fools, continually confound. Love carries with it a mutuality of feeling, a certainty of joys that nothing can alter, and a too constant exchange of pleasures, a too complete adherence between hearts, not to exclude all jealousy. Possession is then a means and not an end; an infidelity may cause suffering but not detachment; the soul is not more, nor is it less, ardent or agitated, it is ceaselessly happy; in short, desire, extended by a divine breath from one end to the other of the immensity of time, takes on for us but one tint,—life is as blue as the pure sky. Passion is the presentiment of love and of its infinitudes, to which all suffering souls aspire. Passion is a hope which may be deceived. Passion signifies at once suffering and transition; passion ceases when hope is dead. Men and women can without dishonoring themselves feel more than one passion; it is so natural to reach out towards happiness! but there is in life only one love. All discussions, written or spoken, upon the sentiments, may then be resumed by these two questions: "Is it a passion? Is it love?" As love can not exist without the intimate knowledge of the pleasures which perpetuate it, the duchess was now under the yoke of a passion;

thus she was experiencing the consuming agitations, the involuntary calculations, the parching desires, in short, all that is expressed by the word *passion:* she suffered. Amid these troubles of her soul, rose the tumult stirred up by her vanity, by her self-love, by her pride or by her haughtiness,— all these varieties of egotism are allied to each other. She had said to a man: "I love thee, I am thine!" The Duchesse de Langeais, could she really have uttered these words in vain? Either she must be loved or abdicate her rôle in society. Conscious now of the solitude of her voluptuous bed, in which voluptuousness had not yet set his burning feet, she writhed and twisted in it, repeating to herself:

"I wish to be loved!"

And the faith she still kept in herself gave her hopes of success. The duchess was piqued, the vain Parisian woman was humiliated, the true woman had glimpses of happiness, and her imagination, avenging all the time which nature had caused her to lose, amused itself by making flame before her the inextinguishable fires of pleasure. She well nigh attained to the sensations of love; for, in the doubt of being loved which stung her, she found happiness in saying to herself: "I love him!" God and the world, she had a strong desire to trample them under her feet. Montriveau was now her religion. She passed the following day in a species of moral numbness mixed with bodily agitations that nothing can express. She tore up as many letters as she wrote, and made a thousand impossible conjectures. At the hour in which Montriveau formerly came she tried to believe that he would arrive, and she took pleasure in waiting for him. Her whole being was concentrated in the single sense of hearing. She closed her eyes at times and endeavored to listen through space. Then she wished for the power of annihilating all obstacles between herself and her lover, so that she might obtain that absolute silence which allows sound to reach us from enormous distances. In this concentration of her mind the ticking of her clock was distracting to her, it was so like a sinister chatter that she stopped it. Midnight sounded from the salon.

"My God," she said to herself, "to see him here, that would be happiness. And yet he came formerly drawn by desire. His voice filled this boudoir. And now, nothing!"

Remembering those scenes of coquetry that she had played, and which had driven him from her, tears of despair flowed down her cheeks for a long time.

"Madame la Duchesse is perhaps not aware that it is two o'clock in the morning," said her maid, "I thought that Madame was indisposed."

"Yes, I am going to bed; but remember, Suzette," said Madame de Langeais, wiping away her tears, "never to enter my room unless I ring; I shall not tell you again."

For a week Madame de Langeais went to all the houses where she hoped to meet Monsieur de

Montriveau. Contrary to her custom, she went early and came away late; she gave up dancing and played cards. Useless attempts! she could not succeed in seeing Armand, whose name she no longer dared to pronounce. However, one evening in a moment of desperation she said to Madame de Sérizy with as much indifference as she could assume:

"Have you quarreled with Monsieur de Montriveau? I no longer see him in your house."

"Why, he no longer comes here," replied the countess, laughing. "Moreover, he is not seen anywhere, he is doubtless occupied with some woman."

"I thought," said the duchess, gently, "that the Marquis de Ronquerolles was one of his friends—"

"I never heard my brother say that he even knew him."

Madame de Langeais made no reply. Madame de Sérizy thought that she could now with impunity lash a discreet friendship which had so long been bitter to her, and she resumed:

"You regret, then, that gloomy individual? I have heard shocking things said about him,—wound him, and he never returns, never forgives; love him, and he will put you in chains. And to everything which I have said about him one of those who laud him to the skies replies to me only with this one word: 'He knows how to love!' They never grow tired of repeating to me: 'Montriveau would quit everything for his friend, his is an immense soul.' Ah, bah! society does not require such grand souls. Men of that character are all very well among each other, let them stay there, and leave us to our own pretty pettinesses. What is your opinion, Antoinette?"

In spite of her worldly self-possession the duchess seemed agitated; but she replied, nevertheless, with an ease of manner that deceived her friend:

"I am really sorry not to see him any more, I took a great interest in him and would have given him a sincere friendship. Even if you should think me absurd, dear friend, I love the nobler natures. To give yourself to a fool, is not that to admit distinctly that one has only senses?"

Madame de Sérizy had never *distinguished* any but commonplace men, and was at this moment beloved by a handsome fop, the Marquis d'Aiglemont.

The countess made her visit very brief, it may be believed. Madame de Langeais, seeing some hope in the complete retreat of Armand from the world, wrote him immediately, a tender and humble letter which should bring him back to her if he still loved her. She sent it the next day by her valet de chambre, and when the man returned she asked him if he had given it to Montriveau himself; at his affirmative reply she could not repress an involuntary movement of joy. Armand was in Paris, he was there alone, at home, not going out in the world! She was then loved. During all that day she waited for an answer, and no answer came. In the midst of the reawakened agitations renewed by her impatience Antoinette found constant reasons for this delay,—Armand was hesitating, his reply would come by post; but in the evening she could no longer deceive herself. A frightful day, a tumult of sufferings which brought pleasure, of palpitations which crushed life, heart excesses which shortened life. The next day, she sent to Armand for a reply.

"Monsieur le Marquis sends word that he will come to see Madame la Duchesse," answered Julien.

She turned away so that her happiness might not be seen, she threw herself on her sofa to give way to her first emotions.

"He is coming!"

This thought rent her soul. Unhappy, indeed, are they for whom such waiting is not the most horrible of tempests and the fecundation of the sweetest pleasures, they are devoid of that clear flame which reveals the images of all things and doubles nature for us by presenting us with the pure essence of desired objects as well as their actual reality. In love, to wait, is it not to constantly exhaust a certain hope, to deliver one's self to the terrible flail of passion, happy without the disillusions of the truth? The constant emanation of strength and of desire, expectation, is it not to the human soul what their perfumed exhalations are to certain flowers? We leave the gorgeous and sterile colors of the coreopsis or the tulip to breathe the perfumed thoughts of the orange flower and the volkameria,—two flowers which their native lands have likened involuntarily to youthful fiancées, full of love, lovely in their past, lovely in their future.

The duchess learned the joys of her new life as she felt, with a species of intoxication, the scourgings of love; then, with the change of her feelings, she found new vistas and nobler meanings in the things of life. As she hastened to her dressing-room she understood for the first time the true value of the refinements of the toilet, the delicate minute cares of the person, when dictated by love and not by vanity; already these adornments were aiding her to bear the burden of suspense. Her toilet finished, she fell back into excessive agitation, into the nervous horrors of that dread power which throws all our ideas into a state of fermentation and which is perhaps only a malady the sufferings of which are dear to us. The duchess was dressed and waiting by two o'clock in the afternoon; Monsieur de Montriveau had not yet arrived at half-past eleven at night. To explain the anguish of this woman who might be called the spoiled child of civilization we should need to tell how much poetry the heart can concentrate into one thought, to weigh the force exhaled by the soul at the sound of a bell, or to measure the vital force lost by the prostration caused by a carriage which rolls away and does not stop.

"Can he be trifling with me?" she asked herself as she heard the clock strike midnight.

She turned pale, her teeth chattered, and she struck her hands together as she sprang up quivering in that boudoir where formerly she remembered he had come unasked. Then she resigned herself. Had she not forced him to turn pale and quiver under the cutting darts of her irony? Madame de Langeais now learned the miseries of a woman's destiny, who, deprived of all those means of action which men possess, can only wait when she loves. To seek her lover is a fault which few men will pardon. The greater number of them see degradation in that celestial flattery; but Armand had a great soul, and he should be among the lesser number of those men who know how to reward such excess of love by an eternal love.

"Ah! well, I will go," she said to herself, tossing sleepless on her bed, "I will go to him, I will offer him my hand and never weary of offering it to him. A superior man will see in every step which a woman takes toward him a promise of love and of constancy. Yes, the angels should descend from heaven to come to men, and I will be to him an angel."

On the morrow, she wrote one of those letters in which excels the spirit of the ten thousand Sévignés which Paris now includes. And yet, to know how to ask for pity without humiliation, to fly to him swift-winged and never stoop to self-abasement, to complain but not offend, to rebel with tenderness, to forgive without compromising your personal dignity, to tell all and yet to avow nothing,—surely, it needed to be the Duchesse de Langeais and to have been trained by Madame la Princesse de

Blamont-Chauvry to write this enchanting note. Julien was dispatched with it. Julien was, like all valets de chambre, the victim of the marches and counter-marches of love.

"What answer did Monsieur de Montriveau send?" she asked Julien as carelessly as she could when he returned to give an account of his mission.

"Monsieur le Marquis desired me to say to Madame la Duchesse that it was well."

Frightful reaction of the hoping heart! to receive before inquisitive witnesses this torture of the heart and not to murmur, to be constrained to silence. This is one of the thousand misfortunes of the wealthy.

For twenty-two days Madame de Langeais wrote to Monsieur de Montriveau without obtaining any reply. At last she made the excuse of illness to escape her duties to the princess, of whom she was one of the attendants, and to society. She received only her father, the Duc de Navarreins; her aunt, the Princesse de Blamont-Chauvry; the old Vidame de Pamiers, her maternal great-uncle; and the uncle of her husband, the Duc de Grandlieu. These persons readily believed in Madame de Langeais's illness when they found her day by day paler, thinner, more depressed. The vague ardor of a real love, the irritations of wounded pride, the constant sting of the only disdain that could have reached her, her springing impulses towards those pleasures perpetually desired, perpetually cheated,—all these forces, uselessly excited, undermined her double nature. She was paying the arrears of her wasted life. She went out at last to be present at a review in which Monsieur de Montriveau was to take part. Stationed with the royal family in the balcony of the Tuileries, the duchess witnessed one of those festivals the memory of which lingers long in the soul. She was adorable in her languor, and all eyes saluted her with admiration. She exchanged a few glances with Montriveau, whose presence it was that rendered her so beautiful. The general rode past almost at her feet, in all the splendor of that military costume the effect of which on feminine imaginations is confessed even by the most prudish persons. To a woman deeply in love, who had not seen her lover for two months, this fleeting moment must have seemed like that glimpse in our dreams in which is revealed to our sight the fugitive vision of a land without horizon. Women and very young persons alone can imagine the stupid and yet delirious avidity expressed by the eyes of the duchess. As to men, if, during their youth, they have experienced, in the paroxysms of their first passions, these phenomena of nervous force, they forget them so completely in later years that they come to deny the very existence of these luxurious ecstasies,—the only possible term for these glorious intuitions. Religious ecstasy is the madness of thought released from its corporeal bonds; whereas, in the ecstasy of love, the forces of our dual natures mingle, unite, and embrace each other. When a woman falls a prey to the furious tyrannies under which

Madame de Langeais was now subjugated, her definite resolutions succeed each other so rapidly that it is impossible to render an account of them. Thoughts are born one of another, and rush through the soul like those clouds carried away by the wind across the gray depths which veil the sun. Thenceforward, acts alone will speak. Here then are the facts. The morning after the review, Madame de Langeais sent her carriage and liveries to wait at the door of the Marquis de Montriveau from eight o'clock in the morning till three in the afternoon.

Armand lived in Rue de Tournon, not far from the Chamber of Peers, where there was to be a sitting that day. But long before the peers arrived at their palace some persons had noticed the carriage and the liveries of the duchess. A young officer, scorned by Madame de Langeais and welcomed by Madame de Sérizy, the Baron de Maulincour, was the first who recognized it. He went at once to his mistress to relate to her, under promise of secrecy, this extraordinary folly. Immediately the report spread telegraphically through all the coteries of the Faubourg Saint-Germain, reached the Château, the Élysée-Bourbon, became the news of the day, the topic of all conversation from mid-day until evening. Nearly all the women denied the fact, but in a manner which confirmed the truth of it; and the men believed it in testifying the most indulgent sympathy for Madame de Langeais.

"That savage of a Montriveau has a character of

bronze, he has doubtless exacted this exposure," said some of them, throwing the blame on Armand.

"Well," said others, "Madame de Langeais has committed a most generous imprudence! Before all Paris, to renounce for her lover her world, her rank, her fortune, her good name, is a feminine coup d'Etat as fine as that cut of the peruke-maker's knife which so electrified Canning at the Court of Assizes. Not one of the women who blame the duchess would have made this declaration, worthy the olden time. Madame de Langeais is an heroic woman to proclaim herself thus frankly. After this, she can love no one but Montriveau. Is there not some grandeur in a woman's saying: 'I will have but one passion?'"

"What will become of society, Monsieur, if you thus do honor to open vice, without respect for virtue?" said the wife of the Procureur-Général, the Comtesse de Granville.

While the Château, the Faubourg and the Chaussée-d'Antin were discussing the shipwreck of this aristocratic virtue; while eager young men were hastening on horseback to assure themselves by the sight of the carriage in Rue de Tournon that the duchess was really in Monsieur de Montriveau's house, she was lying palpitating in the depths of her boudoir. Armand, who had not slept at home, was walking in the Tuileries with Monsieur de Marsay. The relatives of Madame de Langeais were visiting each other and appointing a rendezvous at her house to reprimand her and take measures to stop the scandal caused by her conduct. At three o'clock the Duc de Navarreins, the Vidame de Pamiers, the old Princesse de Blamont-Chauvry and the Duc de Grandlieu were assembled in the salon of Madame de Langeais and waiting for her. To them, as to some other inquirers, the servants had stated that their mistress was out. The duchess had made no exception in favor of anyone. These four personages—illustrious in the aristocratic sphere of which the Almanach de Gotha records annually the revolutions and the hereditary pretensions —demand a rapid sketch, without which this social picture would be incomplete.

*

The Princesse de Blamont-Chauvry was in the feminine world the most poetic relic of the reign of Louis XV., to whose surname she had, it was said, in her gay youth contributed her quota. Of her former charms there now remained only a remarkably prominent nose, thin, curved like a Turkish blade, the principal ornament of a face which resembled an old white glove; some crimped and powdered curls; slippers with high heels, a lace cap with ribbon bows, black mittens and the *parfaits contentements*. But, to do her complete justice, it is necessary to add that she had so high an opinion of her ruins that she went décolleté in the evening, wore long gloves, and still painted her cheeks with the classic rouge of Martin. A formidable amiability in her wrinkles, a prodigious fire in her eyes, a portentous dignity in her whole person, a triple dart of malice in her tongue, an infallible memory in her head, made this old woman a veritable power. She held in the parchment of her brain quite as much information as there was in the Cabinet des Chartes, and she knew the alliances of all the princely and ducal houses and even those of the counts of Europe down to the very last descendants of Charlemagne. No usurpation of titles could escape her. Young men anxious to be well thought of, the ambitious, the young women, paid her perpetual homage. Her salon gave the law to the Faubourg Saint-Germain. The words of this female Talleyrand were accepted as final. Certain persons came to her for advice on etiquette and the usages of society, and to receive from her lessons in good taste. Certainly, no other old lady knew so well how to pocket her snuff-box; and she had, when seating herself or when crossing her legs, arrangements of the petticoat of such a precision, such a grace, that the young women, even the most elegant, were reduced to despair. Her voice had remained in her head during the third of her lifetime, but she had not been able to prevent it from descending into the membranes of her nose, which rendered it strangely significant. Of her great fortune there remained to her a hundred and fifty thousand francs in woodland, generously returned to her by Napoléon. Thus, worldly goods and person, everything about her was of importance. This curious antique was seated on a sofa at the corner of the fire-place in conversation with the Vidame de Pamiers, another contemporaneous ruin. This old noble, formerly a commander of the Order of Malta, was a tall, slim and lean man, whose neck was always buckled so tightly that his cheeks fell a little over his cravat and compelled him to carry his head high,—an attitude which would seem consequential in certain persons, but in him was justified by a spirit altogether Voltairian. His prominent eyes seemed to see everything and had, in fact, seen everything He always put cotton in his ears. In short, his person in its entirety offered a perfect model of aristocratic lines, lines slender and fragile, supple and pleasing, which, like those of a serpent, seem to be able to bend or erect themselves at pleasure, to glide or to stiffen.

The Duc de Navarreins was walking up and down the salon with the Duc de Grandlieu. Both were men of fifty-five years of age, still fresh, fat and short, well nourished, rather florid, with weary eyes, the under lips already slightly pendulous. Except for the elegance of their language and the affable courtesy of their manner, their perfect ease, which could in a moment change into insolence, a superficial observer might have taken them for bankers. But any error would have been impossible in listening to their conversation, which was hedged with precautions against those whom they held in awe, dry or empty for their equals, and perfidious for their inferiors,—whom courtiers and statesmen know how to tame with verbal flattery and wound with an unexpected word. Such were the representatives of this great nobility, which chooses to die or to remain quite unchanged, which deserves as much praise as blame, and which will be always misunderstood until some poet shall have portrayed it happy in obeying its king and in perishing by the axe of Richelieu, and despising the guillotine of '89 as a low and contemptible vengeance.

These four personages were remarkable for thin, shrill voices, curiously in harmony with their ideas and their deportment. Moreover, the most perfect equality existed among them. The habit, learned at Court, of concealing their emotions, doubtless restrained them from openly expressing the displeasure caused them by the prank of their young relative.

To prevent the critics from accusing of puerility the commencement of the following scene, perhaps it is necessary to observe here that Locke, when in company with certain English lords renowned for their wit, distinguished as much by their manners as by their political consistency, amused himself maliciously by taking down their conversation by an ingenious method of shorthand, and caused them to shout with laughter in reading it to them afterwards, asking them what they could make of it. The truth is, the upper classes in all nations have a certain jargon of glitter which, when washed in the embers of literary or philosophical thought, leaves a very small residuum of gold in the crucible. In all planes of social life, with the exception of a few Parisian salons, the observer will find the same absurdities, which differ from each other only according to the thickness or transparency of the varnish. Thus, solid conversation is exceptional in society and Bœtian dulness supports habitually the various zones of the gay world. So, consequently, there is a great deal of talk in the upper circles, and very little thought. To think is fatiguing, and the wealthy wish to see their life flow on without much effort. Thus it is, in comparing the great bulk of wit by stages, from the gamin of Paris to the peer of France, that the observer will comprehend the saying of Monsieur de Talleyrand: *Manners are everything,*—an elegant translation of this judicial axiom: "*La forme emporte le fond.*" In the eyes of a poet, the language of the lower classes will always retain a certain advantage from their habit of giving a rough stamp of poetry to their thoughts. This observation will also perhaps explain the barren emptiness of the salons, their want, their little depth, and the repugnance which superior persons feel for the unprofitable interchange of their thoughts which characterizes them.

The duke stopped suddenly, as if struck by a brilliant idea, and said to his companion:

"You have then sold Tornthon?"

"No, he is sick. I am afraid I shall lose him, and I shall be exceedingly sorry: he is a capital hunter. Do you know how the Duchesse de Marigny is?"

"No, I did not call this morning. I was going to see her when you came to tell me about Antoinette. But she was very ill yesterday, they despaired of her life, she received the last sacraments."

"Will her death alter your cousin's prospects?"

"Not at all, she divided her property in her lifetime and kept for herself only a pension which is paid to her by her niece, Madame de Soulanges, to whom she made over her estate of Guébriant for an annuity."

"She will be a great loss to society. She was a good woman. Her family will have one less person whose advice and experience always had weight. Between ourselves, she was the real head of the house. Her son, Marigny, is an amiable man; he is witty, he can talk. He is agreeable, very agreeable,—oh! as for agreeable, that's not to be denied; but—no idea whatever of conducting himself. Still, it is extraordinary, he is very clever. The other day, he was dining at the club with all those rich fellows of the Chaussée d'Antin, and your uncle—who is always there for his game of whist—saw him. Surprised to meet him there, he asked him if he were a member of the club. 'Yes, I don't go into society any longer, I live with the bankers.' You know why?" said the marquis, looking at the duke with a sly smile.

"No."

"He is infatuated with a young bride, that little Madame Keller, the daughter of Gondreville, a woman whom they say is all the fashion among that set."

"Antoinette is not boring herself, it would seem," said the old vidame.

"The affection I feel for that little woman is obliging me to spend my time at present in a singular manner," the princess answered him, pocketing her snuff-box.

"My dear aunt," said the duke, stopping before her, "I am in despair. Only one of those Bonaparte men would be capable of exacting from a respectable woman such impropriety. Between ourselves, Antoinette might have made a better choice."

"My dear," answered the princess, "the Montriveaus are an ancient family and very well connected, they are related to all the high nobility of Burgundy. If the Rivaudoults of Arschoot, of the Dulmen branch, should come to an end in Gallicia, the Montriveaus will succeed to the estates and to the titles of Arschoot; they inherit them through their great-grandfather."

"You are sure of it?—"

"I know it better than the father of this man, whom I often saw, and to whom I told it. Though a knight of several orders, he ridiculed them all; he was an 'Encyclopedist.' But his brother profited greatly during the emigration. I have heard that his relatives at the north behaved admirably to him.—"

"Yes, that is true. The Comte de Montriveau died at St. Petersburg, where I met him," said the vidame. "He was a large man, with an incredible passion for oysters."

"How many could he eat?" said the Duc de Grandlieu.

"Ten dozen every day."

"Without indigestion?"

"Not the least."

"Oh! but that is most extraordinary! Did they not give him the stone or gout, or some other inconvenience?"

"No, he had perfect health, he died from an accident."

"An accident! Nature prompted him to eat oysters, they were probably necessary to him; for up to a certain point our predominant tastes are the conditions of our existence."

"I am of your opinion," said the princess, smiling.

"Madame, you always take things a little maliciously," said the marquis.

"I only wished to make you see that these things might be very much misunderstood by a young woman," she replied.

Then she interrupted herself to say:

"But my niece! my niece!"

"Dear aunt," said Monsieur de Navarreins, "I cannot yet believe that she has gone to Monsieur de Montriveau."

"Bah!" said the princess.

"What is your opinion, vidame?" asked the marquis.

"If the duchess were naïve, I should think—"

"But a woman in love becomes naïve, my poor vidame. You are getting old, it seems?"

"What is to be done?" said the duke.

"If my dear niece is wise," replied the princess, "she will go to Court this evening, happily this is Monday, the day of reception; you will take care to have her well surrounded and to give the lie to this ridiculous rumor. There are a thousand ways of explaining things; and if the Marquis de

Montriveau is a gallant man, he will lend himself to any of them. We will make these children listen to reason—"

"But it would be difficult to break a lance with Monsieur de Montriveau, dear aunt, he is a pupil of Bonaparte, and he has a position. Bless me! he is a *seigneur* of these days, he has an important command in the Guard, where he is very useful. He has not the slightest ambition. At the first word which displeased him, he is just the man to say to the king: 'There is my resignation, leave me in peace.'"

"What are his opinions?"

"Very bad ones."

"In fact," said the princess, "the king is what he always was,—a Jacobin, fleur-de-lysed."

"Oh! somewhat modified," said the vidame.

"No, I know him of old. The man who said to his wife, the day on which she was first present at the first grand repast: 'There are our servants,' indicating to her the Court, can be nothing but a black scoundrel. I recognize perfectly MONSIEUR in the king. The wicked brother who voted so badly in his bureau of the Constituent Assembly probably conspires now with the Liberals, consults them, discusses with them. This philosophical bigot will be quite as dangerous for his younger brother as he was for the elder; for I do not see how his successor will be able to get out of the troubles which this big man with little wit has been pleased to create for him; besides, he hates him, and would be happy to be able to say to himself on his deathbed: 'He will not reign long.'"

"My dear aunt, he is the king, I have the honor to serve him, and—"

"But, my dear nephew, does your office deprive you of the right of free speech? You are of as good a house as that of the Bourbons. If the Guises had had a shade more resolution, His Majesty would only be a poor gentleman to-day. I am going to leave the world at a good time, nobility is dead. Yes, everything is at an end for you, my children," she added, looking at the vidame. "Is the conduct of my niece to be made the talk of the town? She has done wrong, I don't approve of her, a useless scandal is a fault; so that I still have my doubts of this lack of the proprieties, I brought her up and I know that—"

At this moment the duchess emerged from her boudoir. She had recognized her aunt's voice and had heard the name of Montriveau. She was in morning dishabille; and, as she came into the room, Monsieur de Grandlieu, who was looking carelessly out of the window, saw her carriage return without her.

"My dear daughter," said the duke, taking her head and kissing her on the forehead, "do you know what is going on?"

"Is anything extraordinary going on, dear father?"

"But all Paris thinks you are with Monsieur de Montriveau."

"My dear Antoinette, you have not been out, have you?" said the princess, offering her hand, which the duchess kissed with respectful affection.

"No, dear mother, I have not been out. And," she added, turning to salute the vidame and the marquis, "I intended that all Paris should think me with Monsieur de Montriveau."

The duke raised his hands to heaven, struck them together despairingly and folded his arms.

"But do you not know what will be the result of this rash action?" he said at last.

The old princess rose suddenly on her heels and looked at the duchess, who blushed and lowered her eyes; Madame de Chauvry drew her gently to her and said:

"Let me kiss you, my little angel."

Then she kissed her forehead very affectionately, pressed her hand and added smiling:

"We are no longer under the Valois, my dear daughter. You have compromised your husband, your position in the world; however, we will take measures to undo all that."

"But, my dear aunt, I want nothing undone. I wish all Paris to think or to say that I was this morning with Monsieur de Montriveau. Destroy that belief, false as it is, and you will do me the greatest harm."

"My daughter, do you wish, then, to be lost, and to grieve your family?"

"My dear father, my family, in sacrificing me to its own interest, gave me over, without intending it, to irreparable misery. You may blame me for seeking to soften my fate, but certainly you must pity me."

"To give yourself a thousand troubles in order to establish your daughters suitably!" murmured Monsieur de Navarreins to the vidame.

"Dear child," said the princess, shaking off the grains of snuff that had fallen on her dress, "be happy if you can; it is not a question of hindering your happiness, but of making it accord with ordinary customs. We all know, here, that marriage is a defective institution modified by love. But is it necessary in taking a lover to make your bed on the Carrousel? Come now, be reasonable, listen to us."

"I am listening."

"Madame la Duchesse," said the Duc de Grandlieu, "if uncles were obliged to take care of their nieces, there would be but one business in life; and society would owe them honors, rewards and incomes, such as it gives to the king's employés. Therefore, I have not come to talk to you of my nephew, but of your interests. Let us consider. If you are resolved to make an open break, I know the Sieur Langeais, I don't like him. He is miserly, he has the devil of a character; he will separate from you, he will keep your fortune, he will leave you poor and consequently without position in the world. The hundred thousand francs of income which you have lately inherited from your maternal great-aunt will go to pay for the pleasures of his mistresses, and you will be bound, garroted by the laws, and compelled to say *Amen* to all these arrangements. Suppose Monsieur de Montriveau should leave you! —*Mon Dieu,* dear niece, do not let us get angry, a man will never abandon you while you are young and pretty; but have we not seen enough charming women forsaken, even among princesses, for you to admit of my making this supposition—almost impossible, I readily believe; then, where will you be without a husband? Manage, then, the one you have, just as you take care of your beauty, which is, after all, like the husband himself, the parachute of a woman. I wish you to be always happy and beloved; I will not take into consideration any unfortunate event. This being so, happily or unhappily, you may have children? What will you call them? Montriveau?—Well, they can never inherit their father's fortune. You will wish to give them all yours, and he, all his. *Mon Dieu,* nothing is more natural. You will find the laws forbidding it. How often have we seen suits brought by heirs-at-law to dispossess love children? I have heard of them in all the tribunals of the world. Will you have recourse to some person to whom you will leave your property in trust; if the person in whom you put your confidence deceives you,—in truth, human justice will not interfere, and your children will be ruined. Choose, then, carefully!"

"You see the difficulties in which you are. In every way your children will necessarily be sacrificed to the fancies of your heart, and deprived of their position in the world. *Mon Dieu!* so long as they are little, they will be charming; but they will reproach you one day with having thought more of yourself than of them. We know all about that, we old gentlemen. Children become men, and men are ungrateful. Did I not hear the young de Horn in Germany say, one night after supper: 'If my mother had been an honest woman, I should have been the reigning prince?' But this IF, we have passed our lives in hearing it uttered by the lower classes, and it made the Revolution. When men cannot accuse their father or their mother, they complain to God of their evil fate. To sum up, dear child, we are here to open your eyes to all this. Well, I can resume it all in one word, which you should think over,—a wife should never give her husband reason to condemn her."

"Uncle, I have calculated so much that I did not love. Then I saw, as you do yourself, interest there where now there is no longer for me anything but feeling," said the duchess.

"But, my dearest child, life is altogether a complication of interests and feelings," replied the vidame; "and to be happy, especially in the position in which you are placed, we should try to combine feelings with interest. Let a grisette make love as she likes, that's all very well; but you have a pretty fortune, a family, a title, a place at Court, and you should not throw them all out of the window. To arrange all this, what is it we ask of you? Only, to cleverly conciliate the proprieties, instead of flying in their face. Ah, *Mon Dieu!* I am nearly eighty years old, and I do not remember to have ever met, under any régime, a love which was worth the price which you are ready to pay for that of this fortunate young man."

The duchess silenced the vidame with a look; and if Montriveau could have seen her then he would have pardoned everything.

"This would be a fine theatrical scene," said the Duc de Grandlieu, "and yet signifies nothing when it concerns your property, your position and your independence. You are not grateful, my dear niece. You will not find many families in which the relations are courageous enough to give the lessons of their experience and make the giddy young heads hear the language of common sense. Renounce your salvation in two minutes, if it pleases you to get yourself damned, I am willing! But reflect well when it comes to renouncing your income. I don't know any confessor who can absolve you from the pains of poverty. I think I have the right to speak to you thus; because, if you go to perdition, I alone shall be able to offer you a refuge. I am almost the uncle of Langeais, and I alone can put him in the wrong by so doing."

"My daughter," said the Duc de Navarreins, rousing himself from painful meditation, "as you speak of feelings let me observe to you that a woman who bears your name should have other feelings than those which belong to the common people.

Do you wish to help the cause of the Liberals, of those Jesuits of Robespierre who seek to dishonor the nobility? There are certain things that a Navarreins cannot do without injuring her house. You will not be the only one dishonored."

"Come," said the princess, "do not let us talk of dishonor! My children, do not make so much noise over the promenade of an empty carriage, and leave me alone with Antoinette. You will come and dine with me, all three. I take upon myself to arrange this thing in a proper manner. You don't understand things, you men, you put already too much sharpness in your words, and I do not want you to quarrel with my dear daughter. Do me then the pleasure to go away."

The three gentlemen doubtless divined the intentions of the princess, they bowed to the ladies; and Monsieur de Navarreins kissed his daughter on the forehead, saying to her:

"Come, my dear child, be wise. If you will, there is still time."

"Could we not find in the family some vigorous young fellow who would pick a quarrel with this Montriveau?" said the vidame as they descended the stairs.

*

"My treasure," said the princess, making a sign to her pupil to take a small, low chair near her when they were alone, "I know nothing here below so calumniated as God and the Eighteenth Century, for, as I look back to the days of my youth, I cannot recall a single duchess who trod the proprieties under foot as you are doing. The romance-makers and the scribblers have vilified the reign of Louis XV.; do not believe them. The Du Barry, my dear, was well worth the Widow Scarron, she was a better person. In my day, a woman knew how, in the midst of her gallantries, to keep her dignity. Indiscretions have ruined us. From them comes all the trouble. The philosophers, those nobodies whom we admitted into our salons, have had the impropriety and the ingratitude, in return for our bounty, to make an inventory of our hearts, to decry us as a whole and in detail, to rail against the century. The lower orders, who are very badly situated to judge anything, no matter what, saw the character of things only and not their forms. But, in those times, my dear heart, men and women were quite as remarkable as in any other epoch of the monarchy. Not one of your Werthers, not one of your notables, as they call themselves, not one of your men in yellow gloves and whose pantaloons conceal the leanness of their legs, would have crossed Europe, disguised as a peddler, to shut himself up at the risk of his life and in braving the poniards of the Duc de Modène in the dressing-room of the regent's daughter. Not one of your little consumptives with tortoise-shell eye-glasses would have hid, like Lauzun, in a wardrobe for six weeks to give courage to his mistress in the pains of childbirth. There was more passion in the little finger of Monsieur de Jaucourt than in your whole race of wranglers who leave a woman's side to vote for an amendment. Find me to-day a page who would let himself be hacked to pieces and buried under the floor merely to kiss the gloved fingers of a Kœnismark! To-day, really it would seem that the rôles had been changed, and that women were expected to devote themselves to men. These messieurs are worthless, and estimate themselves as worth more. Believe me, my dear, all those adventures which have become public and which are used to-day to assassinate our good Louis XV. were all at first secret. If it had not been for a crowd of poetasters, sorry rhymsters, moralists, who gossiped with our waiting-women and wrote down their calumnies, our epoch would have held its own in literature as to manners and morals. I am defending the century and not its skirts. There may have been a hundred women of quality who lost themselves, but the fools made a thousand of them, just as the gazettes do when they estimate the enemy's dead on the battle field. Besides, I don't know why the Revolution or the Empire should reproach us,—

those times were licentious enough, without wit, coarse, fie! all that revolts me. These are the bad spots on our history. This preamble, my dear child," she resumed after a pause, "is simply to lead up to telling you that, if you care for Montriveau, you are quite free to love him at your convenience and as much as you can. For myself, I know by experience that—short of locking you up, and we no longer lock up people in these days—you will do what you please; that is what I should have done at your age. Only, my jewel, I should not have abdicated my right to make Ducs de Langeais. So, behave with propriety. The vidame is quite right, no man is worth a single one of the sacrifices with which we are foolish enough to pay for their love. Keep yourself then in the position, if you should be unhappy enough to have to repent, to be able to still remain the wife of Monsieur de Langeais. When you are old, you will be glad enough to hear mass at Court and not in some country convent, there's the whole of it in a nutshell. Imprudence, that means an annuity, a wandering life, being at the mercy of your lover; it means the mortification caused by the impertinences of women who are not worthy of you, simply because they have been very vulgarly clever. It would be a hundred times better to go to Montriveau after dark, in a hackney coach, disguised, than to send your carriage in broad daylight. You are a little goose, my dear child. Your carriage flattered his vanity, your person would have won his heart. I have told you the exact truth, but I am not in the least angry with you. You are two centuries behind the times with your misplaced grandeur. Come, let us arrange the matter, we will say that Montriveau made your servants drunk to gratify his vanity and to compromise you—"

"For heaven's sake, dear aunt," cried the duchess, starting up, "do not calumniate him!"

"Ah! dear child," said the princess, whose eyes lighted up, "I should wish to see you have illusions which were not dangerous for you, but all illusions fade. You would melt my heart, if it were not so old. Come now, do not vex anyone, neither him nor us. I take upon myself to satisfy all parties; but promise me that you will not take after this a single step without consulting me. Tell me everything, I will guide you, perhaps safely."

"Dear aunt, I promise you—"

"To tell me all?"

"Yes, all, that is all that can be told."

"But, dear heart, it is precisely that which cannot be told that I wish to know. Let us understand each other thoroughly. Come, permit me to press my dry lips on your beautiful brow. No, let me do it, I forbid you to kiss my bones. Old people have a politeness of their own.—Come, take me down to my carriage," she said after having embraced her niece.

"Dear aunt, I can then go to him disguised?"

"Why yes, that can always be denied," said the old woman.

The duchess had definitely caught this idea alone from the sermon which the princess had preached to her. When Madame de Chauvry was safely seated in the corner of her carriage, Madame de Langeais bade her a gracious adieu, and remounted, radiant, to her own apartments.

"My presence would have won his heart; my aunt is right, a man could not refuse a pretty woman when she knows well how to offer herself."

That evening, at the reception of Madame la Duchesse de Berri, the Duc de Navarreins, Monsieur de Pamiers, Monsieur de Marsay, Monsieur de Grandlieu and the Duc de Maufrigneuse triumphantly denied the offensive rumors which were current about the Duchesse de Langeais. So many officers and others bore witness to having seen Montriveau walking in the Tuileries during the forenoon that this foolish story was laid to the door of chance, which takes all that is given to it. Therefore, the next day the reputation of the duchess became, in spite of the stationing of her carriage, as spotless and bright as Mambrino's helmet after Sancho had polished it. Only at two o'clock in the afternoon, in the Bois de Boulogne, Monsieur de Ronquerolles passing by Montriveau in a secluded alley said to him smiling:

"She is well, your duchess."

"Just as usual," he added, applying a significant stroke of the whip to his mare, which dashed away like a bullet.

Two days after this futile explosion Madame de

Langeais wrote to Monsieur de Montriveau a letter, which remained unanswered like all its predecessors. This time, however, she had taken her measures and bribed Auguste, Armand's valet de chambre. At eight o'clock that evening, therefore, she was introduced into Montriveau's apartment, into a room altogether different from the one in which the former secret scene had been enacted. There the duchess learned that the general would not return that evening. Had he two domiciles? The valet would not reply. Madame de Langeais had bought the key of the room, and not all the integrity of this man. Left alone she saw her fourteen letters lying on an old round table; they were still sealed, unopened; not one had been read. At this sight she fell into an arm-chair, and for a moment lost consciousness. When she came to herself she found Auguste holding vinegar to her face.

"A carriage, quick," she said.

When it came, she ran down stairs with convulsive rapidity, returned home, went to bed and denied herself to everyone. She remained twenty-four hours in her bed, letting no one approach her but her waiting-maid, who brought her from time to time a cup of orange-flower water. Suzette heard her mistress uttering some complaints and saw tears in her eyes, brilliant, though surrounded by dark circles. The third day, after having meditated in tears of despair on the course which she wished to take, Madame de Langeais had a conference with her man of business and doubtless gave him instructions to make certain preparations. Then she sent for the old Vidame de Pamiers. While waiting for him, she wrote to Monsieur de Montriveau. The vidame was punctual. He found his young cousin pale, dejected, but resigned. It was about two in the afternoon. Never had this divine creature been more poetic than she was now in the languor of her anguish.

"My dear cousin," she said to the vidame, "your eighty years have obtained for you this rendezvous. Oh! do not smile, I pray you, before a poor woman who is in the deepest grief. You are a gallant man, and the adventures of your youth, I like to believe, have inspired you with some indulgence for women."

"Not the least," he said.

"Really!"

"They are happy with everything," he answered.

"Ah! well, you are in the heart of my family; you will be perhaps the last relative, the last friend, whose hand I shall ever press; I may then ask of you a favor. Do me, my dear vidame, a service which I cannot ask from my father, nor from my uncle Grandlieu, nor from any woman. You will understand me. I entreat you to obey me, and to forget that you have obeyed me, whatever may be the issue of your action. It is to go with this letter to Monsieur de Montriveau, to see him, to show it to him, to ask him as one man can ask of another, —for you have between yourselves an integrity, certain feelings, which you forget with us,—to ask him if he will read it, not in your presence, men wish to hide certain emotions. I authorize you, to enable him to decide and if you judge it necessary, to say to him that it is a matter of life or death to me. If he deigns—"

"Deigns!" exclaimed the commander.

"If he deigns to read it," continued the duchess, with dignity, "say to him one last word. You will see him at five o'clock, he dines at that hour at home to-day, I know this; well, he should, for sole answer, come and see me. If, three hours later, if at eight o'clock, he has not left home, all will be over. The Duchesse de Langeais will have disappeared from this world. I shall not be dead, my dear, no; but no human power will ever find me again on this earth. Come and dine with me, I shall have at least one friend beside me in my last agonies. Yes, to-night, my dear cousin, my life will be decided; and which ever way it is it can only be cruelly fervid. Go now. Silence, I can listen to nothing which resembles either comments or advice.—Come, let us talk, let us laugh," she said, holding out to him a hand which he kissed. "Let us be like two old philosophers who know how to enjoy life up to the moment of their death. I will adorn myself, will be very coquettish for you. You will be, perhaps, the last man that sees the Duchesse de Langeais."

The vidame made no reply, he bowed, took the letter and did his errand. He returned at five o'clock, found his cousin dressed with care, exquisite in fact. The salon was decorated with flowers as if for a fête. The repast was delicious. For this old man the duchess displayed all the brilliancy of her wit and showed herself more attractive than she had ever been. The commander at first tried to see in all these seductions only a young woman's pretty whim; but from time to time the false magic of her charms displayed for him suddenly paled. At times he surprised her shivering with sudden terror; at times she seemed to listen in the silence. Then, if he said to her:

"What is it?"

"Hush," she replied.

At seven o'clock the duchess left the old man, but soon returned dressed as her maid might have been dressed for a journey; she requested the arm of her guest, and asking him to accompany her, they entered a hired coach. At a quarter before eight o'clock they were both before the door of Monsieur de Montriveau.

Armand all this while was meditating over the following letter:

"MY FRIEND,

"I have passed a few moments in your room without your knowledge; I have brought back my letters. Oh, Armand! from you to me this cannot be indifference, and hatred would act otherwise. If you love me, cease this cruel play. You would kill me. Later, you would despair on learning how much you were loved. If I have unfortunately understood you, if you have for me only aversion, aversion means contempt and disgust; then, all hope abandons me: from those two feelings men never return. However terrible it might be, this thought would bring some consolation into my long sorrow. You will have no regrets some day. Regrets! Ah, my Armand! would that I were unacquainted with them! If I have caused you a single one—no, I will not tell you what ravages it would cause in me. I should live, and should no longer be your wife. After giving myself utterly to you, in my thought, to whom must I now give myself?— to God. Yes, the eyes which you loved for a moment shall see no man's face again; and may the glory of God close them! I shall hear no other human voice after having heard yours, so tender at first, so terrible yesterday, for I am still in the morrow of your vengeance; may then the word of God consume me! Between His anger and yours, my friend, there will be for me only tears and prayers. You ask, perhaps, why I write to you. Alas! may I not cling to a last ray of hope, breathe a last sigh toward the happy life before I leave it forever? My situation is a terrible one. I feel in me all the serenity which a supreme resolution communicates to the soul, and yet feel the last upheavals of the storm. In that terrible adventure which first drew me to you, Armand, you went from the desert to the oasis led by a faithful guide. Well, I—I drag myself from the oasis to the desert, and you are for me a pitiless guide. Nevertheless, you alone, my friend, can comprehend the melancholy in the last looks which I give to happiness, and you are the only one to whom I can complain without a blush. If you hear my prayers, I shall be happy; if you are inexorable, I will expiate my wrong doing. After all, is it not natural that a woman should wish to live in the memory of him she loves, clothed with all noble feelings? Oh, my only dear one! Suffer your creature to bury herself in the belief that you will think her noble. Your harshness has compelled me to reflect; and since I have loved you so well, I have come to think myself less guilty than you deem me. Listen to my justification, I owe it to you; and you who are all the world to me, you owe me at least a moment's justice.

"I have learned through my own sorrows how much my coquetries must have made you suffer; but I was then in complete ignorance of love. You, yourself, you know the secret of these tortures, and yet you impose them on me. During the first eight months that you gave to me you did not make yourself loved. Why, my friend? I can no more tell you than I can now explain to you why I love you. Ah! certainly I was flattered to find myself the object of your passionate discourses, to receive your burning glances; yet you left me cold and without desires. No, I was not a woman, I conceived nothing, either of the devotion or of the happiness of our sex. Whose was the fault? Would you not have despised me if I had given myself up without impulse? Perhaps it is one of the sublime qualities of our sex to give ourselves without receiving any pleasure; perhaps there is no merit in abandoning one's self to delights known and ardently desired. Alas, my friend, I may say it to you, these thoughts came to me when I was so coquettish with you; but you seemed to me so noble that I could not wish that you should win me through mere pity.—What have I written? Ah! I have taken away from you all my letters, I have thrown them into the fire! They are burning. You will never know what they revealed of love, of passion, of madness—. I will be silent, Armand, I stop, I will say no more to you of my feelings. If my prayers have not communicated from my soul to yours, neither can I, a woman, owe your love only to your pity. I would be loved irresistibly or cast off ruthlessly. If you refuse to read this letter, it will be burned. If, after having read it, you are not within three hours my only husband forever, I shall have no shame in knowing that it is in your hands; the pride of my despair will protect my memory from all insult, and my end shall be worthy of my love. You yourself, meeting me no more in this world, though I shall still be living, you will not think without a shudder of the woman who within three hours will breathe only to cover you with her tenderness, of a woman consumed by love without hope, and faithful, not to shared pleasures, but to misunderstood feeling. The Duchesse de la Vallière wept a lost happiness, her vanished power; while the Duchesse de Langeais will be happy because of her tears, and will still remain a power for you. Yes, you will regret me. I am conscious that I was not made for this world, and I thank you for having proved it to me. Adieu, you cannot touch my axe; yours was that of the executioner, mine is that of God; yours kills, and mine saves. Your love was mortal, it could not support either disdain or ridicule; mine can endure everything without weakening, it lives immortally. Ah! I feel a dreary joy in overcoming you, you who feel yourself so great, in humbling you with the calm and protecting smile of the feeble angels who obtain, in sitting at the feet of God, the right and the power to watch over men in His name. You have had only passing desires; while the poor nun will ceaselessly lighten your path with her ardent prayers and cover you forever with the wings of divine love. I foresee your answer, Armand, and I give you a rendezvous—in heaven. Friend, strength and weakness are both admitted there; both are sufferings. This thought soothes the agitations of my last trial. Now I am so calm that I should fear I no longer loved thee, were it not for thee that I quit the world.

"ANTOINETTE."

"Dear vidame," said the duchess when they reached Montriveau's house, "do me the kindness to ask at the door if he is at home."

The commander, obeying after the manner of the men of the Eighteenth Century, got out of the carriage and presently returned to his cousin with a yes which made her shiver. At this word she took his hand, pressed it, permitted him to kiss her on both cheeks and begged him to go away without watching her or seeking to protect her.

"But the passers-by?" he said.

"No one could show me disrespect," she answered.

This was the last word of the woman of the world and the duchess. The commander went away. Madame de Langeais remained on the threshold of this door wrapt in her mantle, waiting till the hour of eight. The clock struck. This unhappy woman gave herself ten minutes more, a quarter of an hour; finally she saw a new humiliation in this delay and hope abandoned her. She could not repress one cry : "Oh my God!" then she left the fatal threshold. It was the first word of the Carmelite.

*

Montriveau had a conference that evening with several of his friends, he urged them to bring it to a close, but his clock was slow and he only left his house to go to the Hôtel de Langeais at the moment when the duchess, carried away by a cold rage, was flying on foot through the streets of Paris. She was weeping when she reached the Boulevard d'Enfer. There, for the last time, she looked at Paris, smoking, noisy, covered by the reddish atmosphere produced by its lights; then she entered a hired carriage and quitted this city, never to enter it again. When the Marquis de Montriveau reached the Hôtel de Langeais he did not find his mistress there, and thought himself tricked. Then he rushed to the vidame, and was received at the moment when that worthy man was putting on his dressing-gown and thinking of the happiness of his pretty cousin. Montriveau threw at him that terrible look whose electric shock affected equally men and women.

"Monsieur, have you lent yourself to a cruel jest?" he cried. "I have just come from the Hôtel de Langeais, and the servants say the duchess is out."

"There has doubtless happened, through your fault, a great misfortune!" replied the vidame. "I left the duchess at your door—"

"At what hour?"

"At a quarter to eight."

"Good evening," said Montriveau and returned home precipitately to ask his porter if he had seen in the evening, a lady at the door.

"Yes, Monsieur, a beautiful lady, who seemed in much trouble. She was crying like a Madeleine, without making any noise, and standing up straight like a picket. At last she said, *'Oh my God!'* and went away, so that, begging your pardon, my wife and I, who were close by without her seeing us, it made our hearts ache."

These few words made this strong man turn pale. He wrote a line to Monsieur de Ronquerolles and sent it to him immediately, then he went up to his own apartment. Towards midnight Ronquerolles arrived.

"What is the matter, my good friend?" he said on seeing the general.

Armand gave him the duchess's letter to read.

"Well?" asked Ronquerolles.

"She was at my door at eight o'clock, and at a quarter past eight she disappeared. I have lost her and I love her! Ah! if my life belonged to me, I would have already blown out my brains!"

"Bah! bah!" said Ronquerolles, "calm yourself. duchesses do not fly away like milkmaids. She cannot do more than three leagues an hour; tomorrow we will do six, all of us. Ah! plague on it!" he added, "Madame de Langeais is not an ordinary woman. We will all be on horseback to-morrow morning. In the course of the day we will know through the police where she has gone. She must have a carriage, these angels have no wings. Whether she is on the road, or hidden in Paris, we will find her. Have we not the telegraph to stop her, without following her? You will yet be happy. But, my dear brother, you have committed the error of which all men with your strength are more or less guilty. You judge of others by yourself, and never know when human nature will break under the strain which you are putting on it. Why did not you consult me a little earlier? I should have said to you: 'Be punctual.' —Till to-morrow then," he added, grasping the hand of Montriveau, who stood silent. "Sleep now, if you can."

But the greatest resources with which statesmen, sovereigns, ministers, bankers, in short, all human powers, were ever invested were employed in vain. Neither Montriveau nor his friends could find any trace of the duchess. She was evidently cloistered. Montriveau resolved to search, or to have searched, every convent in the world. He would have the duchess even though it cost the lives of a whole city. To do justice to this extraordinary man, we must state that his passionate ardor rose day after day with the same fire, and that it lasted for five years. It was not until 1829 that the Duc de Navarreins learned by chance that his daughter had gone to Spain, as waiting-maid to Lady Julia Hopwood, and that she had left the latter at Cadiz without

Lady Julia's having any suspicion that Mademoiselle Caroline was the illustrious duchess whose disappearance had excited so much interest in the upper circles of Parisian society.

The feelings with which these two lovers met at last at the iron grating of the Carmelites and in the presence of a Mother Superior, can now be understood in all their intensity; and their violence, reawakened on both sides, will doubtless explain the final scenes of this history.

The Duc de Langeais having died in 1823, his wife was free. Antoinette de Navarreins was living, consumed by love, on a rock of the Mediterranean; but the Pope might annul the vows of Sister Thérèse. Happiness bought by so much love might yet blossom for these two lovers. These thoughts carried Montriveau from Cadiz to Marseilles, from Marseilles to Paris. Some months after his arrival in France a merchant brig, armed, left the port of Marseilles for Spain. This vessel carried a number of distinguished men, nearly all French, who, filled with a desire to see the Orient, wished to visit those countries. The intimate knowledge which Montriveau possessed of the manners and customs of these lands made him a most desirable traveling companion for these gentlemen, who entreated him to join them, and he consented. The Minister of War appointed him Lieutenant-General, and placed him on the Committee of Artillery, that he might be free to join this party of pleasure.

The brig dropped anchor twenty-four hours after

her departure, to the north-west of an island in sight of the coasts of Spain. The vessel which had been selected was sufficiently slender of keel and light of mast to permit her to anchor without danger within half a league of the reefs which on this side effectively defend the approach to the island. If the fishing vessels or the inhabitants perceived the brig at her anchorage, they would scarcely have their suspicions aroused; and, in addition, her presence could be readily explained. Before arriving in sight of the island Montriveau had run up the flag of the United States. The seamen engaged for the voyage were all Americans and could speak nothing but English. One of Montriveau's companions took them all ashore in a long-boat and conducted them to the inn of the little town, where he kept them at a degree of drunkenness which deprived them of the free use of their tongues. He himself gave out that the brig was chartered by treasure-seekers, a class well enough known in the United States for their superstitions, and of whom one of the writers of that country has compiled a history. Thus the presence of the vessel outside the reefs was sufficiently explained. The owners and the passengers were searching, said the pretended boatswain, for the wreck of a galleon lost in 1778, with treasures brought from Mexico. The innkeepers and the authorities inquired no further.

Armand and the devoted friends who were seconding him in his difficult enterprise concluded at once that neither fraud nor force would enable them to assure the deliverance or the carrying away of Sister Thérèse by the town approach to the convent. Therefore, with a common accord, these audacious men resolved to take the bull by the horns. They determined to construct a path to the convent on the very side where all access seemed impossible, and to vanquish nature as General Lamarque had vanquished it at the assault of Capri. In the present instance, the perpendicular granite cliffs at the edge of the island offered less foothold than the cliffs of Capri had offered to Montriveau, who was in that incredible expedition, and the nuns seemed to him more redoubtable than had been Sir Hudson Lowe. To carry off the duchess with noise and disturbance would have covered these men with confusion. They might as well have laid siege to the town and the convent, and not left alive a single witness of their victory, after the manner of pirates. For them, this enterprise had but two aspects. Either, some conflagration, some feat of arms, which might terrify Europe without revealing the cause of the crime; or some aërial, mysterious carrying-off which would persuade the nuns that the devil had paid them a visit. This last plan had carried the day in the secret council held at Paris, before the departure. Moreover, everything had been foreseen for the success of an enterprise which offered to these men, wearied with the pleasures of Paris, a genuine amusement.

A species of pirogue, of an excessive lightness, constructed at Marseilles after a Malay model, permitted them to navigate among the reefs to a point beyond which navigation became quite impossible. Two cables of iron wire, stretched parallel for a distance of some feet on an inward incline, and along which traveled baskets also made of iron wire, served for a bridge, as in China, on which to pass from one rock to another. The reefs were thus connected together by a series of cables and baskets which resembled the threads on which certain spiders travel and in which they envelop the branches of a tree,—a work of instinct which the Chinese, that people of born imitators, were the first, historically speaking, to copy. Neither the waves nor any of the caprices of the sea could affect these frail constructions. The cables had elasticity and play enough to offer to the fury of the waves that curve—studied by an engineer, the late Cachin, the immortal creator of the port of Cherbourg—the scientific line of which limits the power of the angry waves; a curve established by a law won from the secrets of nature by the genius of observation, which is almost the whole of human genius.

The companions of Monsieur de Montriveau were alone upon the vessel. No eye of man could reach them. The best glasses, leveled from the upper decks of the passing merchant vessels, could not have discovered these cables lost among the reefs, nor the men hidden among the rocks. After eleven days of preparatory toil, these thirteen human demons reached the foot of the promontory, which rose to a height of thirty fathoms above the sea, a cliff as difficult for men to climb as would be the polished sides of a porcelain vase for a mouse. This table of granite was fortunately cracked. Its fissure, whose edges were two straight lines, allowed them to drive in, at the distance of a foot apart, stout wooden wedges in which these bold workmen fastened cramping-irons. These irons, prepared in advance, terminated at one end with perforated iron plates into which they fixed steps made of very thin fir plank, which also fitted into notches made in a mast the exact height of the promontory, and which was firmly set into the rock at the foot of the cliff. With an art worthy of these men of action, one of them, a profound mathematician, had calculated the angle at which to space the steps gradually from the top to the bottom of the mast, so as to bring at its exact middle the point from which the steps of the upper half should widen like a fan till they reached the top of the rock; while the steps of the lower half widened in like manner, only in a reversed direction, to the bottom. This staircase of incredible lightness, and perfectly firm, cost twenty-two days of work. A steel and phosphorus, a night, and the breakers of the sea, would suffice to obliterate all traces of it. Thus no revelation was possible, and no search for the violators of the convent could be successful.

On the summit of the rock was a platform, surrounded on every side by the perpendicular precipice. The thirteen strangers, examining the ground with their telescopes from the top of their mast, were satisfied that, in spite of some difficulties, they could easily reach the gardens of the convent, the trees of which were sufficiently thick to offer secure cover. There, they could doubtless come to an ultimate decision as to the best means of seizing the nun. After such great efforts they were unwilling to compromise the success of their enterprise by running any risk of discovery, and they were obliged to wait till after the last quarter of the moon.

Montriveau remained for two nights wrapped in his cloak, lying on the bare rock. The chants of the evening and those of the morning filled him with inexpressible delights. He went to the foot of the wall to hear the notes of the organ, and endeavored to distinguish one voice in this volume of voices. But, in spite of the silence, the distance was too great for any but the confused sounds of the music to reach his ear. They were mellow harmonies, in which all defects of execution disappeared, and from which the pure thought of art disengaged itself and filled the listener's soul, requiring of him no efforts of attention, nor the weariness of listening. Terrible memories for Armand, whose love blossomed afresh in its entirety in this breeze of music in which he wished to find aërial promises of happiness. On the morning of the last night he descended before sunrise, after having remained several hours with his eyes fixed on the unbarred window of a cell. Bars were not necessary to the windows looking out over these abysses. He had seen there a light throughout the night. And that instinct of the heart, which deceives as often as it speaks true, had cried to him: "She is there."

"She is certainly there, and to-morrow she will be mine," he said to himself, mingling his joyous thoughts with the sounds of a bell ringing slowly.

Strange capriciousness of heart! He loved with more passion the nun, wasted away in the raptures of love, consumed by tears, fastings, vigils, and prayer, the woman of twenty-nine so sorely tried, than he had loved the light young girl, the sylph, the woman of twenty-four! But the men of vigorous soul, are they not naturally moved by an impulse which draws them towards the sublime expressions which noble griefs, or the impetuous flow of thought, have imprinted upon the face of a woman? The beauty of a sorrowful woman, is it not the most attaching of all to a man who feels in his heart an inexhaustible treasure of consolations and of tenderness to expend on a creature, tender in weakness and strong through feeling. The fresh beauty, florid, smooth, the *pretty* in a word, is a commonplace charm which attracts the common run of men. Montriveau was one of those to love a face in which love reveals itself amid the lines of grief and the blight of melancholy. Should not a lover suffice to bring forth, at the voice of his puissant desire, a new being, young, palpitating, breaking forth for him alone from the worn shell so beautiful to his eyes yet defaced for all others?

Does he not possess two women,—one who shows herself to the world pale, discolored, sad; and that other one of his heart, whom no one sees, an angel who comprehends life through her feelings and who only appears in all her glory for the solemnities of love? Before quitting his post, the general heard faint harmonies which issued from that cell, soft voices full of tenderness. When he descended to his friends stationed at the bottom of the rock he told them in a few words, imprinted with that passion, communicative yet discreet, whose imposing expression men always respect, that never in his life had he experienced such captivating felicity.

In the evening of the next day, eleven devoted comrades mounted in the darkness up the precipice, having each one a poniard, a provision of chocolate, and all the instruments necessary for the trade of a burglar. When they reached the enclosing wall of the convent, they scaled it by means of ladders which they had made, and found themselves in the cemetery of the convent. Montriveau recognized both the long vaulted gallery through which he had recently passed on his way to the parlor and the windows of that apartment. His plan was at once formed and adopted. To enter by the window of that parlor which opened into the part occupied by the nuns, to penetrate into the corridors, to see if the names were inscribed on each cell, to go to that of Sister Thérèse, to surprise her there and gag her during her sleep, bind her and carry her away, all this part of the work would be easy for men who, to the audacity, to the expertness of galley-slaves, joined the special knowledge of men of the world, and to whom it was indifferent whether the stroke of a poniard should be necessary to purchase silence.

The bars of the window were sawed in two in two hours. Three men remained as sentries without, two others watched in the parlor. The rest, bare-footed, stationed themselves at certain distances along the cloister which Montriveau entered, hidden behind a young man, the most dexterous of them all, Henri de Marsay, who, as a matter of precaution, was dressed in the habit of the Carmelites, precisely like that worn in the convent. The clock struck three as Montriveau and the false nun reached the dormitories. They soon made out the position of the cells. Then, hearing no noise, they began to read by the light of a dark lantern the names fortunately inscribed on each door together with those mystical devices, portraits of saints, male or female, which each nun wrote like an epigraph over the new dispensation of her life, and in which she revealed the last thought of her past. When they reached the cell of Sister Thérèse, Montriveau read this inscription: *Sub invocatione sanctæ matris Theresæ,* The motto was: *Adoremus in æternum.* Suddenly his companion laid a hand upon his shoulder and showed him a bright light shining on the flagstones of the corridor through the chink of the door. At this moment Monsieur de Ronquerolles joined them.

"All the nuns are in the church, and are commencing the Office of the Dead," he said.

"I remain here," replied Montriveau; "fall back, all of you, to the parlor and close the door of this corridor."

He entered quickly, preceded by the pretended nun who put down his veil. They saw then, in the antechamber of the cell, the dead body of the duchess lying on the floor upon a plank of her bed and lighted by two wax tapers. Neither Montriveau nor de Marsay said a word, nor uttered a cry; but they looked at each other. Then the general made a sign which meant: "We will carry her away!"

"Save yourselves," cried Ronquerolles, "the procession of nuns is returning, you will be seen."

With that magical rapidity which a passionate desire infuses into movements, the body of the duchess was carried into the parlor, passed through the window and conveyed to the foot of the wall just as the abbess, followed by the nuns, reached the cell to take the body of Sister Thérèse. The nun, whose duty it was to watch with the dead, had had the imprudence to leave her charge, to search the inner cell for the secrets of its occupant, and was so intent upon this purpose that she heard nothing, and was thunderstruck when she came out and found the body gone. Before these stupefied women thought of making any search, the duchess had been lowered by ropes to the foot of the rocks and the companions of Montriveau had destroyed their work. At nine o'clock in the morning no trace remained of the stairway, nor of the cable bridges; the body of Sister Thérèse was on board; the brig came into port to embark her men, and disappeared in the course of the day. Montriveau remained alone in his cabin with Antoinette de Navarreins, whose countenance, during several hours, shone mercifully for him, resplendent with the sublime beauty which the peculiar calm of death lends to our mortal remains.

"Come," said Ronquerolles to Montriveau when the latter reappeared on deck, "she was a woman, now she is nothing. Let us fasten a cannon ball to each of her feet, throw her into the sea, and think no more of her than we do a book read in our childhood."

"Yes," said Montriveau, "for it is no longer anything but a poem."

"Now you are wise. Henceforth, have passions; but, as for love, it is well to know where to place it, and it is only the last love of a woman that should satisfy the first love of a man."

Geneva, Pre-Lévêque, January 26, 1834.

BOOK JUNGLE

Bringing Classics to Life

www.bookjungle.com email: sales@bookjungle.com fax: 630-214-0564 mail: Book Jungle PO Box 2226 Champaign, IL 61825

The Two Babylons
Alexander Hislop

You may be surprised to learn that many traditions of Roman Catholicism in fact don't come from Christ's teachings but from an ancient Babylonian "Mystery" religion that was centered on Nimrod, his wife Semiramis, and a child Tammuz. This book shows how this ancient religion transformed itself as it incorporated Christ into its teachings....

QTY

Religion/History   Pages: 358

ISBN: *1-59462-010-5*   MSRP *$22.95*

The Power Of Concentration
Theron Q. Dumont

It is of the utmost value to learn how to concentrate. To make the greatest success of anything you must be able to concentrate your entire thought upon the idea you are working on. The person that is able to concentrate utilizes all constructive thoughts and shuts out all destructive ones...

Self Help/Inspirational   Pages: 196

ISBN: *1-59462-141-1*   MSRP *$14.95*

Rightly Dividing The Word
Clarence Larkin

The "Fundamental Doctrines" of the Christian Faith are clearly outlined in numerous books on Theology, but they are not available to the average reader and were mainly written for students. The Author has made it the work of his ministry to preach the "Fundamental Doctrines." To this end he has aimed to express them in the simplest and clearest manner..

Religion   Pages: 352

ISBN: *1-59462-334-1*   MSRP *$23.45*

The Law of Psychic Phenomena
Thomson Jay Hudson

"I do not expect this book to stand upon its literary merits; for if it is unsound in principle, felicity of diction cannot save it, and if sound, homeliness of expression cannot destroy it. My primary object in offering it to the public is to assist in bringing Psychology within the domain of the exact sciences. That this has never been accomplished..."

New Age   Pages: 420

ISBN: *1-59462-124-1*   MSRP *$29.95*

Beautiful Joe
Marshall Saunders

When Marshall visited the Moore family in 1892, she discovered Joe, a dog they had nursed back to health from his previous abusive home to live a happy life. So moved was she, that she wrote this classic masterpiece which won accolades and was recognized as a heartwarming symbol for humane animal treatment...

Fiction   Pages: 256

ISBN: *1-59462-261-2*   MSRP *$18.45*

Bringing Classics to Life

BOOK JUNGLE

www.bookjungle.com email: sales@bookjungle.com fax: 630-214-0564 mail: Book Jungle PO Box 2226 Champaign, IL 61825

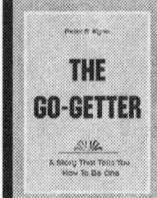

The Go-Getter
Kyne B. Peter

QTY

The Go Getter is the story of William Peck. He was a war veteran and amputee who will not be refused what he wants. Peck not only fights to find employment but continually proves himself more than competent at the many difficult test that are throw his way in the course of his early days with the Ricks Lumber Company...

Business/Self Help/Inspirational   Pages:68

ISBN: *1-59462-186-1*   MSRP *$8.95*

Self Mastery
Emile Coue

Emile Coue came up with novel way to improve the lives of people. He was a pharmacist by trade and often saw ailing people. This lead him to develop autosuggestion, a form of self-hypnosis. At the time his theories weren't popular but over the years evidence is mounting that he was indeed right all along...

New Age/Self Help   Pages:98

ISBN: *1-59462-189-6*   MSRP *$7.95*

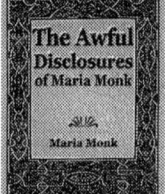

The Awful Disclosures Of Maria Monk

"I cannot banish the scenes and characters of this book from my memory. To me it can never appear like an amusing fable, or lose its interest and importance. The story is one which is continually before me, and must return fresh to my mind with painful emotions as long as I live..."

Religion   Pages:232

ISBN: *1-59462-160-8*   MSRP *$17.95*

As a Man Thinketh
James Allen

"This little volume (the result of meditation and experience) is not intended as an exhaustive treatise on the much-written-upon subject of the power of thought. It is suggestive rather than explanatory, its object being to stimulate men and women to the discovery and perception of the truth that by virtue of the thoughts which they choose and encourage..."

Inspirational/Self Help   Pages:80

ISBN: *1-59462-231-0*   MSRP *$9.45*

The Enchanted April
Elizabeth Von Arnim

It began in a woman's club in London on a February afternoon, an uncomfortable club, and a miserable afternoon when Mrs. Wilkins, who had come down from Hampstead to shop and had lunched at her club, took up The Times from the table in the smoking-room...

Fiction   Pages:368

ISBN: *1-59462-150-0*   MSRP *$23.45*

Bringing Classics to Life   BOOK JUNGLE

www.bookjungle.com email: sales@bookjungle.com fax: 630-214-0564 mail: Book Jungle PO Box 2226 Champaign, IL 61825

The Codes Of Hammurabi And Moses - W. W. Davies

The discovery of the Hammurabi Code is one of the greatest achievements of archaeology, and is of paramount interest, not only to the student of the Bible, but also to all those interested in ancient history...

Religion   Pages: 132
ISBN: *1-59462-338-4*   MSRP *$12.95*

The Thirty-Six Dramatic Situations
Georges Polti

An incredibly useful guide for aspiring authors and playwrights. This volume categorizes every dramatic situation which could occur in a story and describes them in a list of 36 situations. A great aid to help inspire or formalize the creative writing process...

Self Help/Reference   Pages: 204
ISBN: *1-59462-134-9*   MSRP *$15.95*

Holland - The History Of Netherlands
Thomas Colley Grattan

Thomas Grattan was a prestigious writer from Dublin who served as British Consul to the US. Among his works is an authoritative look at the history of Holland. A colorful and interesting look at history....

History/Politics   Pages: 408
ISBN: *1-59462-137-3*   MSRP *$26.95*

A Concise Dictionary of Middle English
A. L. Mayhew
Walter W. Skeat

The present work is intended to meet, in some measure, the requirements of those who wish to make some study of Middle-English, and who find a difficulty in obtaining such assistance as will enable them to find out the meanings and etymologies of the words most essential to their purpose...

Reference/History   Pages: 332
ISBN: *1-59462-119-5*   MSRP *$29.95*

The Witch-Cult in Western Europe   QTY
Margaret Murray

The mass of existing material on this subject is so great that I have not attempted to make a survey of the whole of European "Witchcraft" but have confined myself to an intensive study of the cult in Great Britain. In order, however, to obtain a clearer understanding of the ritual and beliefs I have had recourse to French and Flemish sources...

Occult   Pages: 308
ISBN: *1-59462-126-8*   MSRP *$22.45*

Bringing Classics to Life   BOOK JUNGLE

www.bookjungle.com *email:* sales@bookjungle.com *fax:* 630-214-0564 *mail:* Book Jungle PO Box 2226 Champaign, IL 61825

Name	
Email	
Telephone	
Address	
City, State ZIP	

☐ **Credit Card**   ☐ **Check / Money Order**

Credit Card Number	
Expiration Date	
Signature	

Please Mail to: Book Jungle
                  PO Box 2226
                  Champaign, IL 61825
or Fax to: 630-214-0564

ORDERING INFORMATION

web: *www.bookjungle.com*
email: *sales@bookjungle.com*
fax: *630-214-0564*
mail: *Book Jungle PO Box 2226 Champaign, IL 61825*
or PayPal *to sales@bookjungle.com*

Please contact us for bulk discounts
DIRECT-ORDER TERMS

**20% Discount if You Order
Two or More Books**
Free Domestic Shipping!

www.ingramcontent.com/pod-product-compliance
Lightning Source LLC
Chambersburg PA
CBHW082103230426
43671CB00015B/2597